ARNOBIUS OF SICCA

THE CASE AGAINST THE PAGANS

ADVERSUS NATIONES

ANCIENT CHRISTIAN WRITERS

THE WORKS OF THE FATHERS IN TRANSLATION

EDITED BY

JOHANNES QUASTEN, S. T. D.
*Professor of Ancient Church History
and Christian Archaeology*

JOSEPH C. PLUMPE, Ph. D.
*Professor of New Testament Greek
and Ecclesiastical Latin*

The Catholic University of America
Washington, D. C.

No. 8

ARNOBIUS OF SICCA
THE CASE AGAINST THE PAGANS

NEWLY TRANSLATED AND ANNOTATED

BY

GEORGE E. McCRACKEN, Ph. D., F. A. A. R.

Professor of Classics
Drake University, Des Moines, Iowa

VOLUME TWO

BOOKS FOUR – SEVEN

NEWMAN PRESS

New York, N.Y./Ramsey, N.J.

Nihil Obstat:
Johannes Quasten, S.T.D.
Censor Deputatus

Imprimatur:
Patricius A. O'Boyle, D.D.
Archiepiscopus Washingtonensis
die 18 Maii 1949

COPYRIGHT 1949
BY
REV. JOHANNES QUASTEN
AND
REV. JOSEPH C. PLUMPE

Library of Congress
Catalog Card Number: 78-62458

ISBN: 0-8091-0249-8

PUBLISHED BY PAULIST PRESS
Editorial Office: 1865 Broadway, New York, N.Y. 10023
Business Office: 545 Island Road, Ramsey, N.J. 07446

PRINTED AND BOUND IN THE UNITED STATES OF AMERICA

CONTENTS

Volume Two

	PAGE
TEXT	373
Book Four: Criticisms of Various Gods	375
Book Five: Jupiter Elicius, Attis, and the Mysteries	409
Book Six: Temples and Images	452
Book Seven: Sacrifices and Ceremonials	481
NOTES	541
Book Four	543
Book Five	566
Book Six	584
Book Seven	603
INDEX	621

ARNOBIUS OF SICCA

THE CASE
AGAINST THE PAGANS

BOOK FOUR

CRITICISMS OF VARIOUS PAGAN GODS

Deifications of abstract qualities.

1. We should like to ask you and, especially, you Romans,[1] lords and princes of the world, whether you think Piety,[2] Harmony, Safety, Honor, Virtue, and Happiness, and all other such names[3] to which we see you have built altars with splendid shrines, have divine power and live in the precinct of heaven; or have you thus placed them on the list of the gods above for the sake of form as usual, because we[4] desire and want the good things for which they stand to come our way? If you think they are mere words and names without substance and yet deify them in sacred areas, you will have to consider whether it is a childish joke or is calculated to bring mockery to your divinities[5] by equating and identifying them with the fictions of meaningless words.[6] But if, on the other hand, you really think they are gods and honor[7] them with temples and couches, we beg you to teach our ignorance, for what reason and in what way Victory, Peace, Equity, and those others which were mentioned before can be gods and belong to the assembly of the gods above.

2. For we—unless, indeed, you deny us common sense[8] altogether—feel and see that none of these "deities" has divine power or exists in any form properly its own; but they are the manliness[9] of a man, the safety of the safe, the honor of the honored, the victor's victory, the harmony of the harmonious, the piety of the pious, the mindfulness of the

mindful, the happy fortune of one who lives truly in happiness and without any misfortunes.

Now it is easy to see we really speak the truth when we note the contrary qualities opposed to them: unhappiness, discord, forgetfulness, injustice, impiety, cowardice of heart and unfortunate state of health. As these things befall men and depend on the deeds of men by accidental circumstances, so the opposite of each ⟨and what⟩ is named for more agreeable qualities must be inherent in others; and out of this complexion of things, the figurative representation of names has been conceived.

3. As for the fact that you introduce hordes of others stamped [10] as gods, we cannot determine whether you do it seriously and with the conviction that you have found out the truth, or whether playing with empty fictions you indulge your unbridled imagination.

"Varro,"[11] it is said, "is authority for the statement that a goddess was called Luperca [12] because the she-wolf, not given to gentleness, spared the castaway infants."

It was, then, from the course of events, and not from nature itself that that goddess made her appearance? And only after the horrid beast restrained itself from using its savage fangs, the goddess herself began to exist and received the identification of her name? Or if she was a goddess long before Romulus and his brother were born, show us what her name and title were.

Praestana [13] became a name, as you say, because in throwing the javelin Quirinus [14] excelled all others in strength; and because Titus Tatius [15] was permitted to open up [16] and make passable a road to take the Capitoline Hill, a goddess was called Panda [17] or Pantica. Before this happened, then, these divinities, too, never existed, and had Romulus

BOOK FOUR: CRITICISMS OF VARIOUS PAGAN GODS 377

not held the Palatine[18] through hurling of the weapon[19] and if the Sabine king had been unable to take the Tarpeian rock,[20] there would have been no Pantica, no Praestana?[21] And if you say they existed before the occasion arose that gave them their special name, a point which has been discussed in an earlier chapter,[22] then tell us also what they were called.

4. "Pellonia[23] is a goddess powerful in repelling enemies."

Whose enemies, tell me, if it is not asking too much? Opposing sides come into combat and fighting together hand to hand decide the issue with clash of arms; and to one this side is an enemy and that is hostile to the other.[24] Whom, therefore, will Pellonia repel, when fighting takes place on both sides, or in whose favor will she yield, seeing that she is under obligation to give to each side the might and services of her name?[25] But if she does so—that is, if she gives her favor and good will to both sides—she without fail destroys the force of her name which was created to signify the repulsion of one side.

But perhaps you will say: "She is goddess only of the Romans and siding with the Quirites[26] alone, is ever ready with her gracious assistance." We wish, indeed, this were so, because we like the name, but the matter posits a real problem. Yes, tell me, do the Romans possess gods peculiar to themselves who are not the gods of other nations?[27] And how can they be gods if they will not show all nations existing anywhere the impartiality of their name? And where, I ask, was this Pellonia long ago when the national honor was brought under the yoke at the Caudine Forks;[28] when at the Trasimene Lake[29] blood ran in torrents; when the plains of Diomedes[30] were piled high with the corpses of Romans;

when a thousand other wounds were received in the countless disasters of battles? Was she sleeping, was she snoring, or, as worthless knaves [31] commonly do, had she fled to the enemy's camp?

The gods on the left.

5. The gods [32] on the left preside only over regions on the left and are hostile to the right side.[33] But for what reason or with what meaning this is said, we do not ourselves follow and we are certain that you cannot clarify the matter for the ordinary understanding. First of all, the world itself has in itself for itself neither right nor left nor upper regions nor lower nor front nor after parts. To illustrate: whatever is round and surrounded on all sides by the curve of a solid sphere, has no beginning, no end; and where there is no end or beginning, there can be no part with a name of its own [and a beginning].[34] And so when we say: this direction is right and that left, we speak not with relation to the character of the world, which is everywhere quite the same, but we refer to our own position and station, being so constituted that some things are said to be on our right, others on our left. Yet these very things which we call left and right [35] have no permanence, no fixity, but just as chance and the accident of the moment has placed us, so they derive their representations from our sides. If I look to the rising sun, the polar regions become the left; if I turn my face to that direction, on my left will be the west which was thought behind my back when I looked at the sun. But again, if I cast my glance at the region of the setting sun, the south then takes on the designation of left, and if a momentary exigency turns me in that direction, the east becomes the left owing to the changed position of the body.

And from this it can be gathered at once that nothing at

all is by nature right or left but relative according to position and time and as the location of our body results from the attendant circumstances. And since this is the case, by what cause, in what manner, can there be gods of the left when it is evident that the same directions now become right, now left? Or what have the regions on the right done to deserve from the immortal gods that they should be without any guardians, even though it is these they have ordained should be fortunate and ever possessed of favorable omens?

Other curious divinities.

6. "Lateranus," [36] as you say, "is god and genius of hearths and was given this name because men construct that kind of fireplace out of unbaked *laterculi*." [37]

Well, now, if hearths are made of burned clay or any other kind of material, will they not have genii, and will Lateranus, whoever the fellow is, withdraw from his office of protector because his kingdom has not been constructed of clay blocks? And for what purpose, I ask, has that god been charged with the guardianship of hearths? Through the kitchens of mankind he runs, looking and examining to see with what kinds of wood the heat is generated on his hearths. He puts earthen vessels into such a condition as not to crack under the power of the flames. He takes care that the savors of things in their unspoiled state may reach the palate with all their delights, and he performs the function and part of a taster to see whether the sauces have been properly seasoned. Is this not unseemly? Indeed, to put it more truly, is it not disgraceful, impious, to have only this in view when introducing some certain fictions of gods—not to venerate them with worthy honors but to put them in charge of shameful things and disreputable activity?

7. And, pray, does not Venus Militaris[38] preside over vice in the army camps and over pederasty? Yes, is there not one Perfica[39] of the tribe of divinities who perfects those obscene and dirty pleasures and causes them to proceed to the end with undisturbed delight? And is there not Pertunda[40] who stands by husbands in the act of defloration? Is there not also Tutunus?[41] But if the facts themselves bring you to no understanding of the truth, can you not at least from the names themselves understand that they are the inventions of a most inane superstition and false gods created by the imagination?

"Puta," you say, "is in charge of the pruning[42] of trees, Peta, of petitions. The god of groves[43] is Nemestrinus. Patellana[44] is a divinity and so is Patella, of which the one is placed over things already made patent, the other of things yet to be disclosed. Nodutis[45] is said to be a god who brings to the knots[46] things already sown; and she who presides over the treading out of grain, Noduterensis.[47] When we become lost on the roads, the goddess Upibilia[48] extricates us. Parents bereft of their children are in the care of Orbona;[49] those who are near death, in that of Nenia.[50] But[51] she who hardens and strengthens the bones of little children is herself called Ossipago.[52] Mellonia[53] is a goddess whose very special province bees are, caring for and guarding the sweetness of honey.

Criticism of the worship of such divinities.

8. Now please do tell me—and may Peta, Puta, Patella graciously favor you—if there were no bees at all on earth, or if we members of the human ⟨race⟩ were born like worms without bones,[54] would there be no goddess Mellonia or would Ossipago, the solidifier of bones, not have her special

BOOK FOUR: CRITICISMS OF VARIOUS PAGAN GODS 381

name? I ask and keep on asking: whether you think the gods are more ancient in nature, time, antiquity, or human beings, or bees, crops, shrubs, and the rest? No man will doubt that you will say that the gods precede by countless ages, centuries, all things that exist. But if so, how can it happen in the natural order of things that from things created at a later time things which in point of time are earlier received their names? Or that the gods were given the protection of things which were not yet produced and made available for the use of mortals? Or is it that the gods were for long without names, and after things began to spring forth and exist on earth, you deemed them worthy to be named by these signs and titles? And whence could you have known what names to give to each since you were totally unaware of their existence or that they possessed certain powers? For you were equally uninformed as to which had any power and over what he ought to be placed with reference to his divine power.

9. "What?" you say, "Are you stating that these gods are nowhere and are the products of false opinions?"

Not we alone but the voice of truth says that, and so does reason, and that common sense[55] which is in all mortals. Who is there who would believe that there are gods called Lucrii[56] and that they preside over the pursuit of gain, knowing as we do that most frequently it comes from base causes and always consists of loss to others?[57] Who believes that Libentina,[58] who that Burnus[59] has the guardianship of those lusts which wisdom bids us flee and which in a thousand forms shameless obscenity submits to and practices? Who that Limentinus,[60] who that Lima,[61] bear the guardianship of thresholds and discharge the duties of doorkeepers, when every day we see ⟨the thresholds⟩ of shrines and of private homes wrecked and ruined, and that the approaches to shameful brothels are not without them? Who, that the Limi [62] are the caretakers of slopes, who that Saturn [63] is the protector of sowing, who that Montinus [64] is the protector of mountains, who that Murcida [65] is the protectress of the lazy? Who, finally, would believe that there is a goddess Pecunia [66] who, as if she were the greatest divinity, your writings say gives golden rings,[67] choice seats in the games and shows, the very highest of honors, the distinction of magistracy, and—a thing the lazy like most of all—the security of ease through riches?

10. But if bones, honies, and thresholds, and all the rest which we have either run through cursorily or have omitted to touch upon from a desire to avoid wearisome prolixity, possess, enthroned, their own peculiar protectors, then in like manner we may introduce a thousand other gods who ought to furnish care and guardianship to things without number. Why should there be a god over honey alone, not one over gourds, turnips, marjoram, cress, vetch, beets, cabbages? Why have bones alone deserved protection, not nails, hairs, and all the rest that are located in covered places and the private parts? They are exposed to many dangers and need the diligent care of the gods even more. Or if you say that these parts also function under the care of their own tutelary deities, you will have the beginning of as many gods as there are things; and no reason will be advanced why the divine care should not watch over everything, if you are going to say that there are certain things over which the divinities preside and watch.

Book Four: Criticisms of Various Pagan Gods 383

Such divinities cannot exist.

11. What do you say, my dear fathers of new [68] religions, of new powers? Do you strain your voice and multiply complaints that we profane these gods [69] and neglect them with sacrilegious contempt: Lateranus, the genius of hearths; Limentinus, the protector of thresholds; Pertunda, Perfica, Noduterensis? And because we do not fall on our knees before Mutunus [70] and Tutunus, do you say that things have fallen into ruin and that the world itself has changed its laws and constitution? And yet be sure to watch out lest, while you imagine such monstrous things and devise them, you offend those gods which have the surest title to existence [71] —provided there are any who deserve to bear and possess the distinction of this name—and for an added reason those evils, which you mention, rage and grow stronger each day.

"Why, then," perhaps one of you will say, "is it not true [72] that these gods exist? Yet when they are invoked by the soothsayers, they respond; when summoned by their names, they come; when they are consulted, they give true answers."

We can show that this statement is false,[73] both because the whole business is one great mass of conjectures, and because we daily see many of their predictions either turning out otherwise or twisted into contrary outcomes and the thing hoped for unrealized.

12. But let them,[74] as you assert, be true! How, however, will you make us believe that Mellonia, for example, or Limentinus, introduce themselves into the viscera [75] or that they accommodate themselves to the interpretation of the things which you ask? Did you ever see their face, conduct, countenance, or can these same things be seen in lungs or livers? Can it not happen, come to pass—though this you cleverly

conceal—that the one should take the other's place, deceiving, deluding, tricking, and taking on the appearance of the divinity invoked? If the magicians, brothers of the soothsayers, report how in their invocations pseudo-deities [76] often steal in taking the place of those invoked, and in addition that some of these are spirits of grosser substance who pretend that they are gods, and delude the ignorant by their lying pretenses, why should not we similarly believe that here also others substitute themselves for those they are not, so that they may both encourage your fancies and rejoice that victims are slaughtered to them under names of others?

Criticism of multiple divinities.

13. Or if you refuse to accept this because of the novelty [77] of the thing, how can you know whether there is not some one being who comes in place of all those gods and 'fathers' [78] whom you invoke, and substituting himself for the local and regional gods, offers to you the appearance of many gods and powers?

"Who is that one?" perhaps he will ask.

On information gained from truthful authors, we could tell you, but since you might be unwilling to believe us, let him ask the Egyptians, Persians, Indians, Chaldaeans, Armenians, and all those others who saw and learned these things by esoteric arts. Now, assuredly, you will learn who the One God is or who the many under Him are who pretend themselves gods and poke fun at the lack of wisdom in the human race.

For a long time we have been ashamed to come to this point at which not only youngsters and the flippant cannot restrain their laughter but even the serious and those hardened by crabbed sternness. While we have all heard it tra-

Book Four: Criticisms of Various Pagan Gods 385

ditionally taught by our teachers that the declensions of the gods' names have no plurals because gods are individuals and the name of an individual cannot commonly belong to many,[79] you, having forgetfully laid aside the memory of what you learned as boys, endow several gods with the same names, and though otherwise you are more conservative as to their number, have again multiplied them by the association of names. This subject men of acute judgment and keen intelligence have long since explained both in the language of Italy[80] and in Greek,[81] a fact which might have netted us a saving of effort, did we not see that some people are ignorant of those books: the discussion which we have begun forces us also to say something on these topics, although it has already been taken up and treated by them.

14. Your theologians,[82] then, and the writers on antiquarian subjects say that there are in the universe three Jupiters,[83] of whom one was begotten by his father Aether, another by Caelus, and the third by Saturn, both buried and born in the island of Crete;[84] five Suns[85] and five Mercuries,[86] of whom, as they relate, the first Sun is called the son of Jupiter and is believed to be the grandson of Aether. The second is likewise the son of Jupiter and of the mother Hyperiona.[87] The third, the son of Vulcan—not the Lemnian[88] but the one who was the son of the Nile; the fourth, the father of Ialysus whom Acantho in the heroic age bore on Rhodes; while the fifth is regarded as the ⟨father⟩ of a Scythian king[89] and of Circe the changer of shapes.[90] Now the first Mercury, who is said to have lusted after Proserpina, is descended from Caelus who is over all; the second is beneath the earth, and boasts himself to be Trophonius; the third was born of Maia and the third Jupiter; the fourth is descendant of the Nile whose name the Egyptian race dreads

and fears to express; the fifth is the slayer of Argus,[91] a fugitive and exile and inventor of letters [92] in Egypt.[93]

But there are also five Minervas,[94] according to them, as there are five Suns and Mercuries; the first of whom is no virgin [95] but the mother of Apollo by Vulcan; the second,[96] the offspring of the Nile and who is called the Egyptian; the third is descended from Saturn [97] and is the one who devised the use of arms; the fourth, whom the Messenians name Coryphasia,[98] is the descendant of Jupiter; and she who slew her father Pallas when he sought for incestuous love is the fifth.[99]

15. And lest it seem too wearisome and prolix to propose to go through each of them in detail,[100] the same theologians [101] say that there are four Vulcans [102] and three Dianas,[103] as many Aesculapiuses [104] and five Dionysuses,[105] six Hercules [106] and four Venuses,[107] three kinds of Castors [108] and the same number of Muses,[109] sets of three feathered Cupids [110] and sets of four [111] Apollinarian deities, [112] whose fathers they name in like manner, their mothers in like manner, the places where they were born, and they point out the origin of each with their families.[113] Now, if this is true and certain and is demonstrated from the testimony of acknowledged fact, either none of them is a god, since several cannot exist under the same name, as we have heard, or if any one of them does exist he will not be known and recognized because he is obscured by the confusing similarity of the names. And so it comes to pass that, however much you may dislike it, through your own doing religion becomes confused [114] and stumbles and has no fixed end to which it can turn, even if the errors involved in its equivocacy did not spell its frustration.[115]

16. Suppose [116] that we, moved either by your prestige or by violent fear of you, had taken it into our head to be ready to worship Minerva, for example, with the rites you hold

BOOK FOUR: CRITICISMS OF VARIOUS PAGAN GODS 387

sacred and the usual ceremonial; that as we make ready to approach the divine objects and to render her the established tributes on the blazing altars, all the Minervas should flit hither and contending for the right to that name, should each demand for herself that the offerings prepared should be given her. Caught like this, what are we poor creatures going to do? Or to which party shall we give preference in tendering piety's offering?

Perhaps the first one we have mentioned will say:

"The name Minerva is mine, mine is the divinity, who bore Apollo, bore Diana, and with the fruit of my womb enriched heaven with divinities, and multiplied the number of gods."

"What? You—you are it," the fifth Minerva will say, "who are a wife and so often in childbirth have lost the holiness of pure chastity? Do you not see that in all the Capitols the images of the Minervas are virgin, and that all the artisans give them the forms of ⟨un⟩married girls? Therefore stop appropriating to yourself a name not rightfully yours. That I am Minerva, daughter of my father Pallas, the entire chorus of the poets is witness, who name me Pallas after my father's name." [117]

"What are you saying?" the second will say on hearing this, "So you want to bear the name of Minerva—an impudent parricide and one polluted by the stain of incestuous love, who, while you decked yourself with rouge and the harlot's arts, aroused the mind of even your father and filled it with maddened lusts for yourself? [118] Away with you, therefore! Seek some other name for yourself, for this one belongs to me whom the Nile, the greatest of rivers, begot from among his flowing waters and brought to maidenhood from the condensing of dew." [119] But if you ask about the credibility of this fact, I will also call the Egyptians to witness, in whose language ⟨I am⟩ Neith, as the *Timaeus*[120] of Plato attests."

What do you suppose will happen now? Will she stand back and not say that she is Minerva, she whose name is Coryphasia, derived from the name of Coryphe, her mother, or because from the top of Jupiter's head[121] she sprang forth, bearing a shield and girt with terrible weapons? Or that she who is third, will quietly surrender the name, and will not, in the face of what has been said, render an account of herself and oppose the arrogance of the first ones?

"So you dare to usurp for yourself the majesty of my name, you who have come, if what is said be true, from mud and were born and developed from slimy whirlpools? And you[122] —do you assume the honor of a goddess belonging to another, you who put out the lie that you were begotten from the head of Jupiter and persuade most gullible mortals that you are reason? He conceive and beget children from his head? And so that the arms you bear could be welded and fashioned, in the hollow of his head was there a blacksmith's shop—anvils, hammers, forges, bellows, coals, and tongs? Or if what you say is true, that you are reason, stop claiming for yourself the name which is mine; for 'reason' which you talk about is not a certain type of divinity but the faculty of understanding obscure causes."

Now then, if, as we have said, the five Minervas should approach us as we apply ourselves to our obligations of religion and they wrangle over the proper ownership of the name and each one asks for herself, either that clouds of incense be offered or that sacrificial wines be poured out from golden cups, by what referee, by what judge are we going to settle such squabbles? Or what investigator, what arbitrator will have the nerve[123] to attempt to give a just

BOOK FOUR: CRITICISMS OF VARIOUS PAGAN GODS   389

decision between such persons or pronounce on their cases as usurped rights? Will he not rather go home and keep away from such business, thinking it safer to have nothing to do with such matters? Otherwise, if he gave to one what belongs to all he would make enemies of the others or, if he referred to all of them what should belong to one, he would incur the charge of being a fool.

17. We can put on this same demonstration regarding the Mercuries, the Suns—yes, regarding all the others whose numbers you stretch and multiply. But it suffices to deduce from a single instance a principle applicable to all; and that our expanding on this may not make you weary of listening, we shall stop dealing with individuals; otherwise, while charging you with excess, we might also ourselves incur the charge of excessive loquacity. What have you to say, you who by torturing the body [124] invite us to the worship of the gods and would force us to undertake the worship of your deities? We cannot be hard to influence if only something worthy of the conception of so great a name be shown us. Show us Mercury, but only one; give us Liber, but only one; a single Venus and likewise a single Diana. For never will you induce us to believe that there are four Apollos and three Jupiters, not even if you were to cite Jupiter himself as witness or make the Pythian [125] your authority.

Human error no excuse for the pagan theologians.

18. But someone from the opposition says: "How do we know whether what the theologians [126] have written was on the basis of knowledge gained from investigation, or whether they have presented this, just as they wished and pleased,[127] with wanton fiction?"

That has nothing to do with the case, nor is the reasonableness of that argument based on this, whether the facts are as the writings of the theologians say they are or whether they are otherwise and differ from them by a great disparity. To us it is enough to speak about things that are public property and not to investigate what the content of truth is, but only to confute, disprove what lies before all and what human thought has taken in. But if those men are liars, you explain what the truth is, and open to us the mystery which suffers no refutation! And how can it be done if the teaching of the written word is set aside? What is there which can be said about the immortal gods which has not reached human thought from the writings of men?[128] Or can you yourselves tell anything about their rites and ceremonials, which has not been consigned to letters and made common knowledge in the treatises of the writers? Or if you think these matters are of no consequence, let all the books which you have about the gods composed by the theologians, pontiffs, and some, too, by persons devoted to philosophy,[129] be done away with. Yes, let us rather suppose that from the beginning of the world no mortal has ever published[130] anything at any time about the gods. We wish to make the experiment and we want to know whether you can make the slightest, the very slightest mention of the gods, or form a mental concept of them without the notion of them as contained in some book producing it. But since it is evident that you have learned about their names and powers by suggestions derived from books, it is unfair to refuse credence to these books by the testimony and authority of which you lend weight to those things which you say.

Attribution of birth to the gods really insults them.

19. But perhaps these things will turn out to be false and what you say prove to be true. By what argument, by what

Book Four: Criticisms of Various Pagan Gods 391

token? For since on both sides those who have said the one thing and those who have said the other were human beings, and by each party the discussion was about doubtful matters, it is arrogant to say that what may please you is true, yet charge what offends your feelings with being arbitrary and false. By the laws of the human race and the common lot of mortality itself, when you hear and read, "That god is sprung from that father and from that mother," are you not impressed with the fact that something is said here which is proper to human nature and proceeds from the lowliness of the earthborn race? Or, while you think this so, do you conceive no anxiety that you may cause some offense to these same gods, whoever they are, because you believe that it was thanks to obscenity, by passion's seed, that they saw the light of day unknown to them before? For we, to prevent any one from happening to think that we do not know or are ignorant of what befits the majesty of that name, hold that the gods ought to be without birth, or if they do have a beginning of some sort, believe and consider that the Lord and Founder of the universe, Himself, by means which He Himself knows, sent them forth—spotless, most chaste, pure, strangers to that horrid thing, coition, and that, too, taking them one and all, after the primordial creation had been completed.[131]

20. But you, on the contrary, unmindful of the great majesty and sublimity involved, attribute births[132] to them and ascribe to them origins which men with more refined thinking regard as both execrable and horrible.

"From Ops," you say, "as his mother and with Saturn as his father, Diespiter was born with his brothers."

Do the gods, then, have wives, and do they enter into the bonds of marriage on terms previously arranged? Do they swear to each other the oaths of the marriage bed by usage, by the cake, or by purchase?[133] Have they sweethearts, have they fiancées, have they brides[134] with the conditions settled? And what can we say about the weddings themselves, when ⟨you dare⟩[135] to state that some have celebrated their marriages and had large crowds of festive attendants and that goddesses sported at these and that, because they had no share[136] in the Fescennine verses,[137] some threw discord[138] into everything and planted the dangerous seeds of ruin for a later generation of human beings?

21. But perhaps in the case of the others this dirty vileness is less apparent. Well, then, did that ruler of the heavens,[139] the father of gods and men, by the nod of his brow moving and shaking heaven,[140] take form from man and woman? And unless both sexes were to abandon ⟨themselves⟩ in disgraceful pleasures by the union of their bodies, would there be no Jupiter, that 'Greatest' one, and even to this day would the divinities have no king and would heaven stand without its lord? But why are we amazed that you keep saying that Jupiter was delivered from the womb of woman, when your authors concoct the story that he both had a nurse[141] and also that he afterward preserved the life imparted to him by nourishment from the breast of another!

What do you say, gentlemen? Did he, then, he—let me repeat it—who thunders, flashes and hurls lightning, and draws together terrifying clouds, suck in the streams of the breasts, squall like a baby, crawl about? And, that he might cease his most senseless crying, was he made to hear the sound of rattles and so became quiet and went to sleep, lying in the softest of cradles and soothed with lullabies?

A holy advocacy of the existence of gods! What demonstration and foreshadowing of the venerable majesty of their awesome sublimity! I ask: is this your version of the genesis

Book Four: Criticisms of Various Pagan Gods 393

of the lordly powers on high? Do your gods issue forth into the light by those same processes of birth by which asses, pigs, dogs, by which all this unclean outpouring of the animal world is conceived and begotten?

The loves of Jupiter.

22. And not satisfied with having ascribed these carnal unions to the dignified Saturn, you even declare that the king of the universe himself begot children more shamefully than he himself was born and created.[142]

"From Hyperiona, his mother," you say, "and from Jupiter the hurler of the thunderbolt, was born the golden and blazing Sun; from Latona and the same were born the Delian archer[143] and Diana, the rouser of the woods; from Leda and the same were born ⟨the brothers whose⟩ name in Greek is Dioscuri;[144] from Alcmene[145] and the same the Theban Hercules whom the club and hide protected; from Semele and the same, Liber, who is called Bromius[146] and was born a second time from the thigh of his father;[147] from the same, again, and Maia, Mercury, eloquent of tongue and the bearer of tame[148] snakes.

Can any more serious slander be visited upon your Jupiter, or is there anything else that so destroys and ruins the authority of the prince of the gods, than that you believe he was at any time overcome by lustful passions and inflamed with the heat of a heart lusting for women? And what did the Saturnian king have to do with unions with other men's wives? Was Juno not enough for him? And could he not stay the force of his desires upon the queen of the divinities, when so great nobility, her looks, countenance, dignity, and the radiance of her arms white as snow and marble[149] graced her? Or did he, not content with just one wife, take delight in concubines, mistresses, and courtesans, and practice his incontinence everywhere, as is the way with young roués—a filthy god—and when gray with years did he restore the ardor of his passions waning after countless liaisons?

What have you to say, you godless ones? What rotten thoughts do you conjure up regarding your Jupiter? Doing so do you not notice, do you not see, with what disgrace you brand him, what a criminal you make of him, or what stigmas of vices, what infamies you heap upon him?

23. Man, though prone to lust and because of natural weakness inclined to sensual attractions, nevertheless has laws according to which he punishes adultery and inflicts capital punishment on those who, they learn, have pre-empted for themselves the rights of another by forcing the marriage bed.[150] What shame, what stigma attaches to the person of the seducer and adulterer, the greatest of rulers did not know! And he who reputedly examines whether we have deserved well or very ill, because he had lost his own principles was unaware of what he could wish with decency!

This abuse you give him could perhaps be borne with, were you to couple him with persons at least of equal rank and if you made out that he had committed adultery with the immortal goddesses. But, I ask, what beauty was there, what charm in human bodies which could arouse, which could captivate the eyes of Jupiter? Skin, flesh, phlegm, and all the filth encased in the intestines—at which not only Lynceus[151] of the piercing gaze could shudder, but the very thought of which any other might try to shun! O marvellous reward of guilt, O worthy and precious delight, for which the Great Jupiter became a swan[152] and bull[153] and a begetter of white eggs![154]

Book Four: Criticisms of Various Pagan Gods

*The pagans, not the Christians, are the authors of
the insults to the gods.*

24. If you will but open the mind's eye and look at the real truth without clinging to any pet idea of your own, you will find that the causes of all the miseries with which, as you say, the human race has long been afflicted, flow from this kind of notions about your gods which you have held from ancient times, and which you have refused to change for the better though the truth has been set before your eyes. Tell us, what have we ever either imagined about them that was improper, or what that was unbecoming have we ever put forth in our writings, that the tribulations of the human race and the lessened comforts of life should be bandied about to our prejudice? Do we say that certain gods were born from eggs like storks, like pigeons?[155] That, formed from the foaming main and the severed members of Caelus, the radiant beauty of Cytherean Venus developed?[156] That because he had committed parricide, Saturn was thrown into chains and was freed and raised up from the weight of chains on fixed days?[157] That through the kindness of the Curetes[158] Jupiter was saved from death? That he drove his father from the kingdom and by violence and deceit he held the sovereign authority rightly belonging to another?[159] Is it our story that the old man when driven out hid in the territories of the Itali,[160] and because he had been saved from his son, gave its name to Latium as a gift?[161] Do we say that Jupiter himself incestuously married his sister,[162] or that in ignorance he breakfasted on the descendant of Lycaon[163] in place of pork when invited to the privilege of the table? That Vulcan limping on one foot practiced the trade of the smith on the island of Lemnos? That because of his greed and avarice, even as Pindar of Boeotia sings,[164] Aesculapius was transfixed by the

thunderbolt?[165] That Apollo, having become rich, deceived by the ambiguity of his reply those very kings with whose treasure and gifts he had enriched himself?[166] Did we publish it abroad that Mercury was a thief?[167] That Laverna[168] is one and together with him presides over secret frauds? Is the writer Myrtilus[169] one of us who claims that the Muses were the handmaids of Megaclo, daughter of Macarius? Have we bruited about that Venus was a harlot, deified by a Cyprian king named Cinyras?[170]

25. Who reported that the Palladium[171] was formed from the remains of Pelops? Was it not you? Who, that Mars was a Spartan? Was it not your writer Epicharmus?[172] Who that he saw the light of day in the Thracian country? Was it not Sophocles[173] the Athenian with the assent of all the theaters? Who, that in Arcadia he was bound for thirteen months?[174] Was it not the son of the river Mela?[175] Who said that dogs were sacrificed to him by the Carians, who, that asses were sacrificed by the Scythians?[176] Was it not above all Apollodorus along with the rest? Who that, while abusing the marriage couch of another, he was caught entangled in snares?[177] Was it not your writings, your plays?

Did[178] we ever write that the gods endured servitude for pay as did Hercules[179] at Sardis because of a wanton love affair; as did the Delian Apollo to Admetus;[180] as did the brother[181] of Jupiter to the Trojan Laomedon; as the Pythian also served the same man but with his uncle; as Minerva,[182] the supplier of light and the trimmer of lamps for those who indulge in secret loves? Is it not that bard[183] of yours who made out Mars and Venus as wounded by the hands of mortals? Is it not Panyassis,[184] one of you, who says that by Hercules Father Dis and Queen Juno were wounded? Do not the writings of your Polemon[185] tell that the virago[186] was

BOOK FOUR: CRITICISMS OF VARIOUS PAGAN GODS 397

beaten, bloodied, harassed by Ornytus? Does Sosibius [187] not declare that Hercules himself suffered the pain of a wound inflicted by the children of Hippocoon?

Is it handed down by us that in the island of Crete Jupiter was given burial?[188] Do we say that the brothers [189] who were united in the cradle were buried in the territories of Sparta and Lacedaemon? Is that writer identified in the titles of his works as Patrocles [190] the Thurine, ours, who relates that the tomb and remains of Saturn are found in the land of Sicily? Is Hieronymus,[191] is Plutarch shown to be one of us, who relate that Hercules, his strength wasted by epilepsy,[192] was reduced to ashes on the top of Mount Oeta?

26. But [193] what shall I say about those love affairs in which according to your literature and your writers the holy dwellers in heaven lusted after women? Is it we that claim that the king of the sea by the ardor of his lust robbed of their virgin purity the Amphitrites, Hippothoes, Amymones, Menalippes, Alcyones? That that spotless one, Apollo, Latona's son, most chaste and pure, sought after, with the passion of a thoughtless heart, Arsinoes,[194] Aethusas, Hypsipyles, Marpessas, Zeuxippas, and Prothoes, Daphnes, and Steropes?

Is it stated in our poems that the old man Saturn,[195] long since covered with white hair and already cold with the weight of years, when caught by his wife in adultery, put on the form of a beast and, neighing loudly, hurried away, in the shape of a steed?

Is Jupiter himself, king of the universe, not notorious among you for having assumed countless shapes and for having covered over by mean deceptions the ardor of his wanton love?[196] Has it ever been set down in writing by us that in order to consummate his stealthy lust, he at one time changed to gold,[197] at another into a sportive satyr, into a snake, into a bird, into a bull, and—a thing that outrivals every kind of disgrace—into a tiny little ant, so that, forsooth, he might make the daughter of Clitor the mother of Myrmidon among the Thessalians? Who made him spend nine long nights with Alcmene?[198] Was it not you? Who made him lie there dallying in love, having deserted his post in heaven? Was it not you? But of course you attribute to him a great service—there was born to you the god Hercules, who in matters such as these was to outstrip and surpass his father's accomplishments:[199] Hercules, holy god that he was, taught the fifty daughters of Thestius to do both—give up the claim of virginity and to bear the burden of mothers!

In addition, not satisfied with having ascribed to the gods passions for the female sex, you even maintain that males have been loved by them! Here some one loves Hylas,[200] there another is fascinated by Hyacinthus; that one burns with desire for Pelops; this one sighs ardently for Chrysippus; Catamitus is kidnapped to serve pleasures and the cups; and Fabius,[201] in order to become the pet of Jupiter, is branded and stamped on the thighs!

27. But now, as you have it, do only the males carry on loves and has the female sex preserved its chastity?[202] Is it not vouched for in your writings that Tithonus was loved by Aurora; that the Moon burned with love for Endymion; the Nereid for Aeacus; Thetis for the father of Achilles; Proserpina for Adonis; her mother Ceres after some rustic Iasion; and after Vulcan, Phaethon, Mars, Venus herself, the mother of the sons of Aeneas and source of Roman domination, for marriage with Anchises? Since, then, without a single exception, you indict with such monstrous outrages and infamies, not some single individual but the entire race of the gods alike in whose existence you believe, do you have the brazen-

BOOK FOUR: CRITICISMS OF VARIOUS PAGAN GODS   399

ness to say without blushing that we are wicked or that you are pious? And this, even though you give them greater cause to be offended because of all the shameful acts which you bring up to malign them than to feel extolled and honored by reason of the official rite of worship? Obviously, either these things which are brought against them individually, insulting their repute and their majesty, are false in their entirety; and this matter is one in which it would be perfectly right for the gods to wipe out entirely the whole race of mortals; or, if these things have been checked and found to be sure and proven beyond any doubt, it adds up to this that, however much you protest, we believe them to be not of a heavenly but of a human race.

28. Plainly, where there are weddings, marriages, childbirths, nurses, arts,[203] debilities; where there is liberty and slavery; where there are wounds, slaughter, bloodshed; where loves, desires, passions; where there is every frame of mind coming from restless emotions—there you have nothing divine, nor can that which is characteristic of a race prone to fall and one of terrestrial frailty[204] be part and parcel of a nature of higher sort. Who can, if he but recognizes and understands what that power stands for, believe that a god had members and was deprived of them by a most shameful mutilation;[205] or that he at one time did away with the children sprung from himself and was chastised by the punishment of chains; or that he, so to speak, engaged in civil war with his father and prevented him from exercising his royal prerogatives; or that he, terrified by the fear of an inferior, was conquered, turned tail, and, like a fugitive and exile, hid himself in the most inaccessible fastnesses?[206]

Who is there, I say, who would believe that a god reclined[207] at the tables of human beings, was slain because of avarice, deceived his suppliants by an ambiguous response, excelled in the tricks of thieves, committed adultery, was a slave, was wounded, and fell in love, and carried on the seduction of impure passions through all the forms of lust? And yet you declare that all those things both were and are in your gods, and you pass over no type of viciousness, evil-doing, aberration, which your rotten imaginations do not bring up as a reproach to your gods. Therefore, you either must search for other gods in whom all these things do not occur—for those in whom they do occur are of a human and earthly race—or if these whose names and character you have declared are the only ones who exist, you erase them by your beliefs. For all the things you relate are mortal.

Even pagan literature attests these charges.

29. And here we can show, of course, that all whom you represent to us and call gods, were men, by consulting Euhemerus of Acragas,[208] whose books Ennius translated into the Italic speech, that all might understand them, or Nicagoras of Cyprus, or Leon of Pella, or Theodorus of Cyrene, or Hippo and Diagoras, both of Melos, or a thousand other authors who with scrupulous diligence and care have brought to light with noble candor things obscured from view. We can, I say, if we wish, discuss the deeds of Jupiter and the wars of Minerva the virgin[209] and of Diana; by what tricks Liber[210] attempted to gain control of the Indian rule; what was the position, the occupation, and the endeavor of Venus; to whom the Great Mother was bound in marriage;[211] what hope, what pleasure was aroused in her by the comely Attis; whence the Egyptian Serapis,[212] whence Isis, or what occasioned the practice of calling them by names.

BOOK FOUR: CRITICISMS OF VARIOUS PAGAN GODS 401

True worship is in the heart, not in sacrifice.

30. It has not been our task or our intention, however, to show and make known who all these were. But because you call us impious and irreligious and maintain, on the other hand, that you are worshippers of the gods, we have set ourselves this task, of clearly demonstrating that no men treat them more shamefully than you do. So, if the very insults prove this so, it follows that you, who either hear or believe such nastiness about them or yourselves fabricate outrageous stories, must be understood to be the ones who rouse the gods to the furies of indignation. No, not he who with scrupulous care selects and slaughters unblemished victims, who contributes piles of incense to be burned with fire, should be thought to worship the gods, or to be the only one who discharges the duties of religion. True worship and a belief worthy of the gods are in the heart, and the offering of blood and gore avails naught, if you believe about them things which are not only far removed and utterly different from their nature but will result in a blot and stain to their majesty and honor.

31. Now, then, we would ask you a question and invite you to reply to our little discussion: do you count [213] it a more serious offense for a person to slaughter no victims to them because he thinks a nature so great neither wishes nor desires such things, or to have such wicked and filthy ideas about them that they could arouse in anyone's mind a mad urge for revenge? If the relative weight of these alternatives be determined, you will find no judge so hostile as not to think it more reprehensible to defame the reputation of anyone by blatant insults than to pass him over in silence. The latter, after all, can be interpreted and believed as having a

rational basis; the former reveals a sacrilegious mentality and an imagination hopelessly blind.

Considering that in your rituals and divine ceremonies there is a place for neglected sacrifices;[214] and that guilt is said to have been contracted, when by an error of inadvertence anyone has made a mistake in a word or in a sacrificial bowl; or again, that in the solemn games or sacred races you all immediately cry out that a violation of the sacred functions has taken place, when the player stands still or the flutist becomes silent,[215] or when the boy, the so-called *patrimus*,[216] through inexperience lets go the lines or fails to stay on his feet:[217] do you dare to deny that the gods are always being wronged by you in sins so serious, when you yourselves admit that in matters of lighter moment they are angered, often with results deleterious to the state?

The fictions of poets.

32. "But all these things," they say, "are the fictions of the poets and idle toyings gotten up for amusement."[218]

It certainly is incredible that men far from stupid, men who directed their research to the most remote antiquity, either[219] put into their poems stories which had not survived in the minds of men and had come to their attention, or that they should have wanted to arrogate to themselves such license as to fabricate in their folly things not far removed from madness, such as could cause them to stand in fear of the gods and in danger of men.

But let us grant that, as you say, the poets are the contrivers and inventors of so many insipidities. Even so you are not free from slandering the gods, you who neglect to punish such slanders or have failed by legislation providing for severe penalties to counteract such temerity and to ordain that henceforth no man was to utter what approached infamy or was unworthy of their majesties, the gods. Whoever suffers the wrongdoer to do wrong, supports him in his temerity; and it is more insulting to brand and mark anyone by false accusations than to inveigh against and upbraid true faults. To be told what you are and feel yourself to be, has a sting less painful, mitigated by the evidence derived from a silent review; but the hurt is a most grievous one when innocence is branded and a fair name and reputation are defamed.

33. Your gods are described as dining, drinking[220] on heavenly couches and in golden halls,[221] and, when they have finished, they are beguiled by the lyre and singing. You fit them with ears most long-suffering and judge it not unseemly to assign to the gods those pleasures by which earthly bodies are supported and which ears enervated by the disintegration of a weakened heart seek after.

Some of these are brought on as lovers, destroyers of chastity, and not only in relations with women but also with men in shameful and criminal intercourse. You do not care what is said about matters so grave and you do not restrain the boldness of your wanton literature even by the fear of punishment. Others through madness, through rage bereave themselves and thus spot themselves with murder of kin as if it were the blood of an enemy. You marvel at these sublimely exalted sacrileges, and what should have been subjected to all punishments, you extol with the stimulus of praise so as to cause effrontery to assert itself all the more proudly. They groan over the wounds of their bereavement, and with unseemly wailings accuse the cruel fates: you are awed at the power of their eloquence and what ought to have been entirely erased from the fellowship of the human race, you study carefully and learn by heart and take care that it not fall into any oblivion. They are spoken of as having been wounded, manhandled, of having made war on each other with hot and furious contests: you enjoy the account and in defense of such insolence on the part of the writers, you advance the excuse that such things are allegories and stand for the principles of natural science.[222]

34. But why do I complain of the indifference in regard to the insults offered to the other divinities? That Jupiter himself, whose name it behooved you not to speak without fear and trembling over your whole body, is described as having confessed his guilt when caught by his wife in a love affair, and, as if he were a fool and a dunce, giving out to the world in his inveterate shamelessness what mistresses, what concubines he preferred to his wife and spouse.

You set forth that those who have uttered such enormities are the princes and kings among the poets, men endowed with godlike genius, most sacred personalities, and so far have you put behind you your devotion to the religion you advocate that the words by which the sublimity of the heavenly ones is profaned are of graver moment to you. So, then, if you had any fear at all of the gods or if you believed with the confidence of a most certain conviction that they exist somewhere, should you not have really prevented, hindered, and forbidden by bills, popular ordinances, by fear of decrees of the Senate,[223] that anybody should wish to speak anywhere at all about the gods except with complete reverence?

And have they not merited at least this honor from you that you should repel wrongs from them by the same laws by which you repulse them from yourselves? Among you such as murmur something derogatory to the rulers are charged with treason.[224] To challenge a magistrate, to abuse a senator you have made a very dangerous thing by decreeing appro-

BOOK FOUR: CRITICISMS OF VARIOUS PAGAN GODS 405

priate penalties. The writing of a libellous poem by which the reputation and life of another is besmirched, you decided in the decrees of the decemvirs [225] should not go unpunished; and that no one might offend your ears with impudent abuse, you formulated legal proceedings for gross affronts. With you the gods alone are without honor—despicable, vile, against whom you have given a right to say whatever anyone wished, and to insult them with any shameful thoughts which frivolity can invent or think of.

And still you do not blush to charge us with want of regard for deities so decried, when it is much better not to believe gods exist than to suppose they are such and of such repute?

The fictions of the dramatists.

35. But [226] is it only the poets whom you were pleased to permit to devise unworthy stories and shameful buffooneries concerning the gods? What do your pantomimists, the actors, that mob of mimes and degenerates, do? Do they not abuse your gods to their own gain and use the wrongs and insults administered to the gods to pander to lust?

At the public shows the colleges of all the priests and magistrates take their seats—the chief pontiffs, and the chief priests of the *curiae*; [227] the *quindecimvirs* crowned with laurel and the *flamines diales* with their mitres take their seats; the augurs, interpreters of the divine thought and will, take their seats; so, too, the chaste Virgins, the replenishers and caretakers of the eternal fire; the whole people and the Senate take their seats; the fathers who have served as consuls; those who are next to the gods and most august—the rulers.[228] And—what should be blasphemy to the ear—that mother of the race of Mars and parent of the master race, Venus, is there dancing the part of an inamorata and is represented as going through the full gamut of passion, playing the wanton in lascivious imitation of the cheap harlot.

And there dances the Great Mother, adorned with her sacred fillets, and—to the disgrace of her age—[229] that Dindymene [230] of Pessinus is shown lusting with shameful passion for the embrace of a certain herdsman; and also in Sophocles' *Trachinian Women* [231] that scion of Jupiter, Hercules, enmeshed in the folds of a death-dealing garment [232] is shown as uttering pitiful moans, broken by the violence of his pain, and utterly wasting away and disintegrating by the corrosion of his vitals.

Yes, in the plays even the greatest ruler of the universe himself is brought in, without any dread at all of his name and majesty, to act the role of adulterers [233] and, [in fear] in order that he might lead astray the purity of the wives of others, putting on the mask of seduction and assuming the appearance of their husbands by counterfeiting a body not his own.

36. Nor is this crime enough. Even into farces and scurrilous plays the characters of the most holy gods are interjected, and to be able to draw a laugh and jollity from the idle spectators, the divinities are buffeted with pungent jibes, the theaters roar and stand up, the entire audience is delirious with clamor and applause. And—a thing for which no expiation is possible—for the debauched scoffers at the gods gifts and prizes are established, freedom from public obligations—exemptions from taxes and military service—together with triumphal crowns.[234]

And after that do you have the front to wonder whence come these ills with which mortality is deluged and oppressed without ceasing, when daily you go over and con daily all these things in which libels of the divinities and slanderous

Book Four: Criticisms of Various Pagan Gods 407

assertions are involved, and whenever you desire your lazy mind to be busied with idle drivelings, you demand that holidays [235] be given you and an exhibition be made of them without interruption?

But if any indignation possessed you in behalf of your religious beliefs, long ago you should rather have burned this literature, you should have destroyed such books, you should rather have torn down these theaters in which the infamies of the gods are daily made public in most shameful plays. Why, indeed, have our writings deserved to be given to the flames? [236] Why should our meeting-places be savagely torn down? In them the Supreme God [237] is prayed to, peace and forgiveness asked for all magistrates, armies, rulers, friends, enemies; for those still living and those freed from the bonds of the body; in which nothing else is said [238] but what makes men kind, what makes men gentle, modest, virtuous, chaste, sharers of their own substance, and united by the bonds of kinship with all on whom the sun shines. [239]

If the divine anger really exists, it is directed against the pagans.

37. But the fact in the case is this, that since you are all-powerful with swords and the might of steel, you deem yourself superior also in the knowledge of the truth and pious before the gods whose might you have been the first to pollute by the foul notions you have regarding them. At this juncture, if your fierceness allows it and your frenzy is patient enough, we ask you to tell us: do you think anger enters into the nature of the gods? Or is the divine blessedness far removed from these emotions? [240] If they fly into such passion and are enraged by the feelings of anger, as your notions suggest—for you say they have often fumed vengeance so

that the lands trembled, and have diseased with pestilential contagion the gentle zephyrs, bringing dire destruction to the people because of games conducted without sufficient care, and because of "dancers" they did not approve of,[241] and because certain premises were desecrated, and because ceremonials were not performed according to ritual—it follows that one should realize that they harbor no small anger on account of the aforesaid opinions.

But if, and this is a necessary conclusion, it be admitted that all these miseries, which for a long time have overwhelmed the human race, flow from fables of this kind; if it is from these causes that the anger of the divinities proceeds, then it is you who are the occasion for such great afflictions because you never cease to offend the spirits of the heaven dwellers and to arouse them to a rage for vengeance. But, if, on the other hand, the race of the gods is not subject to rages of this kind, and does not know at all what it is to be angry, then there is no reason for the assertion that they, who do not know what anger is, are said to be enraged at us, and they are free from its fetters[242] and confusion.

[For[243] by the nature of things it cannot happen that what is one should become two, and that what is by its nature an uncompounded unit should resolve into separate things.][244]

BOOK FIVE

Jupiter Elicius, Attis, and the Mysteries

The myth of Jupiter Elicius.

1. Well, let us grant that all those things have been handed down and ⟨brought in⟩ to the disgrace of the gods by the poets in a spirit of jest. But what of those things which are found in histories, weighty and serious and carefully done, and which are contained in the hidden mysteries handed down—are these mere rogueries devised by the poets? If they seemed to you such absurd stories, you would hardly accord some of them the greatest[1] popularity, nor, as the years rolled by, would you celebrate them as joyous festivals, nor would you preserve them in your sacred ceremonials as harking back to actual events.

Now, then, following a policy of moderation, I shall mention only one example out of so many: the one in which that Jupiter himself is brought out on the stage as an unwary dunce, the dupe of verbal ambiguities.

In the second book of Antias[2]—lest any one think us fabricating accusations, bent on slander—the following tale is recorded: King Numa,[3] not possessing a knowledge of how to avert evil portended by a thunderbolt and being desirous of learning, on the advice of Egeria[4] concealed at a fountain twelve chaste youths who were supplied with fetters, so that when Faunus[5] and Martius Picus[6] should come there[7] to drink—for here they usually came for water—they might fall upon them, seize and bind them. But to expedite matters, the king filled a goodly number of cups with wine and mead and placed them about the approaches to the fountain as a crafty snare in the path of their coming. They, following their usual custom, yielding to their thirst for drink, came to the familiar resting place. But the moment they had gotten a whiff of the cups fragrant with sweet-smelling liquors, they preferred the new to the old. Eagerly they rushed at them. Overpowered by the sweet savor of the drink, they imbibed too freely, and, becoming drowsy, fell asleep. Then the twelve piled upon the sleepers, cast chains around them in their drunken stupor. And when the latter had come to, they forthwith instructed the king by what means and sacrifices Jupiter could be "elicited"[8] to earth; and the king in possession of this knowledge performed the sacred act on the Aventine, "elicited" Jupiter down to the earth, and requested of him the proper ritual of expiating omens.

After long hesitation, Jupiter said,[9] "You shall expiate lightning omens with a head."[10]

"With an onion head,"[11] the king said in turn.

"With a man's," Jupiter rejoined.

"But with a head of hair," the king replied.

"With a living one,"[12] the god protested.

⟨"With a maena,"⟩[13] Pompilius continued.

Then Jupiter, tripped up by the ambiguities set forth, exclaimed as follows: "You have tricked me, for I had decided that evils portended by lightning should be averted by human heads, not by a *maena*, by hair, by an onion. But now that your cleverness has outmaneuvered me, observe the practice which you wished and always undertake the expiation of lightning portents by those means which you have stipulated."[14]

Book Five: Jupiter Elicius, Attis, Mysteries 411

Criticism of this myth.

2. What to take up first, what last, or what should be passed over in silence, is not easy to say nor does any amount of reflection clarify matters. Everything in this story is so concocted and construed as to make it ridiculous, so much so as to make it really incumbent on you to endeavor to have it thought false, even if true, rather than to want it to be taken for the truth, and to suggest, as it were—and this not without disrespect to the divinity itself—that we are in the presence of something extraordinary.

What, then, is it you say, you—?[15] Are we to believe that that Faunus and Martius Picus, if they really belong to the gods and are possessed of that eternal and immortal nature, were once upon a time parched with thirst, and to be able to cool the heat in their veins, went[16] to the flowing fountains? Are we to believe that seduced by wine and enticed by the sweetness of mead, they guzzled the deceitful cups so long that they even got into danger of becoming drunk? Are we to believe that shackled by sleep and immersed in deep slumber's oblivion, they gave earthly creatures an opportunity to put them in bonds? On what parts, moreover, were those bonds flung so as to tie them? Did they have any substance, or did they have hands formed of hard bones, so that they could be bound up by fetters and restrained by the tying of knots? I do not insist on asking whether they were able to say anything as they staggered in their drunken stupor; or whether, even though Jupiter was unwilling, or, rather, unwitting, any one could have made known the ritual for bringing him down to earth. This only I should like to hear: why, if Faunus and Picus are really divine in origin and power, they themselves did not rather answer the query of Numa, the answer to which he sought to hear, at a greater risk, from Jupiter himself?

Or did Jupiter alone have knowledge of this thing? Is it upon him [17] that thunderbolts fall so that he has need of training in some knowledge to avert dangers impending? Or, while he himself hurls these flashes of lightning, is it the business of others to know what means are best adapted to temper his wrathful moods? As a matter of fact it is most stupid to believe that he himself is an expert in the means by which that can be averted which he has decided should take place in human affairs through the hurling of the thunderbolt. This amounts to saying: "By that kind of ceremony you will appease my wrath; and if ever by flashes of lightning I shall make known that something is about to happen, then do this and that, ⟨so that⟩ what I have decided should be done may be cancelled and voided and made to vanish ⟨in virtue⟩ [18] of these sacrificial rites."

3. But let us grant that, as is said, Jupiter himself ordained ways and means against himself by which properly to oppose his own purposes. Are we to believe further that a god of such great power was drawn down to earth and, standing with a miserable man [19] on a petty hillock, entered into a disputatious wrangle? And what divine thing was it, I ask, which forced Jupiter to abandon the great task of propelling the universe and to place himself at the behests of mortals? Salted meal, incense,[20] blood, scent of burning boughs, and the mutterings of dread words? And were all these things more powerful than Jupiter so that they forced him against his will to obey instructions or to surrender of his own accord to their tricks? Tell me, will the conclusion be believed [or] that the son of Saturn was so lacking in foresight that he set down the terms by which he himself was to be ensnared

through equivocations or that he did not know the future, the means by which the craftiness and shrewdness of a mortal would make sport of him?

"You shall expiate," says he, "lightning omens with a head."

The utterance is incomplete and the sense of the statement lacks full precision. Really, one should know whether Diespiter ordains said expiation to be carried out by using a ram's head, a pig's, or an ox's, or some other kind. And when he had not yet specifically settled this point and the decision was still pending and not yet determined, how could Numa know that Jupiter would say the head of a man, ⟨so that⟩ he could anticipate, head him off, and steer his uncertain and ambiguous words into an onion head?

4. Well, perhaps you will say that the king was divine: could he be more divine than Jupiter himself? A mortal man,[21] anticipating what Jupiter would say, outwitted ⟨a god⟩: was the god unable to know how the man was preparing to outwit him? Is it not, then, patent and clear that these are the feeble fancies of puerile inventions, by which a deft wit is accredited to Numa and the greatest lack of intelligence brought in for Jupiter? What betrays so little intelligence as to have been caught by the cleverness of a man's wit, and when you are annoyed at being tricked, to give in to the will of him who bested you and to set aside the antidote which you had offered? If there was a reason and a certain natural propriety why the averting of an evil portended by lightning should be undertaken with a human head, I do not see why the suggestion of an onion head was made by the king; if, however, it could have been settled by an onion head also, there was a case of greedy lusting for human gore. And so on both sides they contradict them-

selves: on the one hand, Numa plainly did not want to know what he wanted [22] and Jupiter evidently was cruel since he said that he wanted what could have been taken care of by a *maena* and an onion head to be averted with human heads.

The myth of Attis.

5. In Timotheus,[23] a man not unknown among theologians, and among others, too, equally learned, the following story is told [24] concerning the origin of the Great Mother of the Gods and concerning her sacrifices as dug up out of obscure books of antiquities and from the most esoteric mysteries, as he himself writes and implies.

In [25] the territory of Phrygia there is, he says, a rock of an unheard-of desolation throughout, the name of which is Agdus, so called by the natives of that region. Stones taken from it, as Themis had enjoined by an oracle,[26] were thrown on the earth, empty of mortals, by Deucalion and Pyrrha;[27] and from these, along with the others, this Great Mother,[28] as she is called, was shaped and given divine breath. Her, resting and sleeping on the very crest of the rock, Jupiter craved for himself with incestuous desires. But in spite of his continued efforts, he failed to accomplish what he had proposed to himself and was defeated. Then the rock conceived and, with many groans going before, in the tenth month, Acdestis [29] is born, so called from his mother's name. In him there was insuperable strength and uncontrollable ferocity of disposition, a lust mad and furious and stimulated by both sexes. Violently he plundered, laid waste, wherever his monstrous spirit led him. He cared not for the gods nor men, nor did he think anything more powerful than himself; he despised earth, heaven, and the stars.

6. When in the councils of the gods the question was

BOOK FIVE: JUPITER ELICIUS, ATTIS, MYSTERIES 415

brought up again and again how his insolence could be either tamed or suppressed, Liber,[30] the rest holding back, takes the task upon himself. With most potent wine he fortifies a spring which that fellow knew well and where he had been wont to slake his burning thirst roused by sport and hunting. On an occasion when he felt the need of it, Acdestis runs hither to drink. He gulps down an immoderate draught into his eager veins. Overcome by this unaccustomed experience, he sinks into a most profound sleep. Liber lurks nearby in ambush.[31] Over his foot he casts the end of a noose woven cunningly of hairs. When the power of the wine had been slept off, he jumps up violently and, straining hard on the knots he himself, by his own strength, robs himself of that by which he had been ⟨a man⟩. There is an immense flow of blood; this is snatched up and swallowed by the earth; thence suddenly is born a pomegranate tree with apples. Nana,[32] daughter of the king or river Sangarius, gazing in astonishment at the beauty of this fruit, plucks and takes some to her bosom. By this she becomes pregnant. As if she had been ravished, her father shuts her up and tries to have her die of starvation. With apples and other food she is supported by the Mother of the Gods. She labors and is delivered of a child, but Sangarius orders it to be exposed. Somebody finds it and takes it,[33] nourishes it on he-goat's[34] milk, and because Lydia[35] calls people who are handsome thus, or because the Phrygians in their dialect name goats *attagi*,[36] it happened that the boy's name Attis was thus derived. Him the Mother of the Gods loved as none other because he was most superb of countenance. Acdestis ⟨loved⟩ him also, his doting companion in his adolescence and who in the only way remaining bound him to himself by his improper attentions, taking him through the wooded glades and giving him many gifts of wild beasts. These the boy Attis at first boasted were the fruit of his own toil and labor; later, under the influence of wine, he admits that he is loved by Acdestis and from him receives woodland gifts as rewards. For this reason it is forbidden for those polluted with wine to enter his sanctuary because it betrayed his silence.

7. Then the king of Pessinus,[37] Midas,[38] desiring to win the boy away from so disgraceful an association, plans to give him his daughter in marriage, and so that no one of sinister omen might break in upon their marriage joys, he caused the town to be closed. But the Mother of the Gods, knowing the youth's fate, and that he would be safe among human beings so long as he was free of a matrimonial alliance, to prevent anything untoward from happening, enters the closed city, having lifted its walls with her head, which began to have towers because of this. As for Acdestis,[39] bursting with anger at having the boy torn from him and brought to have interest in a wife, he inspires all the guests with fury and madness. Terror-stricken, the Phrygians cry out "Adore, adore";[40] the daughter of the concubine[41] of Gallus[42] cuts off her breasts, ⟨in emulation of the self-mutilator⟩. Attis snatches the flute which the one who was goading them to fury was carrying, and being himself full of frenzy, and roving about, hurls himself down at last, and under a pine tree mutilates himself.[43]

With the stream of blood his life flits away. From the blood which flowed, a flower springs up, the violet,[44] and entwines the tree. Thence was derived and arose the custom that even now the sacred pines are veiled and garlanded.[45] The maiden who had been the bride, whom Valerius[46] the pontifex writes was named Ia, covers the breast of the lifeless one with soft wool, sheds tears with Acdestis, and slays herself. When she dies, her blood is changed into purple violets. The Mother of the Gods digs under these,[47] from which an almond grows,

Book Five: Jupiter Elicius, Attis, Mysteries

signifying the bitterness of burial. She then bears away the pine tree under which Attis had robbed himself of his manhood, to her cave, and about the trunk of the motionless tree, joining in lamentations with Acdestis, she beats and wounds her breast.[48] Jupiter refuses Acdestis' request that Attis might come back to life. But what is possible by concession of fate, this he grants without objecting: that his body should not decay, that his hair should ever grow,[49] that the very smallest[50] of his fingers should live and alone react by continued motion. Satisfied with these favors, Acdestis, it is said, consecrated the body in Pessinus, and honored it with annual rites and with a sacred ministry.[51]

Criticism of this myth.

8. If some despiser of the deities and one crazed with a wild sacrilegious heart had intended to revile your gods, would he have the gall to say anything against them more serious than this story brings? And this, as if it were something wonderful, you have reduced to a formal record and, lest time and the long years of antiquity should consign it to oblivion, you have glorified it with honor everlasting! Indeed, what is there asserted or written in it about the gods which, if you should say it about a man of disreputable character and one brought up with all too unrefined training, you would not be subject to a court charge of slander and as a result your wrongs and insults incur hatred accompanied by implacable resentment?

From the stones, you say, which Deucalion and Pyrrha threw, the Mother of the Gods was begotten. O you theologians, you priests of the powers on high! What is this you say? There was no Mother of the Gods anywhere in nature ⟨before⟩ the disaster of the flood? And had not violent downpours of rain taken away the whole race of mortals, then there would have been no cause and occasion of her birth? So she owes it to man that she sees herself existing, and it is to the kindness of Pyrrha she owes the fact that she sees herself possessed of substance. And, of course, if this is true, then, too, it will of necessity be most true that she was human, not divine. Assuredly, if it is certain that men trace their birth to that casting of stones, she also must be believed to have been one of us, begotten as she is by means of like causes. For it was an impossible contradiction in nature that from one and the same type of stones and from an identical method of throwing them, some should be allotted immortality, others a human status.

Varro,[52] that famous Roman, outstanding for the broadness of his learning and a thorough investigator of antiquity, in the first of four books of a work which he has left *On the Race of the Roman People*, shows by careful computations that from the time of the deluge, which we have mentioned above, up to the consulship of Hirtius and Pansa,[53] there are not quite two thousand years. If credence be given him, the Great Mother, too, it must be said, is limited to this number's span for her existence.[54] And so the matter boils down to this that she who is said to be the maternal parent of all the gods is not their mother but their daughter; yes, she is just a baby girl, if indeed, we grant that in the eternal succession of ages the gods have been accorded neither beginnings nor endings.

9. But why should we speak of your having besmirched the Mother of the Gods with earthly lowliness, when you have been unable to pause at all for even a moment's interruption from blaspheming Jupiter himself? While the Mother of the Gods was asleep on the highest point of

BOOK FIVE: JUPITER ELICIUS, ATTIS, MYSTERIES 419

Agdus, her son, you say, tried stealthily to waylay her chastity as she rested.

Having robbed of their chastity countless maidens and matrons, did Jupiter conceive the hope of an unspeakable lust even against his mother? And from that lustful passion was it impossible for him to be turned away by the revulsion with which nature herself and that inborn common instinct has endowed not only human beings[55] but also many of the animals? Or was filial regard and regard for propriety wanting in him who presides over the Capitols, and in the confusion of his crazed mind was he unable to reflect and realize what crime he was bent upon? But, be that as it may, oblivious of his prestige and majesty, he kept sneaking forward toward that shocking theft, trembling and shaking, holding his breath, walking panicky on tiptoe, and wavering between anxiety and hope, touched her, trying to see how soundly his mother was sleeping and what she would allow.

O abominable representation! O shameful figure of Jupiter ready to attempt a filthy struggle! And so that ruler of the world when, because of his heedlessness and haste he was repulsed from his stealthy foray, turned to the use of force, and since he could not steal his pleasure by cunning, violently attacked his mother, and proceeded most openly to tear down the chastity he ought to have revered? Having struggled, then, a long time with her who would not yield, did he give up—beaten, tamed, overcome?[56]

10. Well, perhaps you will say: The human race shuns and abhors intercourse in this kind of union; but among the gods there is no incest.

And why did his mother fight back her son most bitterly when he was trying to force her? Why did she flee from contact with him as if she were avoiding something forbidden in his embraces? If there was nothing wrong in the matter, she should have been just as compliant without showing any reluctance, as he was eager to satisfy the cravings of his passion.[57] And, pray, what followed? Tell us!

"In the inner bosom of the stone and in the hard flint a babe was fashioned and given life, destined to be the great Jupiter's offspring."

It is not an easy matter to raise objections in the presence of conceptions so marvellous and so extraordinary! If, however, according to you the human race is sprung and begotten from stones, one is forced to the belief that the stone had generative organs and conceived and with the lapse of time bore pregnant wombs and at last gave birth, travailing in pain, as women do.

That forces our curiosity to inquire: since you say that after ten months issue was given forth, in what womb of the rock was it enclosed during that period? With what foods, with what liquids was it sustained? Or what nourishment could it draw from the hard stone, such as unborn infants normally do from their mothers?

"Not yet," he says, "had he reached the light of day and already he was bellowing and imitating and reproducing his father's thunderings."

And once it was given to him to look upon heaven and day, he attacked and laid waste whatever crossed his path and was confident that he could evict even the gods themselves from heaven's realm. Yes, how cautious and foresighted the Mother of the Gods! She, that she might not load upon herself the hatred stirred up by so insolent a son, or that his bellowing, while still unborn, might not disturb her slumbers or interrupt her rest, took herself away and put far from her the most ruinous venom of that seed and passed it on to the jagged rocks!

11. The tide of opinion flowed back and forth in the councils of the gods: how was that unyielding fierceness to be subdued? And when no other means remained, recourse was had to one unique—that he should be swilled with a great dosage of wine and deprived of his virility through castration. As if, indeed, those who have been subjected to such mutilation of body become less brazen, and as if we do not daily see them becoming more wanton and laying aside every restraint of shame and modesty breaking forth into filthy vileness, making open admission of their abominable conduct.[58]

I should like, however, to have seen—had it been granted me to be born in those times—how that Father Liber, the subduer of the Acdestian fierceness, gliding down from the pinnacles of heaven after the most august session of the gods, bobbing the tails of old nags,[59] braiding flexible nooses, inebriating[60] the pure innocent water with a great quantity of sheer wine; how then, when drunkenness ⟨had sunk Acdestis⟩ who had imbibed all too immoderately ⟨into a most profound sleep⟩,[61] he carefully directed his attention to the things that were doomed to perish.

12. Could anyone, even when tainted by a very low opinion of them, say this about the gods? Or if they did occupy themselves with such activities, considerations, cares, would any wise person believe that they were gods or reckon them even among men? Your fellow Acdestis, pray, whose mutilation was to bring security to the heaven dwellers, was he one of the creatures of earth or some one of the gods and endowed with the dignity of immortality? If he was held to be a sharer of our human lot and station, why was he causing so much fear among the deities? If, however, he was a god, how could be he deceived, or how could anything be severed from[62] a divine body? But on this point we raise no question.

He may have been of divine birth, or one of us, if you think it better to say so. Did a pomegranate also spring up from the flow of blood? Or because the earth's power covered in its bosom so great a thing, did it lay hold of the ground with a root, spring up into a mighty tree, shoot forth branches loaded with wild pomegranate blossoms and in a moment of time bear mellow apples, perfectly and completely ripe? And because these sprang from red blood, is their color, therefore, purple [63] tinged with a touch of golden light? [64] Say also that they are for this reason juicy, for this reason wine-tart, because they derive their origin from the blood of one soaked in wine,[65] and you have completed a right pretty tale!

O Abdera,[66] Abdera, what opportunities ⟨would you give⟩ to mortals for laughing at you if you had concocted such a tale! All the fathers [67] tell it and proud states peruse it, but you are judged to be a nitwit and most hopelessly stupid.

13. "Through her bosom," he says, "Nana conceived a son from an apple."

The explanation is self-evident: where rocks and hard stones give birth, there of necessity apples also have the generative faculty.

"The Berecyntian [68] fed the imprisoned girl on acorns and figs."

Properly and rightly, for she who was made a mother by a fruit ought to have lived on fruit.

"After the offspring was delivered, Sangarius ordered it to be cast far away."

What he had long before believed to have been divinely conceived, he disdained to recognize as the offspring of his dear daughter! [69]

"The infant was brought up on he-goat's [70] milk."

What a story, ever hostile and most obnoxious to the male

sex, in which men not only lay aside their manly sex but even male animals become mothers!

"He was outstanding for his singular beauty and his handsomeness was something to talk about."

It is really something that the stench of the goat did not make people shun him and run away!

"The Great Mother loved him."

If as a grandmother, her grandson, there is nothing unusual in that; but if it was as the theaters blare out, the love [71] is infamous and scandalous.

"Acdestis also was his lover and gave him generous gifts from the hunt."

A half-man could not, it is true, be a danger to his purity; but is it not easy for the suspicious to guess what Midas shuddered at? [72]

"The Mother entered in with the very walls." [73]

Here we marvel, indeed, at the mighty powers of the divinity, but then again we blame her for her carelessness because, although she remembered fate's decree, in her heedlessness she laid bare the city to enemies.

"Those celebrating the nuptial vows Acdestis aroused to fury and madness."

If King Midas, who was trying to tie the youth to a wife, had offended him, what had Gallus done, what the concubine's daughter, that he should rob himself of his manhood, she rob herself of the glory of her breasts? [74]

14. What have you to say, you gentiles, you pagans devoted to beliefs of this sort? When such things are put forth, are you not seized with shame and do you not blush in the presence of such indecencies? We are eager to hear and learn from you something worthy of the gods, but no—you keep on handing out stories about mutilations, ragings,

blood, mad frenzies, suicides of maidens, and flowers and trees produced from the blood of the dead.[75]

When you read through such stories, I ask, do you not have the impression that you are listening to girls at the loom beguiling the boredom of a tedious task, or old women [76] trying hard to distract credulous children, and giving out all sorts of fiction under the guise of truth?

"Acdestis spoke with Jupiter to restore life to his beloved. Jupiter refused assent because he was prevented by fates more powerful. But not to be completely hardhearted, he granted one favor: the body was not to undergo any putrefaction, the hair was to continue to grow out, the smallest of the fingers alone was to live in the body, alone was to show constant motion."

Is there anyone who will admit this or support and yield belief to the view that hair grows on the dead;[77] that a part ⟨did not⟩ perish and that freed from the law of putrefaction his mortal body remains even to the present?

It is the pagans, not the Christians, who are at fault.

15. Long ago we might have urged you to test this point if it were not equally stupid to say such things and to demand proofs of them. At any rate this story is false and contains not a particle of truth in it. It matters not to us on whose account you claim the gods have been driven from the earth; whether it is consistent and based on firm belief or, on the contrary, is fashioned with deceit and somehow is a false fabrication. It is enough for us who have today undertaken to make plain that those divinities you bring forth, if they exist anywhere in the world and grow hot with the heat of anger, derive their raging wrath no more from us than from you;[78] and that that story has been reported as a fact and put into written form by

BOOK FIVE: JUPITER ELICIUS, ATTIS, MYSTERIES 425

you, and because you wish this to be daily reading and to be handed down for each succeeding generation in the future.

Now if this is true, we see no reason why the gods who dwell in heaven should be said to be angry at us when we have neither passed on against them such infamies nor committed them to writing nor proclaimed them to be a public witness in the celebration of sacred rites. But on the other hand, if, as you think, it is false and a concatenation of deceptive lies, no man can doubt that you are the cause of the offense since you either have permitted certain people to write such things down or, once written down, have suffered them to endure in the memory of the ages.

The ceremonials of the Mother of the Gods show this.

16. And for all that, how can you assert that representation not to be true when the very rites you continue to practice at each returning anniversary are evidence that you believe it to be true and consider that it has been verified and found worthy of credence? What, for example, does that pine mean which you always introduce on appointed days into the sanctuary of the Mother of the Gods? Is it not symbolic of that tree under which the mad and unhappy youth laid hands on himself and which the parent of the gods consecrated as a solace for her grief? What is the meaning of the fleeces of wool with which you bind and surround the trunk of the tree? Is it not a recollection of the woolens with which Ia covered him who was expiring and believed that she could procure some warmth for his limbs as they grew cold? What is the meaning of the little branches of the tree decked and girt round with garlands of violets? Do they not signify how the Mother adorned the pine with the earliest blossoms, as a

memorial and testimony of her sad misfortune? What is the meaning of the Galli [79] with hair dishevelled, beating their breasts with their hands? Do they not commemorate the sorrow with which the tower-bearing [80] Mother, together with the tearful Acdestis, lamented the boy? What is the meaning of the fasting from bread to which you have given the term *castus*? [81] Is it not an imitation of the time when in the poignancy of her grief the divinity abstained from Ceres' fruit?

17. Or if what we say is not so, speak out, tell us yourselves: those eunuchs and effeminates [82] we see in your midst in the services for that divinity—what is their business there, what their concern, their charge? And why do they like mourners beat their arms and breasts and represent the misfortune of those who experience a woeful lot? What is the meaning of those garlands, those violets, those swathings and coverings of soft wool? Why, finally, is the pine itself, a little while before swaying in the thickets—an utterly inert piece of wood—next set up in the quarters of the Mother of the Gods like some present and most august divinity? Well, either this is the cause—the one we have found in your writings and treatises, and it is clear that you do not practice divine rites but that you are giving a representation of sad events; or, if there is another reason which the obscurity of the mystery has withheld from us, it too, must be involved in the infamy of some disgrace. Indeed, who is there that would believe that there is anything noble in what those worthless Galli put their hands to, what effeminate debauchees perform?

Various mysteries.

18. The importance of the subject as well as the task of the defense itself really demand that we should likewise pur-

BOOK FIVE: JUPITER ELICIUS, ATTIS, MYSTERIES

sue other types of infamy, those which the histories of antiquity supply or those sacred mysteries called "initiations"[83] contain, which you do not divulge to all but hand down to the secrecy of a few. But the countless rituals of these ceremonies and the loathsomeness attaching to each of them prevents us from going through them all one by one. Indeed, to tell the truth, from certain ones we purposely and intentionally turn aside, lest in striving to unfold everything, we be defiled by the pollution of that exposition.[84]

Let us, therefore, pass over Fenta Fatua[85] who is called the "Good Goddess," whom Sextus Clodius[86] in his sixth book in Greek *On the Gods* says was beaten to death by myrtle sticks because without her husband's knowledge she drank a whole jar of wine; and a sign of this becomes evident from the fact that when women conduct divine services in her honor, a covered jar of wine is placed there and it is unlawful to bring in myrtle twigs, as Butas[87] writes in his *Causalia*.

But[88] let us also in like manner ignore and say nothing about the dii Conserentes, whom Flaccus[89] among others writes buried ⟨themselves⟩ in the ash which had been made under a pot of entrails.

19. We shall also pass by the wild Bacchanalia[90] bearing in Greek the name of Omophagia[91] in which with pretended frenzy and with sanity of mind set aside, you bind around you snakes, and to show yourselves full of the divinity and majesty of the god, tear asunder with gory jaws the flesh of loudly-bleating goats.[92] And those hidden mysteries of the Cyprian Venus[93] we pass by also, of whom the founder is said to have been King Cinyras,[94] in which those who take[95] them bring stipulated fees as to a harlot and carry away obscene tokens, given them as a sign of the propitious divinity.[96]

Consign to oblivion also the rites of the Corybantes[97] in

which this holy mystery is handed down: a brother[98] was slain by brothers, from the blood of the murdered parsley sprang up—that plant forbidden to be placed on the tables lest the shades of the dead be unappeasably offended. And we also refrain from speaking of those other Bacchanalia in which a sacred secret which must not even be uttered is revealed and communicated to the initiated: how Liber[99] when busy with boyish pranks was torn asunder by the Titans; how he was cut up, limb by limb, and thrown into pots to be cooked; how Jupiter enticed there by the savory odor, came flying to the meal uninvited; and when he discovered the awful thing, overwhelmed the revellers with his thunderbolt and hurled them into the lowest quarters of Tartarus. As evidence and proof of this, the Thracian[100] in his poems handed down the dice, mirror, spinning tops, wheels, and smooth balls, and the golden apples taken from the virgin Hesperides.

The Sabazian mysteries.

20. We had in mind to pass by, to leave unnoticed also those mysteries into which Phrygia is initiated, and all that race,[101] except for the fact that the name of Jupiter, inserted by them forbids us cursorily to pass by the wrongs and slanders he undergoes; not that we take pleasure in deriding those shameful mysteries, but in order that it may be made clear to you again and again what wrong you heap upon those whose guardians, champions, worshippers you profess yourselves to be.

Once upon a time Diespiter, they say, when he was seething with wicked passions and with lusts illicit for his mother Ceres—for the inhabitants of that region say she is Jupiter's mother—but not daring to seek by plain force what he had conceived in his lewd desire, contrived some clever strategy

BOOK FIVE: JUPITER ELICIUS, ATTIS, MYSTERIES 429

by which to defile his mother without her suspecting any such thing. From being a god he becomes a bull and under the appearance of an animal, concealing reckless design of ambushing her, he suddenly rushes with mad force upon her, unconcerned and unsuspecting; and when his passion betrays his deception, he speeds away, known and recognized. His mother burns, foams, pants, boils with furious wrath, and being unable to repress the howling tempest of her rage, received thereafter the name Brimo[102] from her continued emotion, and she has no concern more urgent than that she should punish the temerity of her son with whatever penalties she can.

21. Jupiter is in trouble, cowed with fear, and cannot think up any means by which to palliate the feelings of the outraged woman. He pleads and pleads and make supplication: the ears of the grief-stricken are closed. The entire galaxy of the gods is delegated to intercede for him: the authority of none is big enough to merit a hearing.[103] At last the son, seeking ways to give satisfaction, hits on the following expedient: he selects a full-blooded ram and mutilates it. Then, sadly approaching his mother with eyes cast down, and as if he had by his own judgment condemned himself, he casts and throws what he had taken, into her lap. She sees the pledge, she takes on a gentler mood and takes an interest in the child she has conceived. After the tenth month she bears a daughter of most fair form, whom the following ages of mortals named sometimes Libera,[104] sometimes Proserpina.[105] When like a wether Jupiter saw her, a picture of health and in the full bloom of life, forgetting what evils and crime and what foolhardiness he had plunged in shortly before, he returns to his former doings; and because it seemed quite impious for a father to consort with his daughter in wifely embrace, he

changes into the fell form of a dragon. He entwines the terrified maiden with his huge coils and in gruesome disguise, sports and caresses her with the gentlest of embraces. As a result she too conceives of most powerful Jupiter, but not on the same terms as her mother, for she bore a daughter resembling herself; but the maiden's issue had the appearance of a bull, a memorial to seduction by Jupiter.[106] Someone will want to know the author of the story: we shall then cite the well-known senarian by the Tarentine[107] which antiquity sings, saying:

> The bull begat a dragon and the dragon a bull.

Lastly, the rites themselves and the ceremonials of the initiation itself which bear the name of Sebadia[108] can witness to their truth: in these a golden snake is let down into the bosom of the initiated[109] and taken away again.

Jupiter is charged with all wickedness.

22. Here, too, I think it unnecessary to make a long story, going individually through all, and to show what baseness and shame well forth from each in particular. What mortal who possesses even a particle of human feeling would not himself see clearly these things for what they are, how wicked, how filthy, and what ignominies the gods bear from the very mystery's rites and from the unseemly origins of the rites?

Jupiter, it is said, burned with love for Ceres. Why, I ask, has that Jupiter, whoever he is, deserved so ill of you that there is no kind of shame, infamy, no adultery, which you do not heap upon his head as if he were some vile and worthless character? Leda[110] betrayed her marriage obligation: Jupiter is said to be responsible for her guilt. Danae could not protect her virginity: Jupiter is said to have stolen it. Europa

Book Five: Jupiter Elicius, Attis, Mysteries 431

hastened to become a woman: the same one, so the story goes, was the conqueror of her chastity. Alcmene, Electra, Latona, Laodamia, a thousand other mothers and with them Catamitus [111] were robbed of their honor, their chastity: everywhere it is always the same story—Jupiter. Nor is there any kind of depravity in which you do not link his name with the lusts associated with them, so that the wretch simply does not seem to have been born for any other reason at all than that he be a headquarters for crimes, a subject for blasphemy, a sort of open place into which filth of every kind should pour itself in the backwash of the stage.[112] Still, were you to say he had commerce with strange women, this would indeed be wicked but a libellous wrong that could be borne with. Did he not lust even after his mother, even after his daughter, with the passions of a maddened heart,[113] and no filial piety, no reverence for his mother, no dread of the child of his own loins, could keep him from the representation of so foul a thought?

The stories show Jupiter does not exist.

23. And so I should like to see Jupiter, that father of the gods, the eternal power of the universe and of men,[114] adorned [115] with oxhorns, shaking his shaggy ears, with his feet compressed into hooves, chewing a cud of green grass, and on his hinder part a tail, hocks, ankles, all smeared with soft dung and bedaubed with intestinal filth. Yes—for this should be mentioned frequently—I should like to see him who turns the stars and who terrifies and frightens nations pale with fear at his thundering, chasing the flocks of wethers, looking over the rams, using that censorial [116] and divine hand with which he was accustomed to shake the gleaming lightnings and to rage with thunderbolts! Then, next, to see him ripping open the insides,[117] and without witnesses, tear-

ing away the membranes, and offering it to his mother, when she was still boiling with rage, as so many fillets of a suppliant for drawing compassion from her; cast down, pale, miserable —faking the torments of pain and to make this plausible, bespattered with the blood of the ram and for a pretense of a wound covered with wool and linen bandages!

And something like this can be heard and read under heaven?[118] And those who deal in these things wish to be thought righteous, holy, and guardians of religion? Is there any greater sacrilege than this, or can any mind be found so imbued with impious ideas as to believe such things or receive them or hand them down in the most secret mystery cults? That Jupiter—whoever he is—if he felt he existed or if he were affected by any sense of wrong—would it not be the proper thing for him, angered and aroused, to take the earth from under our feet, to put out the light of the sun and moon, yes, indeed, to throw all things into one mass as of old?[119]

24. "But," they say, "these are not the rites of our state."

Who makes this statement or rejoinder? A Roman, Gaul, Spaniard, African, German, or Sicilian? And what good does it do your cause, if these stories are not yours, while those who make them up are on your side? Or what difference does it make whether you approve them or not, since what are really your own are found to be either equally foul or even of a type of vileness that outdoes theirs?

The Eleusinian mysteries.

Do you want us to consider, for instance, also those divine mysteries which are called Thesmophoria[120] by the Greeks, in which those holy vigils and solemn night watchings[121] were consecrated by the people of Attica? Do you want us, I say, to see what beginnings or what causes they have, so

Book Five: Jupiter Elicius, Attis, Mysteries

that we may prove also that Athens itself, pre-eminent in the pursuit of the humane arts, says things as insulting against the gods as do others and that things no less blasphemous are bruited abroad by her than are proposed by the rest of you?

Once, they say,[122] when in the Sicilian meadows Proserpina, not yet a woman and still a maiden,[123] was picking purple flowers and when her eagerness to gather them was calling her hither and thither everywhere through the flowery harvest, the King of the Shades, springing out through a cavern of the deep underworld, seizes and bears off the maiden with him and conceals himself again in the caverns of the earth.

Now when Ceres did not know what had happened and had no idea where in the world her daughter was, she determined to seek her lost one over the whole world. She takes a pair of torches kindled with the fires of Etna[124] and with these she lights her way and hastens to go on her quest in all the regions of the earth.

25. In her wandering[125] on that quest she reaches also the territories of Eleusis.[126] That is the name of a district in the Attic region. There were five aborigines[127] who at that time inhabited these parts, and their names were: Baubo,[128] Triptolemus, Eumolpus, Eubuleus, Dysaules; Triptolemus, the yoker of oxen; Dysaules, the herder of goats; Eubuleus, of swine; Eumolpus, of the fleecy flock, from whom issues the family of the Eumolpidae[129] and is derived that name famous among the Cecropians,[130] and those who afterwards flourished as caduceus-bearers,[131] hierophants, and heralds.

Well, then, that Baubo who we said was an inhabitant of the district of Eleusis, hospitably receives[132] Ceres exhausted by many kinds of evils, waits upon her with gentle courtesies, begs her to take care of and refresh her body, proffers for quenching her thirst a drink of wine and spelt[133] which the Greeks call *cyceon*. The goddess in her sorrow turns away and refuses the kindly attentions, and her misfortune does not permit her to remember the ordinary demands of health.[134] But the other begs her and urges her,[135] as is usual in such cases, not to refuse her kindness. Ceres remains absolutely obdurate and keeps tenaciously to her unbending austerity. But when this happened several times and her fixed purpose could not be worn out by any attentions, Baubo changes her tactics; and her whom she could not win by earnestness, she decided to make merry by grotesque jests.[136] She returns to the sad goddess, and to the accompaniment of what one ordinarily says to break and moderate the pangs of grief, she uncovers herself. And so the goddess fixes her gaze and feasts her eyes upon this bizarre form of consolation. Then, having become more relaxed, she laughingly takes the drink she had rejected and drains it, and what Baubo's modesty long was unable to accomplish, the indecency of a shameless action brought about.

26. Should there be anyone who thinks that we are giving out wicked calumnies, let him take the books of the Thracian bard[137] which you remind us are of divine antiquity, and he will find that we are neither cunningly inventing anything nor seeking and contriving ways and means for ridiculing their holinesses, the gods. Indeed, we shall adduce those very verses which the son of Calliope uttered in Greek and published abroad among men to be sung through the ages.[138]

> Thus she spake and straightway drew up her garment.
> Then the goddess, casting down the light of her august eyes,
> Softens a little, lays aside her sadness of soul;
> Then takes the cup in her hand, and with a laugh
> Joyfully quaffs down the whole draught of cyceon.

What have you to say, you bright sons of Erechtheus,[139] you citizens of Minerva?[140] A person is eager to know with what eloquent words you will defend such perilous business, or what arts you have to restore persons so afflicted and diseased. Here there is no false indictment[141] and you are not being assailed with a libellous accusation. These well-known[142] verses display the shameful beginnings of your Eleusinia just as the records of ancient literature and even the very formulas with which you answer, when asked in receiving the sacred things:

> Again I have received, placed in the little box.[143]
> I have fasted and have drunk the cyceon. Out of the box have I taken and into the wicker-basket have I put.

27. Well, then, is it not true, as those holy and secret mysteries say, that your gods are kidnapped and kidnap, that they enter into marriages arranged by underhand dealings, that the honor of virginity is snatched from refusing and unwilling maidens? Wrongs that threaten are unknown to them? What has happened to those who have been kidnapped is unknown? They seek for things lost, as human beings do, and, under the brightest light of the sun, they traverse the earth's vastness with lamps and torches? They are afflicted, they grow sick, they take on the squalor of mourners and the marks of wretchedness? And to make them able to turn their attention to foods and the taking of nourishment, neither reason, nor an opportune moment, nor any serious words or respectable courtesy is used, but a disgraceful indecency of the body is shown and those parts of the body exposed which common shame, which the natural law of modesty bids us conceal, which it is not permissible to name among chaste ears without permission, to speak of without first begging pardon?[144]

What, I ask, was there to see, what was there in Baubo which could make a goddess of the female sex wonder and laugh, which, when exposed to the sight and gaze of the goddess, could make her forget her woes and change her with sudden mirth to a gay mood? O the types, the masses of materials we could have brought forward to scorn at and pasquinade, had not respect for decency [145] and the dignity of literature forbidden!

The Halimuntian mysteries.

28. I must own that for some time I have been hesitating, looking about, turning my back, doubling Tellenian [146] perplexities, while shame keeps me from mentioning those Halimuntian [147] mysteries [148] in which Greece erects human members in honor of Father Liber and the whole region teems with images of the sort. The meaning of this may perhaps be obscure and the reason for it asked. Whosoever of you does not know, let him learn and marvel and with reverent care ever preserve such great things in the purity of his heart!

While Liber, the Nysian [149] and Semelian, [150] so the story goes, still lived among men, he conceived the wish of becoming acquainted with the gods below and to investigate what all went on in the realm of Tartarus. Now this desire of his was impeded by some difficulties because through ignorance of the route he did not know where to go and proceed. A certain Prosumnus [151] turns up, a scoundrel who loved the god and who was much given to wicked lusts. He promises to point out the gate of Dis and the approaches to Acheron if the god will [also] [152] be agreeable and suffer himself to be abused by him. The god agrees and swears that he will put himself in his power and at his disposal, but only after his return from the underworld, upon realizing the expedition desired. Prosumnus obligingly tells him the way and sets him on the very threshold of the lower world. Meanwhile, while Liber surveys the Styx,[153] Cerberus,[154] the Furies, and all the other things with searching curiosity, the one who informed him about the road[155] passes from the number of the living and is buried in the human fashion. Evius[156] comes up from the region of the dead and learns that his guide is dead. In order to discharge his promise and free himself from the obligation of his oath, he hastens to the place of the burial.[157]

Criticism of the myths.

29. And so that no one may think that things so wicked have been fabricated by us, we do not ask him to believe the testimony of Heraclitus[158] nor do we require him to accept what he reads in that man concerning what he felt about such mysteries. Let him ask all Greece what these symbols mean which ancient custom erects and worships through the countryside, through the towns. He will find that the causes are those we say. Or, if they should be ashamed to tell the simple truth, what advantage is there in obscuring, in concealing the cause and origin of the rite, ⟨when⟩ the accusation is valid against the act of worship itself?

What can you say, you peoples, you nations busied in, devoted to, the worship of the temples? Are these the ceremonials to which you would force us by flames, exile, executions, and other kinds of penalties and threat of torture?[159] Are these the gods you would introduce to us, foist and inflict upon us, the like of which you would not wish yourselves to be, nor anyone related to you by blood or ties of friendship? Can you tell your youngsters[160] still wearing the bordered toga[161] the agreements which Liber made with his lovers?[162]

Can you urge upon your daughters-in-law, indeed, those joined with you in marriage, the modesty of Baubo and the chaste pleasures of Ceres? Do you want your young men to know, hear, learn what sort even Jupiter proved himself to be to one mother or another? Do you want your grown-up daughters and your fathers still full of life and vigor to become acquainted with the trick that same fellow played on his daughter? Do you want their own brothers, already sensing passion, and brothers sprung from the same parents as they, to hear that that fellow again was not above lying with his sister?[163]

Therefore, then, should we not flee far from gods of this kind? And that the filthiness of so impure a religion may not creep into our mind, should we not stop our ears altogether against it? What mortal is there so trained in moral purity that the examples[164] of the gods do not entice him to furies of this kind? Or who is there who could restrain his passions from his relatives and persons who should be revered, when he sees that with the gods above nothing is kept sacred in the confusion of their passions? For, when it becomes evident that the first and perfect nature is not strong enough to curb its passion within right limits, why should not a human being throw himself in promiscuous lusts, borne headlong by his innate frailty and encouraged by the teaching of a sacred deity?

The pagans are the true atheists.

30. I must say that for some time[165] as I reflected on monstrosities of this kind it has been my wont to wonder at the fact that you dare say anyone is an atheist,[166] irreligious, sacrilegious, who denies the gods exist at all, or doubts it, or maintains that they were men and because of some power and

merit they were placed among the number of the gods. The fact is, if a true examination be made, it is but fair that no one more than you should be called by these names, who under the pretense of worship pile up on them more blasphemies and accusations than if you had conceived the idea of doing this openly with avowed abuse.

A man who doubts the existence of the gods or who completely denies their existence, although the boldness of his ideas may give him the appearance of following monstrous views, nevertheless without reviling the faith of anyone, merely does not agree to things that are obscure. And one who asserts they were earthborn, although he takes away from them the sublimity of heaven's nobility, yet heaps upon them adventitious honors, since he affirms that they have been deservedly exalted to divinity on account of their good deeds and from recognition of their virtues.[167]

31. But you who assert that you are the champions and protagonists of their immortality, have you passed by, overlooked any single one of them and left him unabused by your maledictions? And is there any kind of insult so damnable in the belief of all that you have hesitated to use it on them, even if restrained solely by the authority of a name?

Who was it that declared that the gods loved transitory and mortal bodies?[168] Was it not you? Who, that they perpetrated those most exquisite thefts on the couches of others? Was it not you? Who, that sons consorted in dire intercourse with their mothers, or again that fathers did so with their own virgin daughters? Was it not you? Who, that handsome boys and even grown-up men of attractive appearance were lusted after? Was it not you? Who said they were made eunuchs, debauched, tricksters, thieves; that they were held by bonds, by chains; that, finally, they were assailed by thunderbolts, wounded, passed away, and even received burial on earth? Was it not you? While, then, you have concocted so many and such grievous charges to slander the gods, are you brazen enough to assert that it is because of us that the minds of the divinities have been offended, when as a matter of fact it has long been clear that it is you who are the provokers of such anger and the instigators of divine wrath?

According to the pagans, the stories should be taken allegorically.

32. "But you err," he says, "and are mistaken, and show by the very criticism of these things that you are quite inexperienced, ignorant, and provincial.[169] At the heart of all these stories which seem to you disgraceful and tending to discredit the gods, there is a content of sacred mysteries, principles marvellously profound, which no one can readily grasp by intellectual acumen. For not what is written and indicated on the surface of the words is what is actually meant and said; but all these things are taken in an allegorical[170] sense and with mystical interpretations. Therefore, he who says, 'Jupiter lay with his mother' does not mean the incestuous and vile embraces of physical love, but instead of 'Jupiter' means rain, instead of 'Ceres,' the earth. And again, whoever says that he practiced debauchery with his daughter, is not speaking of foul pleasures, but in the place of the word 'shower,' he puts 'Jupiter,' and means by his 'daughter' the crop sown. So also he who says that Proserpina was carried off by Father Dis, does not, as you think, mean that the maiden[171] was carried off for base lusts; but the fact that we cover the seed with earth, is what is understood by the goddess going beneath the earth and uniting with Orcus to bring forth progeny. In like manner also in the other stories, one

Book Five: Jupiter Elicius, Attis, Mysteries 441

thing is said, but another is meant, and the common and obvious sense contains an underlying hidden meaning and a profound truth shrouded in mystery."

Criticism of allegory.

33. All this is splitting hairs and straws, as is evident, and quibbling, the usual props that bolster bad cases in the courts; indeed, to put it more accurately, we have here the veneer of sophistic disputes by which not the truth but its image and appearance and shadow are always sought after. Since to accept the accounts literally is shameful, unbecoming, undignified, ⟨recourse is had⟩ to this expedient, that one thing is substituted for another, and by way of interpretation the appearance of decency is forced onto what is foul.

But what difference does it make to us whether other senses and other meanings underlie stories that are nugatory? For us who assert that you treat the gods wickedly and impiously, what is written, what is heard is enough, and we need not bother about what is hidden, since the insult to the divinities is contained not in the hidden meaning but in the sense of the words as they appear on the surface.

And yet, lest we appear to be unwilling to examine just what is said, we first ask you this, if you will but lend us your patience: who taught you or who suggested that these things were written in an allegorical sense or are to be so understood? Did the writers usually take you into conference?[172] Or were you lurking in their bosoms at the time they substituted one thing for another, so as to cover the real truth?[173] Further, if for some reason and because of a religious scruple they decided to shroud these mysteries in dark obscurity, then how great is your temerity to wish to understand what they did not wish you to understand, to know yourselves and to spread before the knowledge of all what they concealed to no avail by words that did not stand for the truth!

34. But supposing we agree with you that in all these stories stags are spoken of in place of Iphigenias,[174] even so how is it clear to you, when ⟨you wish⟩ to explain or to unfold those allegories, that you are giving them the same interpretation or entertain the same ideas which were present with the writers themselves in their silent thoughts, not expressed by words proper to their meaning but to other senses?

You say that the rain falling into the bosom of the earth was referred to as the cohabitation of Jupiter and Ceres: another may more cleverly devise something else and make a conjecture with some approximation of the truth; a third may come with this, a fourth with that, and according as the varying endowments of the minds at thought assert themselves, so each thing can be interpreted in an infinite variety of ways. For if in the presence of obscure things everything is taken as so-called allegory and it possesses no certain bounds within which the meaning of the fact under discussion is fixed and immovable, anyone is free to interpret what he reads as he pleases and to assert as the original meaning what his own conjecture and surmises lead him to adopt. But with this the case, how can you establish as certain what is doubtful and attach only one meaning to an expression when you see that it can be drawn out by countless ways in a variety of interpretations?

35. Finally, returning to our inquiry—if this is agreeable to you—we ask you this too: whether you think that all these stories, that is, each and every one of them in all its parts, have been written with equivocal and double sense and in delusive ways; or that some parts of them do not use ambi-

Book Five: Jupiter Elicius, Attis, Mysteries

guities, while others have manifold senses and are veiled in a cloak of allegory thrown about them. If from beginning to end the whole web of exposition and arrangement has been enshrouded in allegory, then tell us, show us in detail, what we ought to adopt and substitute for each thing which each individual story mentions and what other things and meanings we should take into account.

To take an example: you wish Jupiter to be understood as meaning rain, Ceres as meaning earth, and Libera [175] and Father Dis as signifying the casting and burying of seed; so, too, you ought to say what we should understand by the bull; what to put for the wrath and anger of Ceres; what the word Brimo means; what the entreaty of the anxious Jupiter stands for, the gods sent as his ambassadors but not given a hearing, the mutilated ram; [176] again, what is meant by the dealings with his daughter, with lust still more filthy. So, in the other story, what the grove and flowers of Henna are; what the fire taken from Etna and the torches lit from it, the travelling through the world with these torches lit from it; what the region of Attica, the district of Eleusis, the hut of Baubo and her rustic hospitality; what the drink of cyceon means, the rejection of the drink, the exposure of herself, [177] the shameful pleasure of the sight and the oblivion of bereavement caused by such means. Now, if you will show what substantial changes should be substituted for all these things, we shall grant your assertion; but if you cannot make a substitution in each case, nor accommodate the context ⟨to⟩ [178] another sense, why do you try to dignify with allegorical claptrap what was written in a straightforward manner and given out to be clearly understood by everyone?

36. But perhaps you will say that these allegories are not inherent in the whole body of the story, but certain parts are

written in the ordinary way, while others have a double meaning and are veiled and obscured by ambiguity. That is a nice subtlety, but one that is transparent to the dullest. Because it is quite too difficult for you to transpose, rearrange, and interpret properly all that has been written, you select certain items agreeable to your purpose, and from those you strive to maintain that false and adulterated versions have been superimposed over the basic truth.

Well, let us suppose that we agree these things are as you say: but how do you know or whence do you learn which part of the story is written with literal meanings; which, on the other hand, has been covered with unharmonious and extraneous meanings? For it may well be that your supposition is other than the correct one; that what you believe to be otherwise, is actually set forth in that other sense, contrary to yours. Where within the body of connected matter a part is said to have been written in an allegorical sense, another part in straightforward language to be taken literally, and there is in the thing itself no mark by which the ambiguous statements can be distinguished from the unequivocal, that which contains the natural sense may just as well be thought to be said with a double meaning as what has been written ambiguously may be believed to be encased in obscurities. Indeed, we confess we cannot understand at all how this can be done or believed possible.

37. Let us take an example and examine statements made in this matter.

"Once upon a time," it is said, "in the Hennian grove the maiden Proserpina was gathering flowers."

Up to this point there is no corruption and the matter has been stated straightforwardly, for every one indubitably knows what a grove and flowers are, what Proserpina, what a maiden.

Book Five: Jupiter Elicius, Attis, Mysteries 445

"Summanus [179] sprang forth from the earth, borne along in a four-horse chariot."

This, too, is just as straightforward, for four-horse teams, a chariot, and Summanus need no interpretation.

"Suddenly he carried off Proserpina and took her under the earth with him."

"The burying of the seed," so they say, "is meant by the carrying-off of Proserpina."

What has happeneed, I ask, that the story should suddenly change over into something else, that the seed is called Proserpina, that she who all along was regarded a maiden engaged in the gathering of flowers, once she was carried off and kidnapped began to have the sense of sown seed?

"Jupiter," we are told, "changed into a bull and assaulted his mother Ceres: as was explained above, these are names for the falling rain."

Yes, I see the matter's [180] darksome ambiguities removed by the law of allegory!

"Ceres burned with anger, but received the parts of a ram in lieu of punishment and redress."

Here again I see something put forth in common phrasing, for wrath ⟨and⟩ satisfaction are spoken of in their proper terminology. What, therefore, happened here that from Jupiter called 'rains' and from Ceres called the 'earth,' this sense was transferred to the actual Jupiter and to the simplest possible factual account?

38. Therefore, either everything has been written and composed in the allegorical sense and everything should be so explained by us; or nothing was written in that sense, since what is believed to be a part of the story seems not to be.

"All this is written in the allegorical sense."

No, this does not seem certain by any means.

"Why? For what reason?" you ask.

Because all that has actually taken place and is so established in the testimony of any work cannot be converted to allegory, for neither can that be undone which was done, nor can the character of any act ever change into a different one. Can the Trojan War [181] be turned into the condemnation of Socrates, or the famous battle of Cannae become the cruel proscription of Sulla? A proscription, indeed, as Tullius [182] jests, can be called a battle and be given the name of Cannae; but a battle that has taken place a long time ago, cannot be that same battle and at the same time a proscription; nor can anything which has taken place be anything else, as I have said, than what took place, nor can that which is fixed firmly in its own individual nature and in the characteristics proper to its own kind transform itself into a substance foreign to it.

39. How, then, do we prove that all these stories are records of actual events? From the solemn rites, of course, and the mysteries of initiation, either those which take place at stated times and days or those which the clans hand down in secret, preserving the perpetuity of their customs. For it must not be believed that these are without their origins, take place without reason or cause, having nothing to link them with first beginnings.

That pine [183] which is regularly borne into the sanctuary of the ⟨I⟩daean [184] Mother—is it not a representation of the tree under which Attis unmanned himself and which they say the goddess consecrated to be a solace for her grief? Those male images which Greece worships and celebrates in yearly rites—do they not bring back a representation of that awful deed by which ⟨Liber⟩ freed himself from his obligation? Those Eleusinian mysteries and the secret rites contain the memorial of what? Is it not of that wandering by which Ceres, weary from seeking for her daughter, came to the

Book Five: Jupiter Elicius, Attis, Mysteries 447

shores of Attica, introduced wheat, honored the family of the Nebridae[185] with the skin of the hind, and laughed at that very great sight of Baubo's? And if there is another cause, that is nothing to us, so long as they are all produced by some cause. For it defies belief that these were all undertaken without antecedent causes; or we must judge the people of Attica to be crazy for having conjured up a religious rite for no reason at all. And if this is clear and established, that is to say, if the causes and origins of the mysteries derive from past events, by no metamorphosis can they be changed into allegorical form. What has been done, has taken place, cannot be undone; the nature of things makes that impossible.

40. And, supposing that we grant you that such is the case,[186] that is, that the word contents of the stories give them a certain meaning, but, like soothsayers, say something else: yet do you not notice, do you not see, how slanderous and insulting to the gods that is which is said to be the case? Or can any greater wrong be found than to term and to call earth and rain or anything else—for it makes no difference what change in interpretation takes place—the intercourse of Jupiter and Ceres, and by crimes attributed to the gods to mean the fall of rain from the sky and the moistening of the earth? Can anything be thought or believed more impious than that the kidnapping of Proserpina describes seeds buried in the earth or anything else—for here, too, it makes no difference— and to speak about an agricultural phenomenon by branding Father Dis with infamy? Is it not a thousand times more desirable to become tongueless and mute, than to spout forth that vocal outpouring and strident din of filthy twaddle, than to call the foulest things by the names of the gods; indeed, to designate prosaic goings-on by the shameful deeds of the gods?

41. In times past it was the custom to use allegorical speech to cover up things shameful by perfectly decent connotations and to dress things too ugly to mention with euphemisms. But now at your instance serious matters are given in the language of shame, and what is strictly chaste is involved in filthy terminology, with the result that what dignity, modestly shrinking from what is base, formerly concealed, now is spoken of in a vile and shameful manner: the vocabulary of dignified speech has changed!

"When we speak of Mars and Venus being caught in adultery by the craftiness of Vulcan," he says, "we speak of passion and wrath restrained by the force and counsel of reason."

Well, then, what prevented, what hindered expressing each thing by the words and meanings proper to it? Yes, what urgency was there, when you desired to express some thing or other in written records, that you should not want your meaning to be understood but in the same discussion take up mutually exclusive points of view: the eagerness of one wishing to teach, and the grudging attitude of not wanting to reveal? Or did speaking of adulterous gods involve no risk, whereas the mention of passion and anger would have befouled the tongue and mouth by touching upon the filthy?[187] But if this last were done and the veil of allegorical obscurity were lifted, the matter would be readily understood and the honor of the gods would be preserved unscathed. But as it is, when by the binding of Mars and Venus the meaning is said to be the restraining of the vices, two most perverse things are present simultaneously: an evidently vile thing suggests some noble meaning; and baseness pre-empts the mind before any religious consideration can do so.

42. But perhaps you will say—for this is the only thing

remaining which, so it seems, you can bring forward—that the gods do not wish their mysteries to be known by man and therefore the stories were written in allegorical circumlocutions. And how do you know for sure that the gods above do not wish their mysteries to be made known to man? Whence are *you* acquainted with them? Why are *you* anxious to dilute them by explaining them as allegories? Finally and lastly, what do the gods mean that, while they frown upon decent things being said about themselves, they have no objection if most shameful and most unbecoming things are mentioned?

"When we name Attis," says he, "we mean and speak of, the sun."

But if Attis is the sun, as you refer to him and call him, who is that Attis supposed to be whom your literature records and declares was born in Phrygia, who suffered certain things, likewise did certain things; whom all the theaters [188] know in their stage plays; whom every year we see receiving special and individual veneration in the calendar of sacred cults? Was the transference of his name made from the sun to a man or from a man to the sun? But if that name was derived in the beginning from the sun, what in the world, I ask you, has the golden sun done to merit from you that you make him share his name with a half-man? But if the name is derived from a goat and from Phrygia,[189] of what has the father of Phaethon,[190] the father of this light and brightness, been guilty, that he should appear to deserve to be named for a castrated man and should become more august when marked with the appellation of a mutilated person?

43. But what is actually at the bottom of this is clear to all. Because you are ashamed of such writers and stories, and realize these things cannot be deleted once they have been set down as a matter of record in filthy form, you strive to

ennoble what is base, and by every kind of sophistry you pervert and corrupt the proper sense of words by supposititious interpretations; and as usually happens to the sick whose senses and understanding have been dislodged by the ravages of disease, you babble confused and vague ideas and are in raptures about the figments of unrealities.

Have it your way: the watering of the earth was meant by the intercourse of Jupiter and Ceres; the burying of the seed by the kidnapping of Father Dis; the vines scattered over the earth by the limbs of Liber torn asunder; the restraining of passion and temerity was spoken of as the fettering of the adulterous Venus and Mars.

44. But if you insist that these fables have been written in an allegorical manner, what is to be done with the rest regarding which we do see how they can be forced into such changes? What [191] shall we substitute for that to which lustful desire forced the descendant of Semele? And what in place of those Ganymedes [192] carried off and set over the direction of passions? What for the metamorphosis into an ant [193] into which the Great Jupiter contracted the infinity of his body? What for the swans [194] and satyrs? [195] What for the showers of gold [196] which the same lecherous god put on with treacherous deceit, amusing himself in changed forms? And, that we may not seem to want to speak about Jupiter only, what allegories can there be in the loves of other divinities? What in their conditions as hired servants and slaves; what in their bonds, bereavements, wailings; what in their torments, wounds, burials?

While in this it was possible for you to get off with single guilt for writing such stuff about the gods, you have added, as the saying goes, a cheap fish to the rich sauce,[197] when you used the names of the gods to label shame, and again defiled the gods with the designations of infamous things.

But if you believed without indubitable conviction that they are here present or that they exist anywhere at all, fear would have put restraint on you in making mention of them, and, as if they were hearing you and understood what you said, so should your belief in them have remained fixed in your thoughts. Plainly, among men devoted to the practice of religion, not only the gods themselves but also the names of the gods ought to be revered, and just as much dignity should attach to their names as to the persons who are connoted under these names.

45. Let us have an honest appraisal and you will be found at fault in this respect, that in your ordinary language you speak of 'Mars' in place of battle; in place of waters, 'Neptune'; 'Father Liber' in place of wine; 'Ceres' in place of bread; 'Minerva' in place of the warp; in place of filthy lusts, 'Venus.' And what reason is there that when things can be accounted for under their own names, they should be called by the names of the gods, and the divinities should be so insulted that not even we would stand for it, if anybody took our names and misapplied them to bagatelles?

"But the language is filthy, if polluted by such words."

What modesty—yes, modesty worthy of commendation! You blush to name bread and wine but to speak of Venus in place of intercourse does not embarrass you!

BOOK SIX

Temples and Images

The Christians show no ceremonial respect to the gods.

1. Now that we have briefly shown what wicked and infamous opinions you have formed about the gods, we must next speak about temples, about images and sacrifices, and about a number of other things associated and closely connected with them. In this respect you have a habit of charging us with the highest of impiety, the fact that we erect no temples[1] in which we may discharge the obligation of worship, set up no image or likeness to any god, build no public or private altars, no shrines, offer the blood of no slaughtered beings,[2] no incense[3] or salted meal, and, finally, do not bring wine flowing in libations from bowls. We do fail to build or do these things, it is true, but not as though harboring wicked and impious attitudes or having conceived any rash desperation and mad contempt for the gods, but because we think and believe that they—provided they are real gods and are endowed with that exalted name—either scorn honors of this kind, if scorn they do, or suffer them as indignities, if they are susceptible to surging emotions of wrath.[4]

The ideal characteristics belonging to gods.

2. To let you learn what we think about that name and what our judgments are, we consider that if they are actually

real gods—to repeat the same again and to satiety—they should possess all the virtues in perfection,[5] be wise, just, dignified—and we are supposing that it is not wrong for us to heap upon them human praises; they should be outstanding for their own peculiar excellences, and should not cast about for support from without with which to perfect the full measure of unimpaired bliss. Immune to every disturbance and every perturbation,[6] they should not seethe with anger, not be aroused by any passions; they should bring misfortune upon none, receive no cruel pleasure from ills suffered by mankind; should not terrify by portents, should menace with no fear-begetting prodigies; should not hold men responsible and liable for the obligations of vows nor demand expiatory sacrifices by threatening signs. They should bring on no pestilential diseases by the contagion of the air; should not burn up the crops with droughts; should not take part in the butchery of wars, in the devastation of cities; should not will adversity to one party and favor the successes of another; but, as is characteristic of the magnanimous, they should weigh all in a just balance and show impartial benevolence to all. For it is characteristic of a transitory race and of human weakness to act by contraries. Besides, the maxims and pronouncements of the wise declare that those who are touched by passion, are subject to suffering, grief, deterioration, and that those who are given to any emotions cannot but be subject to the laws of mortality. Now, such being the case, how can we be judged to hold the gods in contempt, whose divine existence and fellowship with the powers in heaven we deny unless they are above reproach and measure up to the praise that comes from the admiration of great minds?[7]

We build no temples because the gods need none.

3. True, we build no temples to them, and we do not worship their images; we sacrifice no victims, we pour out no incense and wines to them.[8] But what greater honor or distinction can we bestow upon them than to put them in the same place as the Head and Lord of the universe and the Supreme King himself, to whom the gods, in common with us, owe their consciousness of their own existence and that they are possessed of living substance?

Indeed, do we honor Him with shrines or the rearing of temples?[9] Do we slaughter victims to Him? Do we give other things to offer which, to pour which, is not evidence of measured reason but something continued merely through custom? It is utter folly to treat powers greater than you by your[10] own necessities and to give the givers, the gods, things useful to yourself, and to consider this an honor, not an insult.

We ask, therefore: to meet what need of the gods or for what material use of theirs do you say temples have been built or, again, think they ought to be built?

Do they feel the colds of winter and are they scorched by the summer suns? Are they drenched by rainstorms? Do the whirlings of winds beset them? Are they in danger of experiencing hostile attack or furious onslaughts of wild beasts so that it is proper and right to shut them[11] up in fortified buildings or protect them by throwing up a rampart of stones? These temples, what are they? If you ask weak humanity, they are something tremendously big; if you go by the power of the gods, they are just some little caves, and to speak more truly, the tiniest kind of caverns, formed and excogitated by a poverty-stricken brain. And if you seek to know who was their first founder, who their builder, you will find it was either Phoroneus[12] or the Egyptian Merops,[13] ⟨or⟩, as Varro relates in his *Wonders*,[14] Aeacus,[15] the descendant of Jupiter.

They may therefore be built of massive blocks of marble or shine with ceilings coffered in gold,[16] gems may sparkle here and at varying intervals radiate the brilliance of stars; yet all these things are made of earth and compounded of the lowest dregs of baser matter. Even if you value these as worth more, no one should believe that the gods delight in them, or that they do not refuse and scorn to hedge themselves in and to be shut in and confined by these barriers.[17]

"This," says some one, "is the temple of Mars, this of Juno and Venus; this of Hercules, of Apollo, of Dis."

What else is it than to say this is the house of Mars, this of Juno and Venus; here Apollo dwells; in this stays Hercules; in that, Summanus? Is it not, then, the first and greatest insult to think of the gods as confined in habitations, to give them miserable little huts, to build them rooms and cells, and to think necessary for them what is needed by men, by cats; needed by ants and lizards, by scampering timid little mice?

The gods ought to be omnipresent and to hear everyone.

4. "But," he says, "our reason for assigning temples to the gods is not that we wish to keep from them drenching rains, winds, frosts,[18] or the sun's rays, but that we may stand in their presence and look at them from close at hand, address them from very nearby, and engage, so to speak, in reverent conversations with them present."

Yes, if they are invoked under the bare sky and under the canopy of heaven, they, of course, hear nothing, and unless prayers are addressed to them from nearby, they will stand there deaf and motionless, as if nothing were said.[19] And yet we think that every single god, if by virtue of his name he stands for anything, ought to hear, as if he were present, whatever anyone in any part of the world says.[20] Indeed, he ought to grasp in anticipation whatever anyone conceives in the silent twilight of his thoughts. And, what is more, just as the stars, sun, and moon in their courses above the earth are instantly and everywhere present [21] to the gaze of every last person, so it is equally [22] consistent that the ears of the gods should be closed to no language and should ever be attuned to voices however commingling in reaching them from faraway regions. For this is proper to the gods—to fill all things with their power, not to be partly at one place but to be completely present everywhere, not to be present and then absent, not to go to dine with the Ethiopians and after twelve days to return to their own home.[23]

5. If this is not the case, all hope of aid is taken away, and it will be doubtful whether you are heard by the gods or not, when you perform the sacred ceremonies with their due rituals. Let us suppose, to make the matter clear, there is a temple of some divinity in the Canary Islands,[24] another of the same in farthest Thule,[25] another among the Seres,[26] another among the tawny Garamantes,[27] and whatever others there are who are prevented from knowing each other by the seas, mountains, forests, and the four quarters [28] of the world. If they all at one time render sacrifices and ask of the divinity what their several needs urge them to plead for, what hope will all of them have of gaining the favor, if the god does not hear the cry sent up to him from all sides and if there shall be any distance from which the prayer of a suppliant cannot reach? Either he will be present nowhere, if it is possible at any time for him not to be present somewhere, or he will be at one place only, since he cannot furnish a hearing to all without distinction. And so it comes to pass that either the

Book Six: Temples and Images 457

god helps none at all, if, busied with something, he cannot hasten to hear the cries, or only certain ones go away with their prayers heard, the rest accomplishing nothing.

Burials within sanctuaries.

6. What [29] about the fact, attested by the writings of authorities,[30] that many of these temples reared high with golden domes and with lofty roofs, cover ashes and bones and serve as sepulchres of the dead? Is it not manifestly clear that you either worship the dead instead of immortal gods, or that an inexpiable affront is offered the divinities because their shrines and temples stand piled up over the tombs of the dead? [31]

In the ninth book of his *Histories* Antiochus [32] relates that Cecrops was buried in the Minervan precinct [33] at Athens. Again, in the temple of the same goddess on the citadel of Larisa,[34] it is expressly stated that Acrisius [35] was laid; in the sanctuary of Polias,[36] Erichthonius;[37] the brothers Dairas [38] and Immaradus [39] in the Eleusinian precinct [40] which lies below the city.

What about the virgin daughters of Celeus? [41] Are they not said to have been buried in the temple of Ceres at Eleusis? [42] Is it not in the shrine of Diana which was set up in the temple of the Delian Apollo, that Hyperoche [43] and Laodice lie buried who are said to have been brought thither from the country of the Hyperboreans? [44]

Leandrius [45] says that in the Didymaeum [46] at Miletus, Cleochus [47] received the final rites of burial. Zeno [48] of Myndus states and sets forth that the monument of Leucophryne [49] is in the sanctuary of Diana at Magnesia.[50] Do not the writings consistently point out that the prophet Telmessus lies buried under the altar of Apollo which is seen at the town of Telmessus?[51]

Ptolemaeus,[52] son of Agesarchus, in the first book of the treatise which he wrote on Philopator, asserts on literary testimony that Cinyras,[53] king of Paphus, was buried with all his family, yes, with all his kinsfolk, in the temple of Venus. It would be an infinite and endless task to describe in what shrines they all are through the whole earth; nor is there any need of a painstaking inquiry—although Egypt established a penalty against him who should reveal the places in which Apis lay hidden[54]—regarding the temples by which those *Polyandria*[55] of Varro are covered and what burden of massive stone they have piled upon them.

7. But why do I speak of these small items? What man is there who does not know that the Capitol[56] of the imperial people[57] is the tomb of Olus[58] Vulcentanus? Who is there, I say, who does not know that from the place where its foundations were being laid there rolled out a human head buried not very long before, either by itself without the other parts, as some say, or together with the other members? Now, if you demand that this be attested by the witness of authors, Sammonicus,[59] Granius,[60] Valerianus,[61] and Fabius[62] will declare to you whose son Aulus[63] was, of what clan and people, by the hands of what miserable slave he was robbed of life and light, what he did to his fellow citizens that burial was denied to him in his ancestral land.

You will likewise learn, although they pretend to be unwilling to make this public, what was done with the severed head, or in what part of the citadel it was shut up with careful secrecy, for the simple reason that the sealed omen might remain, unaltered and fixed, in its perpetuity. Now, though it was the proper thing that this story be suppressed and concealed by the oblivion of time, the composition of the name [64] made it public and through testimony that could not be effaced made it to endure with the incidents that provoked it, through its allotted time, and the great city, the worshipper of all divinities, did not blush, when it gave a name to the temple, to name it the 'Capitolium' from the head of Olus rather than use a Jovian name.

8. We have therefore sufficiently shown, I think, that temples have been built to the immortal gods either to no purpose or constructed on the basis of views which are to their discredit or are an affront to the power they are believed to possess.

Why do the pagans make images of the gods?

We must next say something about the statues and images which you form with much skill and treat with religious reverence.[65] If in this matter there can be any question of good faith, we can by no amount of reflection determine for ourselves whether you do this in earnest and with serious purpose, or mock those very things and amuse yourselves with childish fancies. For if you are certain of the existence of the gods whom you suppose, and that they live in the lofty regions of heaven, what cause is there, what reason, that you should fashion those images, when you have sure beings to whom you can direct your prayers and request aid in circumstances of need? But, on the other hand, if you do not believe, or, to put it more moderately, are in doubt, even so, what reason is there to fashion and set up images of doubtful things? And why produce an inane imitation of something in whose existence you do not believe? Or do you possibly mean to say that by these images the presence, as it were, of these divinities is represented, and because you have not been given the experience of seeing the gods, they are thus concretely worshipped and paid the official services owed them? The man who says this and asserts it, does not believe the gods exist, and he is convicted of having no faith in his own religious beliefs who needs to see what he holds, afraid that a mystery unseen may, after all, be nothing.

"*The images are representations of the gods.*"

9. "We worship the gods," you say, "by means of the images."[66]

Well, if these images do not exist, do the gods not know that they are worshipped and will they think that you show them no honor at all? It is through certain bypaths, then, and certain so-called proxies that they take and receive your tokens of veneration; and before those to whom that duty is owed perceive the homage, you first sacrifice to images and transmit certain remnants,[67] as it were, to them, through outside influence. And what greater injustice, disgrace, and hardship can there be than to know a god on the one hand and on the other to pray to something else? To hope for aid from a deity and to make supplication to a senseless image? Does not this, I ask, amount to what is said in the popular saws, "to hit the carpenter when you strike at the fuller"[68] and "when you seek a man's advice to ask asses and pigs what to do?"

How can they be true likenesses?

10. And, how, finally, do you know whether all these images you form as substitutions for the immortal gods, reproduce and bear a resemblance to the divine? It may be that one is bearded in heaven who is fashioned by you as beardless. It may be that another is quite advanced in age to whom

Book Six: Temples and Images 461

you give a boy's years. It may be that here one who really has blue eyes has brown ones; that he has a pug nose whom you make and fashion with a pointed nose. And certainly it is not right to speak of, or call, a 'likeness' something which does not derive a uniformity of features from the face that is its prototype—an obvious certainty which can be gathered from manifest realities.

While, for instance, all of us human beings see by the indubitable sight of our eyes that the sun is round, you have given it the countenance of a man and the features of mortal bodies.[69] The moon is ever in motion and in the course of its monthly restoration puts on thirty faces:[70] under your guidance and designing, it is a woman and has but one countenance, she whose physiognomy changes a thousand times each day in the instability that is hers.[71] We understand that all the winds are a flow of air set in motion by physical phenomena: with you they are human forms blowing twisted trumpets, the blasts of air coming from their own insides.[72]

Among your gods we see the fierce face of a lion smeared with pure vermilion and named Frugiferius.[73] If all these images are likenesses of the divinities above, then one must say there dwells also in heaven such a god, whose form and appearance have served as a model for the present; and, of course, as here that figure of yours, so there that divinity himself is merely a mask and face without a corresponding body, growling and opening his fierce jaws, gruesome in his bloody dye, his teeth sunk in an apple and, as street urchins[74] sometimes childishly do, sticking his tongue out of his gaping mouth!

But if it is not so, as all think it is not, how do you explain this brashness—to fashion to yourself whatever form you please and to call it an image of a god whom you cannot prove exists anywhere in the universe?

Various pagan divinities are ridiculous.

11. You[75] laugh at the fact that in ancient times the Persians worshipped rivers,[76] as the written tradition[77] states; the Arabs a shapeless stone;[78] the Scythian nations a sabre;[79] the Thespians[80] a branch instead of Cinxia; the Icarians[81] an unhewn log in place of Diana; the Pessinuntians a piece of flint[82] in place of the Mother of the Gods; the Romans instead of Mars a spear,[83] as the Muses of Varro[84] point out; and, as Aethlius[85] relates, the Samians, before they were acquainted with the statuary's art, a board[86] instead of Juno: and you keep from laughing when instead of the immortal gods you pray to statuettes[87] of men and to human forms? Indeed, you even regard these little statuettes themselves as gods and outside of these you do not believe that anything has divine power.

What do you say, you—?[88] So the gods in heaven have ears and temples, necks, an occiput, spine, loins, sides, knees, buttocks, thighs, ankles, and all the other parts with which we are formed, and which were mentioned in the first part[89] somewhat more fully and described in greater detail? Would that we might peer into your feelings and deep into your minds in which you reflect on and entertain all your most secret thoughts! We should find that you, too, feel the same regarding the physical appearance of the divinities as we do. But what can we do in the face of the obstinate bias of people threatening us with swords and devising new penalties?[90] By your threats you shield a cause, of the bad state of which you are aware, and once you have gone through with something irrational, that you may not leave the impression that on a given occasion you were uninformed, you defend it; and you think it better to have it your way than to give in and consent to acknowledged truth.

12. From[91] causes of this kind it has also resulted with your connivance that the wanton fancy of artisans have played on the bodies of the gods and given them forms which could serve as a laughingstock to anyone, however strait-laced. Thus, in fact, Hammon[92] is formed and fashioned with goats' horns. Saturn[93] with his crooked sickle is guardian of the countryside like some pruner of the too luxurious branches. The son of Maia[94] wears a broad-brimmed hat, as if he were preparing to take to the roads, and protecting himself against the sun and dust. There is Liber with his delicate limbs and utterly enervated by the languor of effeminacy.[95] Venus[96] is naked and uncovered, as if to say that she offered for sale, auctioned off the beauty of her meretricious body. Vulcan[97] has his cap and hammer, and his right hand free and his garment tucked up ready for the smithy. The Delian[98] has his plectrum and his lyre, making the gestures of a guitar player and of an actor about to sing dirges. The King of the Sea[99] holds his trident, as if he had to fight in a gladiatorial contest; and no representation of any divinity can be found which does not have certain characteristics attributed to it by the generosity of its craftsmen.

Now, listen, if without your knowing anything about it some witty and clever ruler were to remove the Sun from the gate[100] and transfer it to the place of Mercury and, conversely, were to carry off Mercury and make him emigrate to the shrine of the Sun—both of them, as you know, are represented by you as beardless and smooth-shaven—and were to give the latter rays and to place on the head of the Sun the little travelling hat, how would you be able to know them apart, whether this one is the Sun or that one Mercury, since their dress, not the facial characteristics, usually identifies the gods for you?

Again, if he were, by a similar transfer, to remove the horns from the unclad Jupiter, and fasten them to the sides of Mars, and strip Mars of his weapons [101] and so again furnish Hammon with them, how can they be distinguished from each other, since he who was Jupiter can be taken to be the same as Mars, and he who was Mavors can assume the appearance of Jupiter Hammon? Such tomfoolery it is to fashion those images of yours, to dedicate names to them as if they were their own: if you took away their trappings, the possibility of recognizing individuals would be eliminated, god would be confused with god, one would seem to be the other—yes, both could be taken to be both.

Some images were modelled on human beings.

13. But why do I laugh at the sickles and tridents given to the gods, the horns, hammers, and caps, realizing as I do, that some images reproduce the shapes of certain men and the features of infamous harlots? Who [102] is there who does not know that the Athenians fashioned those *Hermae* [103] in the likeness of the body of Alcibiades? [104] Who does not know, if he reads Posidippus' [105] ⟨book on Cnidus⟩ [106] that Praxiteles' [107] ingenious devotion fashioned the face of the Cnidian Venus [108] on the model of the harlot Cratina whom the poor man desperately loved?

But is she the only Venus who has been made more beautiful by borrowed grace taken from a strumpet's face? That Phryne [109] of Thespia, as those who have written on Thespian affairs relate,[110] when she was at the acme of her beauty and the prime of her loveliness, is said to have been the model for all the Venuses which have a reputation, whether throughout the cities of Greece or where a predilection and desire for such statues were rampant. And so all the artists who existed

Book Six: Temples and Images 465

in these same times and to whom a sense of real life gave pre-eminence in the portrayal of likenesses, vied with every care and zeal in transferring the features of the prostitute's head to the Cytherean images.[111] The genius of the artists applied itself with enthusiasm and each sought to outdo the other in emulous rivalry, not that Venus should be the more august but that Phryne should stand for Venus. And so it came to this that sacred honors were paid to courtesans in place of the immortal gods, and an unhappy religion was duped by the fabrication of images.

Among sculptors the well-known Phidias[112] takes first place. When[113] this man had executed the form of the Olympian[114] Jupiter in a work of immense proportions, upon the finger of the god he carved:

PANTARCES IS BEAUTIFUL.[115]

This, incidentally, was the name of the boy loved by him and cherished with filthy passion. And it was not fear or religious awe that induced him to call a god by the name of a male harlot, indeed, to call the divinity and image of Jupiter after a debauchee![116]

So farcical is it and childish to form these your statuettes, adoring them as gods, heaping divine honors upon them, when we see the artists themselves amusing themselves in fashioning them, and consecrating them as memorials to their own lusts! Yes, indeed, if you ask me, what reason was there that Phidias should hesitate to amuse himself wantonly when he was aware that a little while before the very Jupiter he had made had been gold, stones, and bones[117]—shapeless, disjoined, confused—and that he himself was the one who gathered them together and united them; that their appearance had been given to them by himself in the carven imitation of limbs; and what is most important of all, that it was by a favor of his own giving that Jupiter himself was born and given worship in human affairs?

Images are made of matter and are nothing more.

14. At this juncture I should like to make just one address, as if all nations on earth were present, and give their ears the benefit of the following, to be noted by all:

Why is it that you people, of your own accord, cheat and deceive yourselves by voluntary blindness when the matters are so clear and evident? At long last do shake off the darkness and return to the light of the mind, take a good look and see what is going on. Let us hope this prerogative is still yours and that you are still amenable to reason and the good sense given you.

Those images [118] which intimidate you and which you adore in all the temples, prostrate upon the ground, are bones, stones, brass, silver, gold, clay, wood taken from a tree, or glue mixed with plaster. They are a congeries coming possibly from the trinkets of harlots or women's toilet tables,[119] from camel bones or the tooth of the Indian beast,[120] from cooking pots and pans, from candlesticks and lamps, or from still more repulsive vessels. They have been melted down and cast into these shapes and forms which you see, baked in potters' kilns, produced from anvils and hammers, reduced with scrapers, ground with rasps and files, cut, hewn, and hollowed out with saws, augers, axes, bored out with the turning of bits, smoothed off with planes.

Is this not then an aberration? Is it not, to use the right term for it, stupidity to believe a god what you yourself form, to fall down on your knees in terror before a thing made by you; and while you know full well that it is the product of your work and fingers, to cast yourself down on your face, to beg aid in supplication, and in misfortunes and hard times to take recourse to its favor as of a propitious divinity?

15. Now look, if someone were to place before you a lump of copper not shaped for any purpose, masses of unwrought silver and unwrought gold, wood, stones, and bones, and all the other things of which statues and images of divinities usually consist; more, if someone were to add the faces of battered gods, images shattered and broken, and should bid you to slay victims to the bits and fragments, and to devote sacred rites and honors to the formless masses, we would like to know from you: would you do this or would you, on the contrary, refuse to do his bidding?

Perhaps you will say—"Why?" Because in human affairs there is no one so stupidly blind as to class among the gods, silver, brass, gold, plaster, ivory, clay, and say that these same objects have and possess in themselves the divine power. What reason is there, then, that they all should lack the power of divinity and celestial dignity as long as they remain untouched and unwrought; but as soon as they receive human forms—ears, noses, cheeks, lips, eyes, eyebrows—straightway they become gods and are entered in the rank and catalogue of the heaven dwellers?[121]

Does fashioning of them add anything new to these bodies, that from this addition you are made to think something divine and majestic has been conferred? Does it change bronze to gold, or compel the cheap earthenware to change into silver? Does it give life and breath to what a moment before was without any sensation?[122] If what is modelled into the likeness of bodies retains all the natural properties that it had previously,[123] what stupidity it is—I do not want to say blindness—to suppose that the natures of things are changed by a configuration and that what in its original body was inert and unreasoning and deprived of sensation receives divinity from its appearance!

16. And so, unmindful and forgetting what the substance and origin of the images is, you men—rational beings [124] and endowed with the gift of wisdom and discretion—sink down before pieces of baked clay, adore metal plates, beg elephant teeth for good health, magistracies, commands, powers, victories, acquisitions, gains, excellent harvests, and the richest vintages; and while it is plain and clear that you are speaking with brutish things, you think that you are heard; and you yourselves, of your own volition, betray yourselves by the deception of empty credulity.[125]

Oh, that you could enter into the hollow interior of some statue! Indeed, that you could lay open and take apart those Olympian and Capitoline Jupiters and look closely at the disassembled and individual parts of which the totality of their bodies is constituted! You would henceforth see that those gods to whom the artificial sheen of a smooth exterior lends majesty are but a framework of thin plates, the joinings of shapeless pieces; that they are kept from falling apart and from danger of dissolution by dovetails and clamps, by hooks and eyelets, and that in all the hollows and seams there runs a line of lead poured in and that this lends the stability which gives the statues permanence.

You would see at once, I say, that they are detached faces without necks, stumps of hands lacking arms, bellies with the sides halved, the soles of the feet incomplete;[126] and this is particularly ridiculous—they have been assembled by a hybrid construction of their bodies, one part wooden but the other stone.

Granted that skillful camouflaging made these things im-

Book Six: Temples and Images

perceptible, still at least the details that are obvious ought to have taught you and warned you that you are accomplishing nothing and devoting the vain efforts of your services to meaningless things. Really, do you not see that these statues, so lifelike that they seem to breathe,[127] whose feet and knees you touch and stroke in prayer, sometimes crumble away under dripping of rain; that again they disintegrate through decay and rot; how vapors and smoke begrime and discolor them and they grow black; how neglect over a long period causes them to lose their appearance because of weathering, and they are eaten away by rust?

Yes, indeed,[128] I say, do you not see that newts, shrews, mice, and light-shunning cockroaches place in them their nests and live at the base of the hollow parts of these your images; that hither they gather all kinds of filth and other things suited to their needs, hard bits of half-gnawed bread, bones dragged in against the future, rags, wool, bits of paper to make their nests soft, to keep their helpless young warm?[129] Do you not sometimes see spiders spinning cobwebs over the face of an image, and treacherous nets wherewith to entangle in their flight buzzing and impudent flies?

Do you not see,[130] finally, swallows full of filth flying around within the very domes of the temples, tossing themselves about and bedaubing[131] now the very faces, now the mouths of the divinities, the beard, eyes, noses, and all other parts on which the outpouring of their emptied fundament falls?

Blush, then, however late, and take your lessons and norms from the dumb animals and let them teach you that there is nothing divine in images, on which they do not fear or scruple to cast filth, following as they do, their own laws and impelled by their unerring natural instinct.

Why should the gods ennoble their material representations?

17. "But you err," says he, "and you are mistaken, for we do not hold the conviction that bronzes or gold or silver, or any other stuff out of which statues are made, are of themselves gods and sacred deities, but in them we worship and reverence those whom the act of sacred dedication introduces and causes to dwell in the fabricated images. Reasoning this is, which is not impious nor despicable, by which anyone, the dullard as well as the greatest sage, can believe that the gods, having left behind their normal residence—that is, heaven—do not shrink from, nor try to evade, entering earthly habitations; indeed, that impelled by the authority of dedication, they accommodate themselves to, and become identical with, images."[132]

Do your gods, then, dwell in plaster and terracotta? Indeed, are the gods the minds, spirits, and souls of the terracottas and the plaster? And to make the meanest of things more august, do they allow themselves to be shut up and to lurk in the confinement of an obscure abode? Here, then, we desire and beg you to tell us: do they do this against their will; that is, drawn forcefully by the authority of dedication, do they enter the dwelling places of the images? Or do they do so with ready compliance, and do you summon them without using force? Do they do this against their will? And how can it be that they are forced to fulfill some obligation without a diminution of their sovereignty? With the assent of voluntary compliance? And what do the gods seek in the terracottas that they prefer them to their seats among the stars?

Book Six: Temples and Images 471

Other difficulties with this pagan view.

⟨But let us grant that they prefer⟩ the terracottas and the other things of which statues are made ⟨to heaven and their seats among the stars⟩:[133]

18. Would you say then that the gods always continue to dwell in such substances and never depart, even though some very important consideration should require them to do so? Or are they free to come and to go anywhere they please and to depart from their seats and images? If they are under obligation to remain, what can be more wretched than they? What greater misery or greater misfortune could befall them than if hooks and leaden clamps[134] should hold them so securely to the plinths, that, ⟨fettered so as to be nearly immobile,⟩[135] they have lost their power as gods? If, however, they hie away as they wish and have an absolute right to leave the images empty, then on some occasions the statues cease to be gods, and it will be a matter of doubt as to when sacrifices should be rendered, when it is right and proper to refrain.

Quite often we see that in some instances the artists make these statues very small and reduced to the size of a hand, in others raised to a gigantic height and built up to a prodigious size. Considering this, then, it follows that we must understand the gods to contract themselves into tiny little statuettes and compress themselves to the likeness of a different body; but on the other hand they stretch themselves immensely and protract themselves to tremendous size.[136] So, then, if this is the case, in sitting statues the gods must be said to be seated and in standing ones to be standing, in those running forward, to be running, in those hurling weapons to be hurling, to fit and adapt themselves to their countenances, and to adjust their likeness to the other characteristics of the body represented.

19. The gods dwell in images: each wholly in each or divided into parts and members? Remember, it is neither possible that any one god be at one and the same time in several images, nor again can he be divided into parts by dismemberment taking place. Let us suppose that in all the world there are ten thousand images of Vulcan: is it possible, as I said, that the one god can be simultaneously in all ten thousand? No, I do not think so.[137] Why? Because things which are naturally individual and single cannot become many and keep the integrity of their simplicity,[138] and still less are they able to do so, if the gods have the form of human beings, as your belief declares.[139] No, indeed, a hand separated from the head or a foot cut from the body cannot replace the sum of the whole; or it must be said that parts are the equal of the whole, when actually the ⟨whole⟩ cannot exist unless it has been compounded by the gathering of the parts. Moreover,[140] if the same divinity is said to be in all the statues, all reasonableness and soundness of truth is lost, the assumption being that one can remain at one and the same time in them all. Or each of the gods must be said to divide himself from himself, so that he is both himself and another, not differentiated by some distinction but the same self and another. But as nature declines and rejects and scorns this, one must either say and confess that there are innumerable Vulcans, if we wish him to exist and reside in all the images, or he will be in none, because he is prevented by nature from being divided among many.

Why do the gods guard their own temples?

20. And yet, you people, if it is clear and plain to you that the gods live and the celestial ones dwell in the interior of the statues, why do you guard[141] them, preserve them, and

Book Six: Temples and Images 473

keep them under the strongest keys and huge locks, under bolts, bars, and other things of this kind, and against the chance of some thief or robber of the night creeping in, protect them with a thousand attendants [142] and a thousand watchmen?

Why do you feed dogs in the Capitols? Why do you feed and keep geese? [143] Indeed, if you are confident that the gods are there and that they never depart from the statues and images, by all means give them the care of themselves, let their shrines be always unlocked and open, and should anything be carried off by reckless fraud, let them show their divine right and let them inflict the sacrilegious robbers with fitting punishment at the very moment [144] the theft is perpetrated. It is an unworthy thing and destructive of power and authority to entrust to the watchfulness of dogs the guardianship of the highest divinities, and when you seek some kind of deterrent to frighten thieves away, not to ask it of the gods themselves but to place and set it on the cackling of geese.

Examples of temple-robbing prove that the gods do not exist.

21. They [145] say that Antiochus [146] of Cyzicus took away from its shrine a golden Jupiter ten [147] cubits high and substituted for it one made of bronze covered with gold leaf. If the gods are present and dwell in their images, what business, what cares preoccupied Jupiter that he was unable to punish the personal injury and avenge his being substituted in cheap metal? That famous Dionysius—the younger, [148] that is—when he robbed Jupiter of his golden robe and in place of it put one of wool, even joked about it with witty jests, saying that the former was cold in winter, the latter warm; the for-

mer a burden in summer time, while again the latter permitted the breezes to come through during the heat. Where was the King of the Universe that he did not show himself present by some terrifying manifestation and call back the jocose buffoon to earnestness by chastising him? Yes, must I recall that the dignity of Aesculapius was laughed at by him?[149] For when he was robbing him of his very full beard, of a goodly weight and thickly matted such as philosophers[150] wear them, he said it was a crime and indignity that the son of Apollo, a father smooth and beardless and quite like a boy, should be represented with such a beard that it was left in doubt which of them was the father, which the son, or rather, indeed, whether they were one and the same clan and family.[151] While all this was going on and while the plunderer was uttering such blasphemous raillery, if the divinity was present in the statue dedicated to his name and majesty, why did he not punish with just and deserved vengeance the affront by stripping his face and disfiguring his countenance, and thus show that he was present and that he kept guard over his temples and images with unceasing watch?

22. But perhaps you will say that the gods do not bother about these vandalisms and do not think it sufficient cause to make themselves felt and to inflict the punishment of violated religion upon the offenders. Then, if such is the case, they themselves do not care to have images which they suffer to be mutilated and plundered with impunity. Indeed, on the contrary, they teach us clearly that they despise those things, because they make no effort to show by any act of retribution when ⟨they⟩ are insulted in them.

Book Six: Temples and Images

A further abuse of statues.

Philostephanus [152] states in his *Cypriaca* that Pygmalion, king of Cyprus, fell in love with an image of Venus, as if it were a woman. It was regarded as holy and venerated by the Cyprians from ancient times. His mind, his soul, the light of his reason, and his judgment were blinded, and in his madness, as if it were his wife, he [153] would lift up the divinity to the couch. Likewise, Posidippus [154] in the book which he mentions he wrote about Cnidus and about its history, relates that a youth of very noble lineage—the name he suppresses—carried away with love for the Venus on account of which Cnidus is renowned, also entertained amatory relations with the statue of the same goddess. [155]

To ask once again the same question—if the powers of the gods on high lurk in bronze and the other materials of which statues have been formed, where in the world were the one Venus and the other, to drive far from themselves the lewd wantonness of the youths and to punish their impious advances with severe chastisement? Or, since the goddesses are gentle and more inclined to be calmly disposed, what effort would it have taken on their part to dissipate the maddening lust of the wretches and to restore them to a healthy mind with a return of their senses?

23. Or perhaps, as you say, the goddesses [156] held these affronts the most pleasing of passions and pleasures, and thought it no crime deserving to be avenged because it brought delight to their own minds also and because they realized they themselves were suggesting it to the human passions.

Certain temples have been destroyed by fire and earthquake.

But[157] granting that the goddesses, the Venuses, endowed with more serene dispositions, decided that they should close an eye to the unfortunate doings of men blind to themselves —when greedy flames so often consumed the Capitol[158] and destroyed Jupiter Capitolinus[159] himself with his wife and daughter,[160] where was the lightning-hurler at such times to keep away that criminal fire and to save from destruction his property and himself and all the family? Where was Queen Juno, when a violent fire destroyed her shrine and the priestess Chrysis in the Argive city?[161] Where was the Egyptian Serapis[162] when by a similar calamity he lay reduced to ashes with all the mysteries and with Isis? Where was Liber Eleutherius[163] when the same happened at Athens? Where was Diana, when this happened at Ephesus?[164] Where was the Dodonian Jupiter when he burned?[165] Where, finally, was Apollo the diviner[166] when by pirates and sea brigands he was so robbed and scorched that of all the many pounds of gold which countless ages had piled up, he did not, as says Varro,[167] that is, the Menippean, have one single grain[168] to show the swallows coming to be his guests?[169]

It would be an endless task to recount what shrines have been wrecked the world over by earthquakes and storms, what ones have been burned by enemies, what ones have been stripped bare by kings and tyrants[170]—yes, by caretakers and priests themselves, turning the suspicion away from themselves, and, finally, by thieves and the men who lift bars by devices unknown,[171] the Caracheni.[172] These would assuredly remain safe and subject to no mischances if the gods actually were present as protectors and showed any interest in their temples, as is said. But now because they are empty and without the protection of inhabitants, they are in the power of Fortune, and the result is inevitable—they are exposed to all misfortunes as are all other things deprived of an inherent motive power.

"The images are intended to impress the rabble."

24. In this same regard even the proponents of the images are wont to say that the ancients were not unaware that the statues have no divinity in them and there is in them no sense capacity. But because of the unruly and ignorant mob[173] which constitutes the predominant element among peoples and states, it was for the good that they formed them and with this in view, that, being made to face a certain semblance, as it were, of the deities, they might from fear shake off their rudeness, and sensing themselves to be acting in the presence of the gods, might cease their impious deeds, and changing their manners adopt civilized ways. And for no other reason were august forms sought for them in gold and silver save that a certain power might be thought to reside in their splendors, not only to fascinate their eyes but to strike terror into their very minds with radiant, awe-inspiring lustre.

Now, this statement might perhaps appear to be in a measure reasonable, if, after the temples of the gods were founded and the images set up, no evil man existed in the world, no wickedness at all; if justice, peace, fidelity possessed the hearts of mortals, and no one on earth was called guilty or guiltless,[174] all being ignorant of wicked deeds. But now when, on the contrary, all things are full of wickedness, the name of innocence has almost perished, and every moment, every second, new swarms of evil deeds are begotten by the wickedness of wrongdoers, how does it square to say that the images of the gods were instituted to strike terror into the mob? When besides innumerable forms of crime and wickedness, we see even the temples themselves attacked in sacrilegious violation by tyrants, by kings, by robbers, and thieves by night, and the gods themselves whom ancient times fashioned and consecrated to cause terror, wandering into the dens of robbers along with their golden and awe-inspiring splendors?

This purpose is frustrated.

25. If you look at the truth without any prejudice, what great thing do those so-called images have in themselves, that antiquity should have rightfully hoped or thought that by beholding them the vices of men could be broken and their wicked morals kept under control?

The sickle,[175] an attribute of Saturn, was of course bound to cast fear upon mortals, so that they should be willing to lead a life of peace and cast away their wicked inclinations! And so the double face of Janus, or that key with the teeth by which he is distinguished! [176] Jupiter with his headpiece [177] and beard, holding in his right hand a stick of kindling wood cut out like a thunderbolt! That cestus [178] of Juno or the slip of a girl lurking under the military helmet! [179] The Mother of the Gods ⟨with⟩ her tympanum,[180] the Muses with their pipes and psalteries! [181] Winged Mercury, the Argus-slayer![182] Aesculapius with his staff! [183] Ceres with immense bosom, or the drinking cup swinging in Liber's right hand! Mulciber [184] with his workman's clothes, or Fortune with her horn filled with apples, figs, and the fruits of autumn! Diana with her half-clad thighs, or Venus naked, voluptuous! The dog-faced Anubis,[185] or Priapus!

26. O fell, dire spectacles of fears and appalling terrors!

Book Six: Temples and Images

Because of these the human race was to be paralyzed forever, to attempt nothing in its stupefaction, to curb itself from every criminal and outrageous act! Sickles, keys, chapeaux,[186] kindling wood, winged sandals, staffs, tympana, pipes, psalteries, bosoms exaggerated and exposed, drinking cups, pincers, horns filled with fruit, naked forms of women and men!

Would it not have been better to dance, to sing, than to put on pretended dignity and sham seriousness and to relate that such cold and foolish images were devised by the ancients for restraining wrongdoing and to inspire fear in the wicked and impious? Were the mortals of that age and time so empty of heart, so void of reason and sense, that like little boys they were restrained from doing wrong by monstrous, grim-looking masks—yes, by grimaces and bugbears? And how did this boomerang into the opposite! Though there are so many temples in the cities full of images of all the gods, with all the legislation and all the different sanctions, the multitude of criminals cannot be coped with. There is no effective means to correct the situation, and wicked deeds multiply by leaps and bounds the more the law and the courts strain to reduce brutalities and to discourage them by penal laws.

But if images inflicted any fears upon mortals, the passing of laws would cease, and so many kinds of torments would not be set up against the audacity of men given to crime. The fact is, however, that because it has been proven and established that belief in fear supposedly inspired by the statues is in reality nothing, there has been recourse to the sanctions of laws, that these might produce most indisputable fear and provide definitely established penalty for guilt. And it is to these that the images themselves owe the fact that they stand unharmed up to now and are protected by the granting of a measure of honor.

27. Since [187] in the course of the exposition it has been sufficiently shown how futile it is to make images, we must next in order speak as briefly as possible and without any equivocation about sacrifices, about the slaughtering and immolation of victims, about wine, about incense, and about all the other things which play a role in that sphere. With respect to this it is your practice to stir up the most violent hatreds against us, to call us atheists; and, because we pay no honors to the gods, you impose upon us capital punishment through the savage tearing of wild beasts.[188] This, of course, we confess that we do, not from contempt or scorn of the divine, but because we think that such powers make no such demand and are possessed of no desires for such things.

BOOK SEVEN

Sacrifices and Ceremonials

Varro's opinion is against sacrifices.

1. "Well, then," some one will say, "is it your opinion that no sacrifices should be performed whatsoever?"

In reply we quote you not our opinion but your Varro's [1]—none.

"Why so?"

"Because," he says, "true gods neither desire nor demand them, and those made of bronze, baked clay, plaster, or marble, care for them much less, for they lack feeling. And no blame will attach to you if you do not perform them, nor any credit, if you do."

No sounder opinion can be found, none truer, and it is one anyone may adopt, however stupid and difficult to convince he may be. For who is so dull-witted as to slay victims to beings having no sensation, or to think that they should be given those who are far removed from them in nature and blessedness?

The definition of a "true god."

2. "Who are the true gods?" you say.

To answer you in common ordinary language, we do not know. For how can we know who those are whom we have never seen? We are accustomed to hear from you that a great many gods exist and are so accounted in the roster of divine beings. If these exist anywhere, as you say, and are real, then, as Terentius believes, they must necessarily correspond to their name, that is, such as we all think they ought to be and such as they must be spoken of in view of that name. Indeed, to put it briefly, they must be such as the Lord and Omnipotent Master of the Universe Himself[2] is, whom we all know and understand that we pronounce Him true God when we take it upon ourselves to mention His name. One god does not differ in any respect from another as to the fact that he is a god, nor can anything generically a unit be more or less in its parts and at the same time preserve the natural uniformity peculiarly its own. Since there is no doubt about this, they ought then to be never-begotten and eternal, seeking nothing from without and not deriving any earthly pleasures from the resources of matter.

Are the gods nourished by the sacrifices?

3. Therefore, if this is so, we desire first to learn this from you: what is the cause, what the reason, why you perform these sacrifices? Next, what gain do the gods themselves derive from this and what advantage results for them? Whatever is done ought to have a motivation of its own and should not be without a reason, so as to be done with aimless efforts and to be dilly-dallying among the delusions of idle nothings.

Are the heavenly gods, perhaps, nourished on these sacrifices and is there a necessity[3] for the supply of some material to keep their constitution from disintegrating? But what man is so utterly ignorant of what a god is, that he thinks they are sustained by any kind of nourishment and that it is the effect of food which makes them live and last for an endless perpetuity? Whatever is supported by objects and things foreign to itself, must indeed be mortal and have a proclivity to peril when something basic for its life will begin to be wanting.

Again,[4] we note that of the things which are brought to the altars, nothing is added to, and enters into, the substance of the divinities. Either incense is offered and is destroyed, melting on the coals, or a living thing[5] is offered as a victim and the blood is licked up by the dogs, or if any flesh be placed on the altars, in like manner it is burned, and is destroyed and reduced to ashes. Perhaps, though, the god devours the souls of the victims, or from the blazing altars snuffs up eagerly the savor and smoke and feeds upon the fatty fumes[6] which the burning flesh belches forth, still wet with blood and dank with the moisture of previous victims.

But, if a god, as is said, has no body and cannot be touched at all, how is it possible that what is bodiless should be nourished on corporeal things; that what is mortal should sustain what is immortal and contribute to the well-being of something with which it cannot come in contact and to which it cannot give vitality? Hence, justification for the sacrifices, as it seems, is not valid and no one can say that sacrifices are held because the divinities are nourished by them and supported by feeding on them.

Are the sacrifices intended to give the gods pleasure?

4. If perhaps it is not this,[7] is it possible that the victims are slain for the gods and piled on the lighted altars to give them some pleasure and, as is said, to humor them?[8] But what man is there who can persuade himself that the gods relax under the exhilaration of pleasure, that they are eager for the joy of passion and, like a base animal, are affected by wheedling sensations and are fond of momentary tickling of an ephemeral pleasure? For what is overcome by pleasure, must be subject to its opposite, sadness, nor is that which trembles with joy and is exalted by trivial gladness capable of existing free from the anxiety of grief.

The gods, however, ought to be free from either emotion,[9] if we want them to be eternal and without the frailty of mortals. Moreover, every pleasure is, as it were, a kind of flattery to the body and is taken in by the five well-known senses. If the gods above feel this, they must partake also of the bodies which serve as a road for the senses and as a door for the reception of pleasures. Finally, what pleasure is there in taking delight in the slaughter of harmless creatures,[10] to hear constantly the pitiful bellowing, to see the streams of blood, the life fleeting away with the gore, the intestines rolling out with the excrement, as the inwards are laid bare and the hearts still beating with the remaining spark of life and the veins palpitating in the trembling flesh? We half-savage men—indeed, to speak more frankly what is truer and more candid to say, we savages—whom luckless necessity and bad habit[11] have taught to take these as food, are sometimes moved with pity for them. We ourselves accuse ourselves and when the matter is examined and investigated thoroughly, we condemn ourselves, because having neglected the law of humanity, we have broken through the bonds that united us at the beginning.[12]

Will anyone believe that the gods who are kindly, generous, gentle, are delighted and transported with joy at the slaughter of cattle, when these fall and pitifully give up their spirit[13] at their feet? And therefore the cause of pleasure does not, as we see, exist in sacrifices, nor is there a reason why they should be performed, since again there is no ⟨pleasure⟩, and if perchance there is some, it has been shown that it cannot in any way hold true of the gods.

Are the sacrifices intended to appease the gods?

5. We have next to examine also the argument we hear commonly propounded and which enjoys popular accept-

ance: that sacrifices are made to the gods above for this reason that they may lay aside their wrath and anger and become gentle and calm, hushing up the indignation of their fiery spirits. But if we hold to that definition which we should persistently and always remember, namely, that all agitation of spirit is unknown to the gods, the consequence is a conviction that the gods are never angry; indeed, rather, no passion is farther from them than that which, being most like to savage and wild beasts, agitates those who suffer it with stormy feelings [14] and brings them to the danger of destruction. Whatever is harassed by any emotion is evidently capable of suffering and frail. What is subject to suffering and frailty, must necessarily be mortal. But anger harasses and destroys those who suffer from it.[15] Therefore, what is subject to the passion of anger must be called mortal. Now, we know that the gods must be perpetual and possessed of an immortal nature; and if this is certain and clear, anger is far removed from them and from their state of existence.[16] The conclusion is that by no consideration is it proper to wish to appease in the gods above that which you see cannot be reconciled with their blessed state.

6. But let us allow, as you wish, that such a disturbance is common with the gods, and that it is for the sake of placating it that sacrifices take place and the ceremonial solemnities are celebrated. When, then, should these observances be put into effect or at what time should they be given? Before they are angry and provoked or when they have been roused and set in indignation? If to prevent them from becoming angry we must anticipate them, you are proposing to us not gods but wild beasts, to whom it is the custom to toss food for them to vent their mad rage on and to divert their lust to do harm, lest when aroused they rage and burst the bars of

their cages. But if this appeasement of sacrifices is offered to the gods when they are already boiling and burning with indignation, I do not urge the question whether that happy and sublime magnanimity which the divinities possess is disturbed by the offenses of little men and is hurt when a creature blind and ever treading on clouds of ignorance does, says something by which their dignity is impaired.

7. Neither do I insist on this that it be said or that I hear what reasons the gods have for their anger against men, that having taken offense they must be appeased by sacrifices. Did they ever ordain any laws for mortals and was it ever established by them what they should do or not do, what to pursue, what to avoid; or, at least, in what manner they wished themselves to be worshipped, so that they might punish with wrathful vengeance what was done otherwise than had been commanded, and, if treated with scorn, might avenge themselves on the presumptuous transgressors?[17] In my opinion, nothing was ever ordained by them nor given sanction, since they have never at any time been seen[18] nor has it been possible to learn definitely whether there are any. What justice is there, then, that the heavenly gods should for any reason grow angry with those whom they have never deigned at any time to show they existed, or gave or imposed any laws they wished to be respected by them and to be kept with strict observance?

8. But, as I said, skip this and let it pass, consigned to silence. Only this one thing I ask above all: what is the reason that if I kill a pig, a god changes his mood and lays aside his wrath and fury; that if I burn up a pullet, a calf under his eyes and on his altar, he forgets the wrong and desists utterly from feeling offended? What passes over from the present act to his displeasure? Or of what use is a goose,

Book Seven: Sacrifices and Ceremonials 487

goat, or peacock, that from its gore it should work as a medicine for the angry one? Is the conclusion that the gods sell their wrongs and like little boys, to induce them to spare their hot tempers and to stop their bawling, get little birdies, dolls, hobbyhorses and pieces of bread [19] with which to divert themselves, so also the immortal gods receive these palliatives from you to give up their wrath and anger and be on good terms again with those who offend them?

But I thought the gods, if it is right at all to believe that they are disturbed by sentiments of anger, stop their anger and wrath and forgive the offenses of the sinners without any price or fees. For it is a characteristic of divinities to be liberal in granting pardon and to grant favors for no more than thanks. But if this cannot be so, it would be much wiser policy for them to stand doggedly by their anger than to grow lenient under the corruption of bribery. For the multitude of sinners increases when there is hope of buying off the sin, and the road to wickedness is easy when the favor of the pardoners is for sale.

Why should innocent animals be sacrificed for guilty humans?

9. Suppose an ox, or whatever animal you please, slain to appease and soothe the fury of the deities, were to take the voice of a man and speak out in these words:

"O Jupiter, or whatever other god thou art, is this, then, humane or right, or is it to be regarded as fair at all, that when someone else has sinned, I should be killed and from my blood thou shouldst allow satisfaction to be given thee— I who never wronged thee, never knowingly or unknowingly violated thy divinity and majesty, being, as thou knowest, a dumb animal, following my guileless instinct and not prone to the vagaries of a fickle character? [20] Have I ever celebrated thy games in an unholy or negligent fashion? Have I, before they began, dragged across a "dancer" [21] to offend thy divinity? Have I sworn false by thee? Have I carried off and despoiled thee in sacrilegious theft of the gifts made thee? [22] Have I uprooted thy most sacred groves or profaned them with private constructions? [23] What, then, is the reason that another's crime should be washed away in my blood and for a wrong not done by me my innocent life is put on the block? Is it because I am a lowly animal and do not have reason and intelligence, as those declare who call themselves men but by their ferocity outstrip the beasts? Did not the same nature in the beginning create even me? Is it not one and the same spirit which guides both them and me? Am I not affected by the same system of breathing, of seeing, and of the other senses? They have livers, lungs, hearts, intestines, bellies: and has not the same number of parts been assigned to me? They love their young and come together for the begetting of children: do I not also take care to procure offspring? And am I not delighted when it has been begotten?

"Of course, they are possessed of reason and use articulate speech. But how do they know whether I, too, do not do what I do by a reasoning of my own and whether the sound which I utter is not my own method of language and one understood by us alone? [24]

"Ask Piety whether it is more just that I be slain, done away with, or that man should be pardoned and be free from punishment for what he has done. Who formed iron into a sword? [25] Was it not man? Who brought disaster upon races, slavery upon nations? Was it not man? Who mixed deadly poisons and offered them to parents, brothers, to wives, to friends?[26] Was it not man? Who conceived or devised so many misdeeds that they can scarcely be set forth in ten thousand annals[27] or days? Was it not man? Is not this, then, bestial, monstrous, savage, does it not seem to thee, O Jupiter, unjust and barbarous for me to be killed, for me to be slain, that thou mightest be appeased and that acquittal rest on the guilty?"

Therefore, it is established that in vain are sacrifices offered to placate the angered divinities. For reason has taught us that the gods never become angry and that they do not wish one thing to be destroyed on another's behalf and that amnesty for wrongdoing should be obtained from innocent blood.

Are the sacrifices intended to emphasize prayers for favors?

10. But perhaps someone will say: "The reason we give the gods sacrifices and the other gifts is that, having become companionable after a fashion through our prayers, they may grant us good fortune and may avert evils from us, cause us to live constantly with joy, and drive away sadness and the threats of misfortunes unforeseen."

This point requires not a little attention and it is not usual to hear or believe a statement so easily made. For presently that whole tribe of most learned scholars will swoop down on us, asserting and demonstrating that whatever happens, happens through fate,[28] and snatch this your view from us and charge us with putting our trust in vain beliefs. Whatever has been done, is now being done, and is to be done in the world, they will say, has already been determined and fixed long ago, and has an immovable causality by which things are linked together and fashion an unbreakable chain of necessity between the past and the future.

If this is actually determined and fixed, then the evil or good which is bound to come each man's way, is already certain. And if this is certain and fixed, all aid from the gods is out of the question; their hatred, their favors are out of the question. They are no more able to do for you what cannot be done than to prevent from happening what is fated to take place—apart from the fact that they [29] will be able, if they wish, to discount that view of yours still more forcibly, so as to say that even the gods themselves are worshipped by you in vain and the supplications made to them are to no purpose. Yes, seeing that the gods are unable to turn aside or change the order of what has been established by fate,[30] of what use is it, what reason is there to wish to weary and deafen the ears of those on whose assistance in desperate situations you have no reliance?

11. Finally, if the gods drive away sadness and distress; if they graciously grant joy and pleasure, whence come so many, so countless many wretches in the world? Whence come so many unhappy folk, leading a life of sorrow in a most desperate lot? Why are not those who every moment, every second, load and pile up the altars with sacrifices, free from calamities?

"Do we not see," they say,[31] "that some of them are the homes of diseases, the light of their eyes extinguished and their ears stopped; their feet unable to walk; living, mere trunks, without their hands; some sunk, overwhelmed, destroyed by fire, shipwreck, and ruin; turned out of great inheritances, supporting themselves by labor for hire—begging, finally, for alms; exiled, proscribed; ever living in grief, broken-hearted by the loss of their children, harassed by other misfortunes of which the kinds and types no enumeration can list?"

But certainly this would not happen if the gods, obligated by virtue of the sacrifices, could repel, could turn aside, those evils. But now because there is no place among them for misfortunes, but all things happen as the result of inexorable necessity, the prescribed course of events proceeds and it carries out what has once been decreed.

12. Or the heaven dwellers would have to be called unsympathetic, if, even though they have the power to prevent it, they suffer an unhappy race to be involved in so many sufferings and calamities.[32] And perhaps some would utter this as something momentous, which ought not to be heard by ears deceitful, fickle, and scornful. But this point we hurry by because it would take us too far afield and require too much discussion. We leave it undeveloped and untouched, satisfied to have done no more than state that you assign to your gods ignoble reputations if you deny that they grant what is good and prevent what is injurious, without first being bought by the blood of goats and sheep and the other things which are put on the altars. For, to begin with, it is improper to believe that the celestial divinities in their power and sublimity keep their favors for sale, first receiving payment and bestowing accordingly; that, further—and this is much more disgraceful—unless they are paid, they give help to none and suffer most pitiful wretches to undergo misfortunes with their perils, when they might assist them in warding these off.

Let us suppose two men sacrificing, the one sin-laden but rich, the other possessed of a poor lar but praiseworthy for his integrity and goodness. If the former should slaughter a hundred oxen and as many dams with their lambkins, while the poor man burns a little incense and a tiny piece of some fragrant substance—does not logic force us to believe that if the divinities bestow nothing except for prices prepaid, they will bestow their favor upon the rich man, while turning their gaze from the poor little fellow who gave sparingly not because he was so minded but because of his limited means?[33] Evidently when the bestower of favors is venal and mercenary, there the favor must necessarily be granted in proportion to the size of the bribe, and the ballot must tend towards the one from whom the greater fee and graft pours in to him who grants this favor.

Further, let us take two nations arrayed against each other in hostile armament, enriching the altars of the gods on high with the same sacrifices, and the one asking bestowal of strength and aid against the other. Must we not believe again that, assuming the gods are won over by gifts to show favor, they must be in a dilemma over the two sides, stand helpless, and fail to find a solution, realizing as they do that their favor has been pledged by the acceptance of the sacrifices?

Either they will lend their favor to both sides—something impossible, for then they themselves will be fighting against themselves, striving against themselves, striving against their own favor and wishes—or they will fail to render aid to either people, a great crime after the price has been paid and received.[34]

And so the conclusion is that all this infamy should be removed far from the gods and it must not be said at all that they are attracted by gifts and payments to confer blessings and to prevent their opposites—provided, at least, they are true gods and should be described by this name. For either whatever happens, happens through fate, and there is no occasion for currying favor in the case of gods; or if fate has no place and is thrown out, it does not become the celestial dignity to sell the favors of its good offices and the conferring of its bounties.

Are the sacrifices intended to honor the gods?

13. We have sufficiently shown, I think, that victims and the things that go with them are offered to the immortal gods in vain. They are neither nourished by them nor do they derive any pleasure from them; nor [35] do they give up their wrath or animosity so as to give prosperity or drive away and avert [36] the contrary.

Next we must examine a point commonly asserted by many and applied to the forms of ceremony. They say that these sacred rites were established to do honor to the gods in heaven, and they do what they do, in order to honor and to exalt in them the powers of the divinities. What if they were likewise to say they keep awake and sleep, walk around and stand still, write something and read, in order to honor the gods and to enhance their dignity? For what is added to them from the blood of the cattle, and from the other things done in sacrificing? What power is added and accrues to them?

Plainly, every honor said to be given by anyone and attributed out of respect for a higher being is of a kind relative to another and is made up of two elements, one from the grant of the giver and the other from the profit of the recipient. If, for instance, some person upon seeing a man of the highest distinction and authority, gets out of the road, rises, uncovers his head, jumps from his carriage, then greets him with a bow, acting the servile part of a petty slave and with trembling agitation, I see what this kind of respect accomplishes. By the humble bearing of the one, very great honor is given to the other, and he is made to appear great whom the respect of an inferior exalts and places above his own rank.

14. But all this granting and ascribing of honor about which we are speaking has its place only among human beings whom a natural weakness and love of standing higher teaches to delight in haughtiness and in being preferred above others. But, I ask, where is there room for honor among the gods above, or what eminence is found to accrue to them from the performance of sacrifices? Do they become more august, more powerful by virtue of cattle that are slaughtered? Do they get anything out of this, or do they begin to be gods the more by an amplification of their divinity? On the contrary, I personally judge it close to slander, indeed plain slander, when it is said that a god is honored by man and glorified by the offering of some gift. For if respect increases and augments the glory of the one to whom it is given, that means that a god becomes greater by reason of the man who has given the gift and respect. And so it boils down to this that the god who is exalted by human honors is the inferior, but the man who increases the power of the divinity is the more sublime.

15. "Well, now," some one will say, "do you think no honor at all should be given to the gods?"

If you propose to us gods such as, if they exist, they ought to be, and such as we all feel we speak about when we mention that name, how can we but give them the greatest honor, since we have been taught by the higher commands [37] to honor even human beings, of whatever rank and of whatever fortune they may be?

"What is that greatest honor?"

One much more dutiful than is shown by you and established on a profounder basis.

A true opinion about the gods.

"Give us," you say, "an opinion about the gods[38] that is worthy, correct, and honorable, and not vitiated by the ugly features of something sordid."

In the first place, you must not believe that they have any likeness to man,[39] nor look for anything that comes from outside and is foreign to them. Secondly, and this has been stated repeatedly, they do not burn with the fires of anger; they are not given to physical passion; their assistance cannot be solicited with bribes; they cannot be provoked to do harm; their kindness and favor are not for sale; they do not rejoice in honor conferred upon them, they are not angry or nettled when it is not given. But this *is* characteristic of the divine— they know of themselves what they are and they do not appraise themselves by adulations coming from elsewhere.

And now that we may see the nature of what is discussed, what sort of honor is it to bind a wether, a ram, a bull under the face of a god and to slay them in his sight? What sort of honor is it to invite a god to blood you see him take and share with dogs? What sort of honor is it to light piles of wood and to becloud the sky with smoke, and to darken with funereal black the images of the gods?

If, then, we decide to appraise facts by what they are, and not according to preconceived notions, those altars of which you speak, and even those beautiful monumental altars are only crematories,[40] funeral pyres, and mounds for consuming the unhappy race of animals, constructed for a most ungainly purpose and built to be a center of stench.

Why not sacrifice other animals and even plants?

16. What do you people have to say? Is that stench which rises and is emitted from burning hides, which comes from

bones, from bristles, from the wool of lambs and the feathers of hens—is that a gift and an honor for a god? And are they glorified whose temples, when you are disposed to go, you approach pure from every stain, washed spotlessly clean?[41] And what could be more polluted than these, more stinking,[42] dirtier, than that their senses should give them a natural predilection for such savagery and a penchant for foul odors which not even the officiants at the sacrifices can bear nor delicate noses can suffer to take in?[43]

And if you think the minds of the gods above are honored and affected by the blood of living creatures, why do you not also sacrifice to them mules and elephants and asses?[44] Why not also dogs, bears, and foxes, camels and hyenas and lions?[45] And since you include birds also among the victims, why not vultures, eagles, storks, falcons, hawks, crows, sparrowhawks, owls, and along with them, salamanders, water snakes, vipers, blindworms? For they also have blood in them and they are likewise animated with the breath of life. What is there in the former to make them more effective or in the latter to give them less aptitude,[46] so that the latter do not contribute to, yet the former do enhance, the glory of the gods above?

"Because it is right," so it is said, "to honor the gods with those things upon which we ourselves feed, are sustained, and live, things which they have in their divine kindness deigned to grant us for our own living."

But the same gods have given to you cumin,[47] cress, turnips, onions, parsley, artichokes, radishes, gourds, rue, mint, basil, pennyroyal, and chives, and bade you to use them as part of your food. Why, then, do you not put these on the altars and scatter over them borage that is fed to oxen, and mix in strong onions?

Book Seven: Sacrifices and Ceremonials

If you were gods, what would you do?

17. Look now, suppose dogs—for we must get up some example[48] to make the matter clearer—suppose, I say, dogs and asses and along with them water wagtails, twittering swallows and with them pigs, were to be endowed with a measure of human[49] feeling and think and believe you to be gods.[50] If, then, they proposed to render you sacrifices in your honor, not consisting of materials or things other than those which make up their customary nourishment and the staples of their natural appetite, we want to know from you: would you consider it a compliment or rather a plain insult, if the swallows slaughtered and dedicated to you flies, wagtails, ants; if the asses were to place hay on your altars and pour out libations of chaff; if the dogs placed bones there and burned human excrement at your shrines; if, finally, the dear little pigs were to pour out the mire taken from their horrid wallows and from dirty mudholes?

Would your anger not blaze up that your dignity should be thus despised and would not you account it an atrocious wrong to be received with dung? Yet you honor[51] the gods with the bodies of bulls and with the slaughter of other living creatures. And how does this act differ from that other, seeing that these same sacrifices will presently be dung too, if they are not already that, and after the passing of a very short time will rot? At long last stop placing fire on your altars. To be sure, you will[52] presently see that consecrated flesh of bulls, with which you extol the honor of the gods, swelling and heaving with worms, tainting and corrupting the atmosphere and infecting the neighboring areas with sickening[53] odors.

If the gods were to enjoin you to turn this carrion[54] into nourishment for yourselves, to lunch and dine upon such sacrifices in the usual way, you would flee far away, and execrating the odor, ask pardon from the gods above and would swear never to offer such sacrifices to them.

Is it not mockery, then, is not this a confession, an admission, that you do not know what a god is, nor to what power the force and title of this name ought to be attached or applied? You magnify the gods with counterfeit[55] foods; you ennoble them with fatty fumes; and just because the things which nourish you are pleasing and agreeable to you, you believe that the gods, too, are transported by the pleasures they give and, like barking dogs, lay aside their savagery for sops and often even fawn upon those who offer them.

Variety of ceremonials argues against the gods' existence.

18. And since we now have to do with the subject of victims, what cause, what reason is there that while the immortal gods—for, so far as we are concerned, let them be whatsoever they are believed to be—are or should be of a single essence or single nature, of one and the same kind and condition, not all are appeased by all the victims but certain ones according to certain prescribed sacrifices? What cause is there, to repeat the same question once more, that one god is honored with bulls, another with kids or sheep; this one with suckling pigs, another with unshorn lambs; this with virgin heifers, that with horned goats; this with barren cows, but that one with pregnant sows; this with white, that with dark, one with female, and another with male creatures? Really, if victims are slaughtered to honor and reverence the gods, what difference is there or what does it matter by what animal's life a given trespass is washed away, what ⟨divinity⟩ renounces its

wrath and displeasure? Or is the blood of one victim [less] [56] especially pleasing and agreeable to one god, while another god is filled with pleasure and joy by another? Or, following custom, does one abstain from the flesh of goats because of some reverence or religious scruple? Is another squeamish about touching pork, while still another finds mutton nauseating? And to avoid overtaxing a weak stomach, does this one pass over tough beef and choose tender sucklings to ease his digestion?

19. "But there you are stumbling into error," he says, "for in sacrificing female victims to the female deities and males to the males, there is a hidden and esoteric reason, one that escapes the common understanding."

My problem, my inquiry is not what the regulations of the sacrifices teach or what they contain; but if reason has its way and the truth is accepted that there is no difference of gender among the gods and that they are not distinguished by any sexes,[57] must not all these reasonings be set at naught and the proof and discovery result that they have been believed under the most foolish delusions?

I shall not summon the opinions of scholars who cannot keep from laughing when they hear difference of sex attributed to the immortal gods. I ask any man at random whether he personally believes in his own mind and is personally convinced that the race of the gods is marked out male and female, and has been formed with an arrangement of members suitable for producing offspring.

But if the laws of the sacrifices prescribe that like sexes should be slain to like, that is, female victims to female, male to male gods, what significance is there in the colors that it is fitting and right that to some [58] white, to others dark and pitch-black, should be slain?

"Because," it is said, "the cheerful color and the one which promises luck on account of the pleasant appearance of white, is popular with the gods above and with those who possess control of favorable omens; but, on the other hand, to the gods of ill omen [59] and those who live in the underworld the dusky color and that tinged with gloomy hues is more pleasing." [60]

But if, again, the reasoning holds good that the word 'underworld' is utterly vain and meaningless and that under the earth there are no Plutonian kingdoms or abodes,[61] this negates the idea you have about the black cattle and the gods beneath the earth. And if there are no infernal regions, there must also be no gods of the shades. For how is it possible that, when there are no such regions, there should be said to be inhabitants of the non-existent?

20. But let us agree, as you wish, that there are both lower regions and the shades and that in them some sort of gods not favorable of omen live and are in charge of unfavorable circumstances. Now then, what cause, what reason is there that dark victims and those of the blackest hue should be brought to them?

"Because black things suit black and gloomy things please things that are the same."

Well, now, do you not see—you will permit us to joke nonsensically with you as you do—that the flesh, bones, teeth, fat, the caul along with the brains and the soft marrow in the bones of the victims, are white?

"But the fleeces are black and the bristles of the animals are black."

Therefore, sacrifice only wool to the gods and little bristles plucked from the victims. Let the poor unhappy cattle, however plundered and shorn they may be, draw in the breath

Book Seven: Sacrifices and Ceremonials 501

of heaven and rest in perfect innocence upon their pastures. And if you think that what is black and dark in color is pleasing to the gods of the nether world, why do you not see to it that all the other things which are ordinarily brought to their sacrifices are black and smoky and lugubrious of color? Dye the incense if that is what is offered, the salted meal[62] and all the libations. Pour soot and ashes into the milk, oil, and blood, that the last-mentioned may give up its scarlet color and the others become ghastly-hued. But if you have no misgivings about bringing some things which are white and retain their brightness, you yourselves do away with your own scruples and principles, since in the work of performing the sacrifices you do not preserve any consistency.

21. But here it also behooves us to learn from you regarding the following. If a goat which is ordinarily sacrificed to Liber and Mercury is slain to Jupiter, or if a barren heifer which is prescribed in the Tuscan rite and usage to be given to Proserpina is offered to Unxia, what misdeed will there be in this, what touch of evil or crime, when it makes no difference to the worship, what animal it is from whose head that obligation of bestowing honor is discharged?

"To confuse these things," it is said, "is unlawful and it is no small crime to mix up the ritualistic and expiatory functions."

Explain the reason, please.

"Because it is prescribed to consecrate victims of a certain kind to certain divinities and that certain forms of homage should be observed."

And what, again, is the reason it is prescribed to consecrate victims of a certain kind to certain divinities and that certain forms of homage should be followed? For such a prescription must itself have its own cause and begin and proceed from certain considerations. Are you going to appeal to antiquity and custom? You are quoting human statutes to me and the inventions of a blind creature. I, however, when I ask a reason to be quoted to me, expect to hear either that something has fallen from heaven or—something the subject rather requires—what relation Jupiter has to a bull's blood that it should be sacrificed to him, and not to Mercury, to Liber. Or what is the nature of a goat that it in turn is suited to the latter but should not be agreeable to the Jovian sacrifices? Did the gods divide up the animals among themselves? Was some compromise settlement made by the terms of which the former was to keep away from the victim of the latter, and the latter party was to stop usurping the blood rights of the other? Are they, like jealous little boys, unwilling to allow others to share a taste of their cattle? Or, as the story goes concerning peoples of very different customs, are the things which these use for eating rejected as food by the others?

22. If, then, these things are vain nothings and have no firm basis in any reason, the entire system of the sacrifices is to no purpose. How can that which follows have a suitable cause, when that very first thing from which the second flows is found to be utterly vain and empty and based on no firm foundation?

"To Mother Earth," they say, "is sacrificed a teeming and pregnant sow, but to Minerva, a virgin, a virgin heifer is slain, never plied by goads to exercise its body in toil."

Just the same, in our opinion virgin should not be sacrificed to virgin lest in the animal the virginity be violated which is the goddess' special province, nor should the pregnant and the gravid be sacrificed to Earth out of respect[63] for her fruitfulness, a thing which we all desire and wish to continue always in never-ending fertility. If, because the

Tritonian[64] is a virgin, it is therefore fitting that virgin victims be sacrificed to her, and because the Earth is a mother, she in like manner must be treated to pregnant sows, then Apollo, because he is a musician, should be honored with sacrifice of musicians, and because Aesculapius[65] is a physician, with physicians, and because Vulcan is a smith, with smiths, and because Mercury is eloquent, with the eloquent and most fluent. If it is crazy to say this, or to put it moderately, crude, it is much greater madness to slaughter pregnant animals to Earth, because she is even more prolific; to Minerva, chaste and virgin animals, because she is pure and of untouched virginity.

Nor do the sinister gods exist.

23. As[66] to what we hear you say—that some of the gods are good, others, however, bad and all too prone to indulge their passion for mischief, and that the customary rites are paid to the former to make them helpful, but to the latter to keep them from harming—with what reason this is said, we confess we cannot understand. For to say that the gods are most benevolent and have gentle natures, is a matter of religious virtue and truth, while that they are evil and sinister should under no circumstances be accepted for the simple reason that the divine essence is utterly alien to a spirit of harmfulness; and whatever is capable of producing a cause for harm, should first be looked into for its nature and should then be completely disassociated from the title of god.

And so, if we were to agree with you that the gods are promoters of good luck and bad, not even so is there any reason why you should induce some to give you prosperity, while coaxing others with the sacrifices and bribes not to harm you: first, because the good gods cannot do evil even if they have not received any token of honor, for whatever is mild and placid by nature is far removed from the doing and scheming of mischief; on the other hand, the evil god does not know how to restrain his ferocity, though he be enticed by a thousand flocks and a thousand altars. Bitterness simply cannot turn itself into sweetness or dryness into moisture, the heat of fire into cold; nor can that which is the opposite of anything take and change its opposite into its own nature.

If, for instance, you should stroke a viper with your hand or caress a poisonous scorpion, the former will seek to bite you, the latter, drawing itself together, will fix its sting in you, and your humoring them will do no good, since both are aroused to harm you not by the stings of anger, but by a certain natural pecularity. In like manner, it does no good to wish to deserve well of the sinister gods by offering victims,[67] because whether you do so or, on the contrary, do not, they act ⟨according⟩ to their own nature, and by innate laws and a kind of necessity they are impelled to do those things which they keep on doing.

Moreover, in this way both kinds of gods cease to retain their own powers and their own character. If divine sacrifice is made to the good to make them helpful, and, on the other hand, homage is offered in the same way to the evil to keep them from being harmful, it must then be recognized that the propitious deities will grant no help if they receive no gifts, and from this fact turn out to be bad; and the bad divinities, if they do receive such, will lay thought of harm aside and thus become good. And so the result is that neither are the first propitious nor the second unpropitious, or, what cannot be, that both are at the same time both propitious and unpropitious.

BOOK SEVEN: SACRIFICES AND CEREMONIALS   505

Curious features present in the sacrifices.

24. But well and good [68]—let us grant that the poor unfortunate cattle are not sacrificed at the temples of the gods without some religious obligation and that what has been done according to some customary practice possesses some rational cause. But if that seems a wonderful and a great thing to slay bulls to the gods, to burn the flesh of animals undiminished and as a compact mass, what do the other things mean that have to do with the arts of the Magi and to which they have given a new position, to rank as pontifical mysteries in the recondite laws of the sacrifices, and to which they have assigned a place in the divine services?

What, I say, do these things mean: *apexaones, hirciae, silicernia, longavi?* [69] These are named for certain kinds of sausages, some filled with goat's blood, others with chopped lungs.

What is the meaning of *taedae, neniae, offae,* not the common variety but those known by the specific name of *penitae?* [70] Of these the first is suet cut into very small pieces after the manner of dainties. The second is the extension of the intestine through which the excrement is drawn off after the extraction of all life-giving juices. The *offa penita* is the animal's tail cut off with a piece of the flesh.

What is the meaning of *polimina, omenta, palasea* or, as some call it, *plasea?* [71] Of these the name *omentum* is given to a certain part which lines the gastric cavities and keeps them in place. The *plasea* is an oxtail rolled in wheat flour and blood. The *polimina*, again, are those parts which we call with more modesty the *proles*; by the common people, however, [72] they are usually called by the name of *testes*.

What is the meaning of *fitilla*, of *frumen*, of *africia*, of *gratilla, catumeum, cumspolium, cubula?* [73] Of these the first two are names of pottages but differing in kind and quality, while those following are designations of cakes of different shapes.

We do not care to mention the *caro strebula*[74] which is taken from the haunches of bulls, nor the pieces of meat roasted, the sweetbreads heated on spits over the coals[75] and then roasted on the embers, nor finally the pickles which are a mixture made of four kinds of vegetables. Likewise, we do not want to mention the *fendicae* which are the same as *hirae* and which the language of the man in the street usually calls *ilia*;[76] nor in the same way the *rumae*[77] which are the first orifice at the base of the gullet, where it is the nature of the ruminating tribes to swallow and regurgitate their food; nor the *magmenta*, the *augmina*,[78] nor the thousand kinds of sausages or pottages, to which you have given unintelligible names and that for the purpose that the common people might reverence them more.

25. If whatever men do, particularly in the realm of religion, must have its causes—and nothing should be done without reason in all their occupations and activity—explain and tell us the cause and reason that these things also are given to the gods and burned on the holy altars. Here, regarding this cause, we must pause, we must doggedly urge our point: we want to know what a god has to do with pottages, with cakes, with different kinds of sausages prepared according to a complex ritual out of a variety of ingredients.

Are the divinities susceptible to sumptuous banquets or dinners, so that we should arrange for them feasts ⟨without⟩ number? Do they suffer from delicate stomachs and to relieve them of their squeamishness must we look for different recipes and serve them meats sometimes well-done, sometimes rare, and, again, medium-done and half-raw? And if the gods

Book Seven: Sacrifices and Ceremonials

love to receive all those parts which you call *praesiciae*,[79] and they are gratified by them from a sensation of pleasure or delight, what prevents you, what keeps you from offering all these things at one time along with the bulk of the animals?

What cause, what reason is there that the *caro strebula* should be treated separately, separately the gullet, the tail,[80] and the *plasea*, that the *hirae* and the *omentum* should be thrown in, each alone, to provide the *augmenta*? Are the gods in heaven taken in by a variety of relishes that, as is the vogue following the gourmandizing of the rich and opulent, they take these little tidbits as tasty delicacies, not to appease their hunger with them but to rouse their relaxing palate and to incite in themselves, with their full stomachs, a gluttonous appetite? O remarkable greatness of the gods, incomprehensible to all men, beyond the understanding of all creatures! Yes, indeed, if their favor may be purchased with the testes and gullets of cattle and they will not relent their wrath and indignation except they see the *neniae* burned and the *offae penitae* offered to them!

Incense in the sacrifices.

26. Next we must briefly say something about incense[81] and about wine, for these also are associated with the ceremonies and hold an important place in the religious worship. In the first place, we want to know and ask particularly concerning the incense, where or when you were able to become acquainted with it and to know it, so that you rightly think that it should be given to the gods or is most acceptable to their desires. In fact, it is almost a novelty, and there has been no endless succession of years since knowledge of it came to these regions and it won its way into the divine shrines.

Neither in the so-called heroic age was incense known, as is proved by the fact that in the books of ancient writers no mention of it is found,[82] nor did the parent and mother of superstition, Etruria,[83] have any knowledge or inkling of it, as the rites of the little shrines prove, nor in the four hundred years that the government at Alba flourished was its use introduced by anyone in performing sacrifices, nor did Romulus himself or that skilled expert in concocting religious observances, Numa, know of it as existing or originating, as is shown by the sacred grits[84] with which it was the custom to perform the functions of the usual sacrifices.

From what source, then, was its use first introduced? What innovation descended upon ancient and old custom, so that what was unneeded in so many ages took first place in the ceremonies?[85] It is evident that ⟨if⟩ without the presence of incense there is a hitch in the performance of a rite, and its efficacy is necessary to make the heaven dwellers propitious and benevolent to men, the ancients sinned. Indeed, their whole life was full of sins, for they negligently overlooked the offering of what was most conducive to the pleasure of the gods. But if in ancient times neither men nor gods sought for this stuff contained in incense, we have proof that what antiquity did not believe necessary and modern times introduced without any reason at all, is today also offered uselessly and in vain.

27. Finally, to adhere always to the rule and definition by which it has been shown and established that any act of man must have its own causes, here we shall abide by it also; so we ask you, for what cause, for what reason incense is thrown on the altars before the statues of the divinities and why at its burning they are thought to become friendly and benevolent. What do they get out of such an act or what affects their

minds to justify the opinion that these things are rightly expended and not burned in vain and to no purpose? As you should show why you give incense to the gods, so, too, it is but logical that you should make clear that the gods have a reason for not rejecting it, indeed, why they are so fond of it.

"We honor the gods with this," perhaps some one will say.

Well, we are not asking about your point of view but about that of the gods; not what you do, but how much they value what is given them as a price for their favor, we ask. And—O piety!—how great is that honor or just what does it consist of, made as it is from the sweat of wood and manufactured from the resin of a tree? Should you not know what this incense is or where it comes from, it is a gum flowing from the barks of trees,[86] from the almond tree, for example, the cherry tree, solidifying in tear-like drops. Does this, then, honor and magnify those dignities on high, or if their displeasure should be incurred, is it dissipated by the fumes of incense and lulled to sleep in the wake of wrath dying down? Why, then, do you fail to burn the gum from any tree, taken from any place, without any distinction? For if the deities are honored and are not displeased when Panchaean[87] gums are burned to them, what difference does it make from what substance smoke is raised on the sacred altars, or from what kind of gum the perfumed clouds billow out?

28. Will anyone say that the only reason incense is given the gods above is because it has a pleasant smell and soothes the nostrils, while other things are acrimonious and are excluded because they might offend? In that case the gods of course have noses with which to breathe in air, they inhale and exhale so that the qualities of different odors can make an impression on them. But if we grant this to be a fact, we yoke them under the laws of mortality and shut them out

from the terms of divinity. Evidently, whatever breathes and draws in alternating draughts of air quickly passing in and out [88] must of necessity be mortal [89] because it is sustained by feeding on the atmosphere. And anything that is sustained by feeding on the atmosphere, must necessarily lose its soul and suffer a deterioration and destruction of its vital principle the moment you take away that on which this life-giving reciprocity depends. Therefore, if the gods also breathe and draw into themselves a smell associated with the accompanying airs, it is not beside the facts to say that they also live on supplementary additions and are liable to die, should the air holes be blocked up.

And whence, finally, do you know whether, if they actually are fascinated by sweet odors, the same things are pleasant to them which delight and stimulate your instincts with a like sensation? May it not be possible that what brings pleasure to you, may seem to them on the other hand harsh and disagreeable? Since the essences of the gods are different and their substances are not identical, how are you going to establish that what is qualitatively different feels and reacts in the same way? Do we not each day see that even among earth-bound creatures the same things are bitter to some and sweet to others, that things are fatal to some which are not essentially harmful to others, that the same things which bring relief to some by their pleasant odors, breathe out exhalations deadly to the bodies of others? But the cause for this phenomenon is not inherent in the things: these cannot at the same time be both deadly and wholesome and at the same time both sweet and bitter. But, as each individual is constituted, so he is affected by contact with something coming from without. A peculiar characteristic is involved which is not the product of the reactions of things but is inherent in his own sense nature and its responses.

But this entire complexion of things is far removed from the gods and they are strangers to it by no small interval. For if it is true, as the sages hold, that the gods are incorporeal and are not supported by the excellence of any physical strength, then, as far as they are concerned, an odor is ineffective nor can any fragrant fumes affect their senses—not if you were to burn a thousand pounds of exquisite [90] incense and the whole sky above us were made dark with the clouds of rising vapors. That which does not have physical strength and substance cannot be affected by physical substance. But an odor is a physical entity, as is shown when it reaches the nose. Therefore, an odor cannot by any means be perceived by a god since he lacks a physical body and is without sense perception.[91]

Wine in the sacrifices.

29. Wine is a companion [92] of incense and regarding it we ask for a like explanation—why it is poured on the burning incense. Unless you show a reason for doing this and the cause is set forth, this is no longer something to be attributed to a ludicrous error, but, to put the truth more drastically, to blind madness and insanity. As has already been stated often, everything done should have its manifest cause and not be enshrouded in any dark obscurity. If, therefore, you have confidence in what is done, open it to us, show us, why that liquid is offered, that is, why wine is poured over the altars. Is the reason perhaps that the bodies of the divinities are parched with thirst, and is it necessary that their dryness be relieved by some moisture? Is it their practice, as we mortals have it, to mix wining with dining? Do they likewise, when they are through the solid food of cakes and pottages and slain victims, soak themselves with many helpings of wine and absorb it the better to dissolve and digest the food?

Do give the immortal gods something to drink—please! Bring on the goblets, cups, bowls, and ladles! And as they gorge themselves with bulls[93] and luxurious messes and rich foods—lest some piece of meat, badly gulped down, should lodge en route to the stomach—come here, hurry! Give wine to Jupiter Optimus Maximus,[94] or he will choke! He wants to belch and cannot, and unless that obstruction slides down and is removed there is the greatest danger that his breathing will be choked off and stopped and that heaven will remain bereft of its directors.[95]

30. "But," he says, "this your horseplay gets you nowhere. We do not pour forth unmixed wine to the gods above for these reasons, as if we thought they are thirsty or drink or take delight in tasting of its sweetness. It is given to them as an honor. That their sublimity may be more exalted, greater, more august, we pour forth libations on their altars; and we raise up sweet smells on the smoldering coals to show our reverence."

And what greater insult can be inflicted on the gods than if you should believe that they may be made propitious on receiving wine? Or if you deem it an attribution of great honor if all you do is throw and sprinkle a few drops of wine on the live coals? We are not talking with men devoid of reason or men without a capacity for truth as it is commonly understood. You, too, possess wisdom, possess sense, and deep down in your hearts you know that we are stating the truth. But what are we to do with people who are unwilling to give profound consideration to the facts themselves, to say what they think? You do what you see is done, not what you are convinced should be done, and the reason is, with you a custom having no basis in reason takes precedence rather than the reality of things looked into and appraised in a search for the truth.

What, indeed, has a god to do with wine, or what or how great is the power that goes with its essence that, when it is poured out, his sublimity is enhanced and his authority is supposed to be honored? What, I say, does a god have to do with wine, which is closely associated with the pursuits of Venus,[96] which weakens the sinews of all virtues, which is the enemy of modesty, shame, and chastity, which has often aroused minds and precipitated them into madness and frenzy, and has forced those gods themselves to abdicate their own authority by maddened blasphemies? Is not this, then, impious and wholly sacrilegious to give as an honor something which, if you take it too eagerly, you do not know what you are doing, you do not realize what you are saying, and end up with deserving the scorn and infamy of being a drunkard, reveller, and debauchee?

31. It is worth-while also to quote the actual words with which, when wine is offered, it is customary to use and make supplication:

BE HONORED WITH THIS WINE OFFERED.[97]

The word 'offered,' says Trebatius,[98] has been added for this purpose that all the wine which is everywhere stored in the cellars and storerooms and from which this wine poured out is taken, may not begin to be sacred and therefore removed from human usage. Well, then, when this word is added, that alone will be sacred which shall be brought, and the rest will not be bound by consecration: what kind of honor is this anyway in which a condition, as it were, is imposed on the gods not to ask for more than is given? Or how greedy is the god himself who, if he were not prevented by the limitation of this word, would extend his appetite farther and rob the suppliant of his stores?

BE HONORED WITH THE WINE OFFERED.

That is an insult, not an honor. What if the deity should wish for more and should not be content with what is brought? Must he not be said to be signally insulted who is forced to accept an honor conditionally? Evidently, if all wine which is in cellars would have to be consecrated except for the limitation that is added, it is manifest that an affront is given to the god, to whom a limit is prescribed against his will; and you yourselves in sacrificing violate the duties of the ceremonials, by not granting the god as much wine as you see he wishes to be offered.

BE HONORED WITH THE WINE OFFERED.

What else is this than to say: be honored as much as I wish; be exalted as much as I order; take as much as I decide you are to have and as I delimit by the limitation of the word?

O surpassing sublimity of the gods, which thou shouldst venerate, shouldst cherish, with all the ceremonial duties, but upon which the worshipper imposes conditions, which he adores with stipulations and formulas, which through fear of one word is kept from immoderate cravings for wine!

Other curious features of the sacrifices.

32. But let there be honor, as you wish, in wine, in incense; by the sacrifice and slaughter of victims let the anger of the divinities and their displeasure be appeased: are the gods moved also by garlands, by wreaths, and by flowers? By the clanging of brass, also, and by the shaking of the cymbals? And by tambourines, by symphoniae?[99] And the clatter of the castanets, does this bring it about that when the divinities hear it, they think that they are honored and stop being boiling mad? And like little brats who forget their silly whining

out of fright induced by the sound of rattles, are the omnipotent deities in the same way hushed up by the sound of pipes, and, their indignation mollified, do they relax at the rhythm of the cymbals?

What is the meaning of those morning ditties [100] which you sing, joining your voices to the music of the pipe? The gods above fall asleep, I suppose, and they are supposed to return to their posts. What about those slumber songs with which you bid them an auspicious good night? They just will not rest and go to sleep, and so that they may be beguiled into doing so, they need to hear soothing lullabies.

"Today," says he, "is the purification of the Mother of the Gods." [101]

Evidently because the gods get dirty and to wash off the filth there is need of bath water and a rubdown with some old ashes.

"Tomorrow is the banquet of Jupiter." [102]

Of course, Jupiter dines and he must have his fill of dishes heaped high: long ere now he has been ravenously hungry, having fasted over the space of a year. [103]

"We are celebrating the vintage festival of Aesculapius." [104]

The gods, you must know, cultivate vineyards and with the help of vintagers hired, press out the wine for their own uses.

"The *lectisternium* [105] of Ceres will be on the coming Ides." [106]

The gods, naturally, have couches, and so that they can lie down on softer spreads, the flattened pillows are taken up and shaken out.

"It is the birthday of Tellus." [107]

Yes, the gods issue from wombs and joyfully keep the days on which it is recorded that they began to draw the breath of life.

The games.

33. Further, the games [108] which you hold, called the Floralia and the Megalensia, and all the other things you determined should be sacred and considered as part of the religious observance—what reason, what cause was there for establishing and founding them and designating them from the nomenclature of the divinities?

"The gods are honored by these things," it is said, "and if they have any recollection of offenses committed by men, they disregard it, get rid of it, and renewing their friendship with us, once again become our patrons."

And what cause is there, again, that they should be made calm, gentle, and kindly, when stupid things are done and people who have nothing else to do sport before the multitude looking on? Does Jupiter give up his wrath if the *Amphitruo* [109] of Plautus is acted and spoken, or if Europa, if Leda, ⟨if⟩ Ganymede or Danae be danced, does he restrain his wrath? Does the Great Mother become calmer, more gentle, if she sees that ancient tale of Attis rehashed by the actors? Will Venus cancel her displeasure if she sees mimics act out the part of Adonis [110] in dancing? Does the anger of Alceus' scion [111] grow weak if the tragedy of Sophocles entitled *The Trachinian Women*, or the *Hercules* [112] of Euripides is acted? Or does Flora think she is treated with respect if in her games she sees a portrayal of shameful things and an exodus from the brothels to the theaters? Is this not, then, a lessening of the dignity of the gods, to dedicate and consecrate to them the most shameful things, things which a stern critic rejects and the performers of which your law has bidden to be dishonored and to be counted infamous? [113]

Yes, unquestionably the gods enjoy the mimes, and that extraordinary being, never comprehended by any human

Book Seven: Sacrifices and Ceremonials 517

nature, lends its ears enthusiastically to hear these things, in the majority of whose plots they know they are involved to furnish material for derision! They take delight—so it is—with the shaved heads of the harlequins,[114] in the sound of the slaps[115] and the applause, in the shameful acts and words.

If they see men throwing off their manhood in exchange for woman's effeminacy,[116] some shouting to no purpose, others running around without cause, and still others, keeping their friendship, knocking each other black and blue and maiming each other with the cruel cestus;[117] others vying in blowing, distending their cheeks with wind and whistling more noisily than the south wind[118]—then the gods raise their hands to heaven, they jump up from their seats awed by such remarkable feats, shout, and rejoin men on terms of affection!

If these things prevail upon the immortal gods to forget their grudges, if the comedies, the Atellan farces,[119] and mimes are for them a source of rapturous delights, why do you hesitate, why do you refrain from saying that the gods themselves play, frisk, dance, compose obscene songs, and weave with quivering haunches? Indeed, what difference is there or what does it matter, whether they do these things themselves, or whether they get pleasure and delight when they are done by others?

The pagan gods are anthropomorphic.

34. What, then, is the source of these depraved ideas, or what are the causes that gave rise to them? Primarily, of course, because of the fact that men, unable to know what a god is, what he stands for—his nature, substance, character—whether he has form or is delimited by no outline of body, whether or not he does anything, is constantly on the alert or sometimes relaxes into slumbers, runs, sits, walks or is free

from such activity and its cessation, being unable, as I said, to know all these things or to discern them by any reasoning faculty, they fell into these notions, with the result that they fashioned gods after themselves and attributed to them a capacity for action, for situations, and for volition such as they themselves possessed. But if they were to recognize in themselves a creature of no account and that there is no appreciable difference between themselves and a tiny ant, they would assuredly cease thinking that they have anything in common with the gods above and would modestly hold themselves to the bounds of their own lowliness.

But, as it is, because they see *themselves* possessed of faces, eyes, heads, cheeks, ears, noses, and other members and parts of flesh, they think of the gods as also fashioned in the same way and as maintaining their individuality in a corporeal organism. And because they see that *they* rejoice at something they associate with joy and become sad in the presence of things producing grief, they think that divinities, too, derive gladness from gladsome circumstances and become dejected in the absence of the gladsome. Because *they* are interested in games, they think the minds of heaven's denizens also are regaled by the enjoyment of games; and because *they* take delight in refreshing themselves with warm baths, they hold that cleansing baths please the gods too.[120] We human beings gather in our vintages—and they suppose and believe that the gods, too, gather and bring in their grapes. We have our birthdays—and they claim that the heavenly powers have natal days. And if they could ascribe to the gods ill health, sicknesses, and bodily diseases, they would promptly say they are splenetic, blear-eyed and ruptured, because they themselves are often splenetic and blear-eyed and weighed down by huge hernias.[121]

Book Seven: Sacrifices and Ceremonials 519

Comparison of pagan and Christian theology.

35 [49].[122] Very well, now that the discussion has brought out squarely these points, let us briefly size up what each has to say and decide whether it is you who have better ideas about the gods above, or whether our beliefs are far more honorable and correct and so as to give and assign to the divine nature the dignity that is its own.

To begin with, you declare that the gods you think or believe have a place in existent things and of whom you have set up images and forms in all the temples, were born and were produced by the practice of intercourse between males and females. But we, on the contrary, hold that if they actually are gods and have the authority, the power and the dignity proper to such title, they are either unbegotten—for this our reverence commands us to believe; or if they have a beginning in birth, it is for the Supreme God[123] to know how He has made them or how many ages there are since He made them participants of the eternity of His own divinity.

You believe that the gods have sex and that some are males and others are of the female kind. We deny emphatically that the heavenly powers are distinguished by sex,[124] since such a distinction has been given to earthly creatures, which by the will of the Author of the universe were to embrace and generate, providing by their passion for offspring. You think they bear the likeness of men and are fashioned with the countenances of mortals. We think these images far removed from them, since form belongs to a mortal body; and if they have any, we swear without hesitation or doubt that no one can understand it. By you they are said each to have his trade, like artisans. We laugh when we hear such things, since it is our firm conviction that the gods have no need of professions;

and as to these, it is clearly established that they have been provided to assist poverty.

36 [50]. You say that there are some of them who cause dissensions,¹²⁵ some who bring pestilences; others, love, madness; others, again, who preside over wars and find pleasure in bloodshed. But we, on the contrary, judge that ⟨things of this kind⟩ are alien to the dispositions of the divinities; or, if there are those who expose and subject wretched mortals to them, we maintain that they have nothing in common with the nature of gods and should not be spoken of by this name. In your appraisal of them the divinities grow angry and perturbed and are given over and subject to the other mental states. We think that such emotions are foreign to them, for they belong to savage beings and those who run the course of mortality.

You think they rejoice in the blood of cattle, in the slaughter and sacrifice of victims; that they are gladdened and are reconciled with men as a result of the quietus put on their offended feelings. We hold that among the heaven dwellers there is no love of blood and that they are not so unfeeling as to part with their wrath only when satiated on the blood of poor animals.

You think honor is given to the gods by wine and incense and that their eminence is thus enhanced. We judge it a monstrous phenomenon that any man at all should believe that a god is made more august by smoke or that by some negligible drops of wine the same should think that he has been implored by men with sufficient reverence and respect.

You are convinced that the gods are delighted and influenced by the clash of brass and the sound of pipes, by horse races and games in the theaters, and that the wrath which they have conceived somewhere along the line is quelled by such satisfaction. We deem it out of place, indeed, incredible, that they who transcend by a thousand degrees every kind of virtue in its very highest form of perfection, should regard as pleasant and be delighted with those things at which the wise man laughs and which no one thinks possessed of charm except little children and such as enjoy only a superficial and ordinary training.

37 [51]. Since this is so, and there is so great a disparity between your opinions and ours, where are we impious on the one hand and you pious on the other, when the proportion of piety and impiety must be weighed on the beliefs of the parties concerned?

It is not the man who makes himself some image to worship as a god or who slaughters a harmless beast and burns it on holy altars, who is to be regarded a devotee of religion. Religion is constituted by critical judgment and the right view about the gods, meaning that you do not regard them as desiring anything contrary to what becomes their own sublimity. Truly, when we see all these things which are offered them consumed here under our very eyes, what else can be said to reach them from us than opinions worthy of the gods and most appropriate to their name? These are the surest gifts, these the true sacrifices; for gruel and incense along with flesh only feed the devouring flames, and go most intimately with the *parentalia*[126] of the dead.

As a result of sacrifices pagan gods are said to have been appeased.

38 [35]. "But if the immortal gods," it is said, "cannot be angry and their nature is not agitated or torn by any passions, what about the histories, the annals, in which we find it written that the gods, harboring many a grievance, brought

on pestilences, droughts, and crop failures and other crises, critical situations upon states and nations, and, again, that they, appeased by sacrifices, dismissed their torrid wrath and gave the skies and the weather a more pleasing complexion? What about the rumblings, the quaking of the earth, which we have heard took place because the games were carelessly performed and their specific forms and character had not received the proper attention, while when they had been reinstated and had been conducted again with careful observance, the terror inspired by the gods subsided and they turned again to caring for, and befriending, man?

"How often, when sacrifice had been made in accordance with the instructions of the seers and the responses of the soothsayers, and certain gods had been brought in from the nations across the sea,[127] and had shrines made for them and certain statues and images had been set on high pillars,[128] have not the fears of imminent dangers been averted and most formidable enemies beaten and the republic extended both by the frequent boon of victories and the acquisition of a string of provinces! Certainly this would not happen if the gods despised the sacrifices, the games, and the other forms of worship and did not think they were honored by these expiations. Hence, if in the presence of these offerings all the burning indignation of the divinities cools off and things which a moment earlier evidently inspired terror are transformed into happy outcomes, it is clear that all this is not done without the will of the gods; and to criticize us for giving these things to them shows conceit and a complete lack of experience."

BOOK SEVEN: SACRIFICES AND CEREMONIALS 523

The story of Jupiter's anger at the "dancer."

39 [36]. In our discussions, then, we have come to the real point at issue, that on which the subject hinges. We have come to the real question around which all else connected revolves, a question deserving that we put aside our superstitious dread[129] and rid ourselves of partisan interests. We should look closely whether there really are gods who, you assert, rage when offended and become gentle as the result of sacrifices, or whether they are something entirely different and should be disassociated from what this title and power stands for. Of course, we do not deny that in the writings of the annalists all these things are found which you have brought forward by way of opposition. Yes, we, too, by the limited endowment and ability that is ours, have read and know the story[130] how once at those very games in the circus which take place for the Great Jupiter, before the show began, a master dragged through the center of the circus a slave really deserving severe punishment, beating him with rods, and afterwards inflicted on him the customary penalty of the cross. Then because of some menacing situation the games were stopped before the races had been concluded. Not long afterwards a pestilence began to rage through the City. And when each day added misfortune to misfortune worse than before, and the people were perishing in droves, Jupiter is said to have appeared in a dream to a certain farmer of obscure estate. He told him to go to the consuls, to inform them that a "dancer"[131] had displeased Jupiter, that things might be better for the City if proper respect were restored to the games and if they were repeated with scrupulous care. And when the fellow completely neglected to do this, either because he thought it an idle dream and that no one who

heard the story would believe him, or because, mindful of his humble birth, he avoided and dreaded approaching such influential persons, Jupiter became angry with the procrastinator and penalized him with the death of his sons. Later, when he threatened the death of the man himself if he did not report his displeasure at the "dancer," the man became terror-stricken by fear of death. As he himself was already infected and was burning with the fever of the plague, he was carried to the Senate House on the advice of his kinsfolk, and when he had related the vision in his dream, the raging pestilence ceased. Then a repetition of the games was decreed and painstaking care given to the shows, and the people recovered their former good health.

Other examples of appeasement.

40 [37]. Neither shall we deny that we know also that once when the city and republic were in sore straits caused by either a terrible plague relentlessly infecting the people and carrying them off, or by powerful enemies who because of their successes in battle were at that time perilously close to robbing them of their liberty, at the bidding and advice of the seers certain gods [132] were summoned from nations across the sea and honored with magnificent temples; and that the malignancy of the plague subsided, and when the forces of the enemy had been crushed, there was many a triumph and the territories of the empire were increased and innumerable provinces fell under your sway and laws.

Nor does it escape our knowledge that we read it recorded that when the Capitol and many objects on it were struck by lightning, even the image of Jupiter, which stood on a lofty column, pitched forward from its place.[133] A response was then given by the soothsayers that cruel misfortunes were portended, arising from conflagrations and murders, from the perishing of laws and the subversion of justice, especially through internal enemies and an impious band of conspirators; and that these things could be averted, indeed, this was the only way in which the criminal designs could be brought to light, if Jupiter were again set up on a higher pedestal, turned to the east and facing the rays of the sun. The response proved truthworthy, for when the pillar was erected and the statue turned to the sun, the intrigues came to light and punishment was meted out for the crimes revealed.

Criticism of these stories.

41 [38]. All these things which have been mentioned have, indeed, the character of the miraculous—rather, they are *believed* to have it—if they come to men's ears just as we have adduced them here; and we do not deny that there is something in them which at first glance, as the saying is,[134] may captivate and deceive us by its resemblance to truth. But if you will take the effort to regard closely the facts, the persons involved and the intentions of these persons, you will find nothing worthy of the gods, and, as has already been said often, nothing that should be referred to the character and dignity of this title.

First of all, who is there that would believe him to have been a god who took idle delight in horse racing and considered it most pleasant to find diversion in this kind of sport? Indeed, who is there who will agree that it was Jupiter, called by you the supreme god and founder of all things, who set out from heaven to see geldings competing in speed and tearing off the seven laps;[135] and that though he himself willed that they should be of unequal agility, nevertheless he rejoiced that they passed, were passed, plunged headlong on their necks, turned up on their backs with their chariots; that others were dragged along and lamed, their legs broken; and that he regarded these as the highest delights—imbecilities consisting of trifles compounded with brutalities, things which any man of joyous character not brought up to look on the serious and weighty side of things, would consider as childishness and would reject as follies?

Who is there, I say, who would believe—to keep right on repeating this topic—that he was of the divine stock who, being irritated when during the games ⟨a slave⟩[136] was driven across the circus to suffer penalty and punishment for his deserts, became embittered and hot with anger and set about taking his own vengeance? If the slave was guilty and should have been punished with that chastisement, why should Jupiter have become excited with indignation at all? After all, nothing was being done unjustly, indeed, a guilty wretch[137] was being punished with condign chastisement. But if he was guiltless and not liable to any charge, Jupiter himself was the cause of the "dancer's" vitiating the games: he might have helped him but failed to do so. Indeed, he was bent upon allowing what he disapproved of and exacting penalties from others for what he had permitted. And why did he then complain and declare that he was wronged by that "dancer" because the fellow was led, cut by rods and whips, through the circus to be crucified?

42 [39]. And what pollution or abomination could have resulted from this fact, either to make the circus less pure or to defile Jupiter, when in a few moments, in a few seconds, he beheld so many thousands throughout the world perishing divers kinds of deaths and in various kinds of agonies?

"He was led across," it is said, "before the games were begun."

If this was from a sacrilegious heart and contempt for religion, we must actually excuse Jupiter for being angry that he was contemned and that no greater care was given to his games in the circus. But if from mistake or mischance that hidden fault was not noticed and recognized, was it not the correct and decent thing for Jupiter to pardon human failings and to grant ready pardon to blind ignorance?

"But the thing had to be punished."

And after this will anyone believe that he was a god who avenged and punished carelessness in the matter of a childish show by the destruction of a state? Was he possessed of any dignity of character or of any firm stability at all, who, to assure himself new races to amuse his passion for pleasure, turned the air men breathed into deadly poison and ordained a holocaust of mortals from the disease of the plague?

If the magistrate[138] who sponsored the games did not care to learn who was led through the circus on that day and guilt was thus contracted, what had the unhappy people done that they with their own life should pay the penalty for another's fault and be cruelly thrust out of existence by pestilence and disease? Indeed, what had the women, whose weaker constitutions kept them from public concerns,[139] the grown-up girls, and the little boys done? What, finally, had the little ones, still dependent on nursing for food, done, that one and the same severity should be visited upon them and that before they could taste the joys of life they should feel the bitterness of death?

43 [40]. ⟨If⟩ Jupiter aimed at greater conscientiousness in the conduct of his games and that they should begin anew; if he sincerely wanted to restore the people to health and the evil which he had provoked to stop and spread no further, was it not the more correct thing for him to go straight to the

consul, to some public priest, the *pontifex maximus* or to his own *flamen Dialis*,[140] and to reveal to *him* through a dream the fault of the "dancer" and the cause of the affliction rampant at the time?

What was the reason that he should choose as the emissary of his will and the spokesman of the satisfaction sought a man living in the country, unknown and obscure of name, unacquainted with city matters, perhaps not even knowing what a "dancer" is? And if he[141] knew, as he certainly did—provided he was divine—that the man would not carry out his mission, would it not have been easier and more becoming for a god to change the mind of the man and instil in him the will to obey, than to try more cruel ways and, like brigands, to vent his rage everywhere without any discrimination?

If the old farmer, not quick-witted enough for action, delayed doing what he had been told because he was impeded by the factors stated above, of what had those unfortunate children of his been guilty that his wrath and indignation should be vented upon them and that they should pay for the sins of others by being robbed of their own life?

And who is there who would believe that he was a god who was so unjust, so wicked, and who does not even keep the laws of mortals, among whom it would be considered a great wrong to strike one for another's fault, and to avenge the misdeeds of some by the necks of others?

"But he did cause the man himself to be seized too by the cruel pestilence."[142]

Would it not have been more effective, then, indeed more fair, if it seemed that this should be done, that terror as a means of coercion should first be applied to the father directly who was the cause of such great passion and whose disobedience caused the delay, than to do violence to the children and

Book Seven: Sacrifices and Ceremonials 529

to injure and destroy innocent persons in order to cause him sorrow?

What sort of savagery was this, this cruelty so great, that when his offspring was dead it afterwards terrified the father because of the peril to his own person? Had he been willing [143] to do this long before, that is, in the first place, not only would the innocent brothers not have been slain but the demands of the offended divinity would have been recognized.

"That is true, but when he had discharged his obligation to convey the information, the disease vanished at once and the man was immediately restored to health."

And what is there remarkable in this if he rescinded the evil which he had inflicted and only vaunted himself with additional pretense? And if you weigh the circumstances thoroughly, the cruelty involved outweighed the gift of restored health; for he preserved the poor man who desired to follow his sons in death, not for the joys of life but to taste loneliness and to feel the torments of bereavement.

44 [41]. In like manner one could go through the other stories and show in these also and in interpretations given them, that something far different from what the gods should be is said in them and about them, as for instance in the one which I shall next relate. I shall combine with this only one or two others, lest giving too much of this beget boredom.

[Of course,[144] we do not deny that in the writings of the annalists all these things are found which you have brought forward by way of opposition. Yes, we, too, by the limited endowment and ability that is ours have read these same things and know that they have been put forth, but the whole of the investigation rests upon this point whether there really are gods who, you assert, rage when offended and become gentle by games and sacrifices, or whether they are entirely different and should be disassociated from what this title and power stands for.

In the first place, who thinks or believes them to be gods who are passionately fond of acting and dancing on the stage, of the idle delight of horse racing; who set out from heaven to gaze upon stupid and lifeless acting and are pained, feeling offended and thinking they are deprived of some of their proper respect, if the player should stand still for a little or the flutist take a little rest when he is tired; who declare that the "dancer" has displeased them if some guilty fellow passes through the circus to pay the supreme penalty for what he has done? If all these things be subjected to a thorough and impartial scrutiny, they will be found to be foreign not only to the gods but to any man of refinement, even though his training does not measure up to the highest ideals of gravity and dignity.

Who in the first place would consider those to be gods, or even believe in their existence, who have sadistic dispositions given to rage, and cast them off again, mollified by a cup of blood and the smoke of incense? Who spend holidays and experience transports of passionate delights at the acting and dancing of stage players, who set out from heaven to look at geldings racing to no purpose and for no reason, and rejoice that they pass, are passed, plunge headlong on their necks, turn up on their backs with their chariots; that others are dragged along and lamed, their legs broken; who declare that the "dancer" has displeased them if some guilty fellow passes across the circus to pay the supreme penalty for what he has done? Who grieve that they are deprived of some of their proper respect if the player should stand still for a little or the flutist take a little rest when he is tired; that a mother's boy [145] happens to fall, stumbling because of some unsteadiness ⟨of the floor⟩?

BOOK SEVEN: SACRIFICES AND CEREMONIALS 531

If all these things be subjected to a thorough and impartial assay, they will be found to be utterly foreign not only to the gods but also ⟨to⟩ a man of common sense, even though he may not have been taught the study of truth by rational thinking.]

The importation of Aesculapius.

"After certain gods," you say, "were brought from across the sea and after temples were established for them, after their altars were piled high with sacrifices, the plague-stricken people regained their strength and recovered; and the pestilential diseases fled when health marched in."

What god, I ask, tell us.

"Aesculapius," you say, "from Epidaurus, the god who presides over good health and is established on the island in the Tiber."[146]

If we were in the mood to deal with those statements of yours more closely, we might demonstrate on your own authority that he was not at all divine who was conceived and born in the womb of a woman, who in the course of years had reached that period of life at which a bolt of lightning, according to statements contained in your books, banished him from life and light.

But we drop that question—let the son of Coronis[147] be numbered, as you wish, among the immortals and endowed with the eternal sublimity in heaven: but what else was brought from Epidaurus than a serpent with great coils?[148] If we trust the annals and grant they report the tested truth, then, as has been recorded—nothing. And now, what shall we say? That Aesculapius, whom you extol, a noble, holy god, the giver of health, the averter, preventer, destroyer of the worst sicknesses, is contained within the shape and contours of a serpent, crawling over the earth like worms born in the mud; with chin and breast he rubs the soil, dragging himself along by sinuous coils, and to enable himself to go forward, he draws his hind part by the efforts of the front.

45 [42]. And as we read that he also used food by which life abides in bodies, he has jaws opened wide through which to gorge down the food craved for with distended mouth. He has a belly to receive it, a place for digesting the flesh he has chewed and swallowed, to supply blood to his body and to reinvigorate his strength. He also has a terminal passageway through which filth passes, relieving his body of a loathsome burden. Whenever he changes his position and prepares to pass from one place to another, he does not, like a god, fly mysteriously through the starry heavens and in a moment of time stand where the situation demands, but like some dumb animal he looks for a conveyance to carry him. He avoids the waves of the deep and that he may arrive safe and unharmed, he embarks on a ship with men and that vaunted god of the public health entrusts himself to frail wood and pieces of timber joined together.

We do not think you can prove and demonstrate that that serpent was Aesculapius, or you may wish to palm off this evasion and say that the god changed himself into a snake so that he might misrepresent himself and prevent anybody from seeing who or what he was.[149]

If you say this, the very inconsistency of the matter will show how weak and feeble your statements are. Thus, if the god tried to avoid being seen by men, then he should not have been willing to be seen in the form of a serpent, since in any form at all he would not be another, but his own self. But if he had intended to let himself be seen[150] and not to deny himself to sight, why did he not show himself such as he knew himself to be and as he realized himself to be vested with the power of his own divinity? This would have been better and far preferable and more befitting his august dignity than to become a beast and change himself into the likeness of a repulsive animal and to give rise to doubts and contradictions as to whether he was a true god or some other thing far removed from the sublimity above.

46 [43]. "But if it was not a god," he says, "why did it, after leaving the ship and crawling to the island in the Tiber, at once disappear and was never seen afterwards?"

Well, how are we to know that there was not some object on the terrain under cover of which it hid itself, or some crevice in the earth? Give an account of it yourselves, you tell us—if you have definite observances for definite personages—what that thing was or what sort of identification it is to receive. Since this is your concern and we are dealing with your deity and your religion, yours is the task to teach us, yours the task to show us what it was, rather than to wish to hear our opinions and to await our decisions. For, as regards us, what else can we say than what took place and was seen, what is handed down in all the records and was observed by eyewitnesses? We, of course, call this thing of very great size and of immense length a snake; or if this term is too commonplace, we can call it an *anguis,* we can give it the name serpent,[151] or any other word sanctified by usage or invented in the growth of language. Certainly, if it crawled like a snake, neither carrying itself on feet nor progressing by movement of lower limbs, but supporting itself on its belly and breast; if flesh was the substance of which it was made and it lay out in an elongate slippery form; if it had a head and a tail, a back covered with scales, a hide spotted with different colors, a mouth bristling with fangs and prepared to bite—

what else can we say than that it was of a terrestrial species, although of huge and excessive size, although it surpassed in length and strength of body that which was slain by Regulus [152] through the might of his army?

This is our alien thinking, however, which makes us subverters and destroyers of the truth! It is therefore for you to explain what it was and of what species, name, and character. How could it have been a god when it had the things we have said, things which gods must not have if they count on being gods and possessing the sublimity that goes with this name?

"After it crawled to the island in the Tiber, it was at once nowhere to be seen. This shows that it was a divinity."

May we then know whether there was something there in the way under cover of which he hid himself or some crevice in the earth,[153] or some caverns and open spaces in masses of rock piled up unevenly, into which it hurried out of sight of those who were watching it? What if it leaped across the river? What if it swam across? What if it made for the dense forests? It is feeble reasoning to suppose from the fact that the serpent withdrew itself from sight with the greatest speed, that therefore it was a god, since by the same reasoning it can, on the other hand, be shown not to have been a god.

47 [44]. "But if that snake was not an actual god, why was its arrival followed by a dissipation of the virus of the pestilence and a restoration of the Roman people to health?"

And we on our part ask the question: if the books of fate [154] and the responses of the soothsayers commanded the god Aesculapius to be invited to the City that he might render it safe and sound from the contagion of the plague and from pestilential diseases, and he came without spurning it, changed, as you say, into the form of a snake, why has the

Book Seven: Sacrifices and Ceremonials 535

city of Rome been so often afflicted by the ravages of this evil, so often—again and again—tortured, harassed, and decimated by countless thousands of deaths of citizens?

Naturally, since the god was said to have been summoned for this purpose, to drive away completely all the causes by which pestilences were set in motion, it followed that the city should have been inviolable and rendered forever immune and unharmed in the face of any ill wind. Yet we see, as has been said above, that very often it has had seasons of mourning because of these diseases and that the stamina of the people has been broken and weakened by severe losses. Where, then, was Aesculapius? Where was he, promised by the venerable oracles? Why, after temples had been founded and shrines built for him, did he suffer a city that had deserved well by him, to continue to be subjected to the plague? And that though he had been summoned for the very purpose that he should cure it of its pressing evils and not permit anything so dreadful to creep upon it in the future?

48 [45]. Perhaps someone will say that the reason why the protection of such a god has been wanting in the more recent ages since then is that the modern way of life is godless and reprehensible; that he brought help, however, to the former ages because they were innocent and not given to contracting any guilt. Now this might have been acceptable and said with some logic, if either in ancient times all men were good without exception or if later times produced only wicked people without any distinction.

But since it is a fact that among great peoples, nations, indeed, even in all cities, the human race has been a composite of natures, inclinations, and habits, and in both former centuries and later ages the good and bad have been able to exist together, it is rather stupid to say that on account of wickedness the later mortals have not received the aid of the divinities. For if on account of the wicked of later centuries the good of recent times have had no protection, then in like manner, because of the ancient evildoers the good people of former times should not have received the favor of the divinities. Conversely, if because of the ancient good folk the ancient evildoers were also preserved, then the following age, too—however reprehensible—ought to have been protected, on account of the later good.

Therefore, either that snake was brought when the force of the plague was already broken and spent,[155] and it gained the reputation of a savior when it had been of no assistance at all, or the hymns of the fates must be said to have strayed far from true predictions, since the remedy given by them is found not to have been given as an aid to all thereafter but to a single age alone.

The importation of the Great Mother of the Gods.

49 [46]. "But also the Great Mother,"[156] he says, "summoned from Phrygian Pessinus in the very same way by the command of the seers, was a cause for safety and great joy to the people. For on the one hand an enemy[157] powerful over a long time was dislodged from the position he held in Italy and on the other, the ancient glory of the City was restored by glorious and famous victories[158] and the boundaries of the empire were extended far and wide, and from countless nations, cities, and peoples the rights of liberty were wrested away and the yoke of slavery placed upon them, and many other things, accomplished both abroad and at home, firmly established the renown and majesty of the people."

If the historical records speak the truth and do not intersperse falsehoods in their accounts, then nothing else is on

BOOK SEVEN: SACRIFICES AND CEREMONIALS   537

record as having been brought from Phrygia, sent by King Attalus, than a certain stone of no great size, which could be carried in a man's hand without exerting any pressure on him, dusky black in color, uneven with some edges[159] projecting, and which we all see today[160] placed in that very image in lieu of a face,[161] rough and uncut, giving to the image a countenance by no means life-like.

50 [47]. Are we to say, then, that the famous Hannibal of Carthage, a formidable, powerful enemy, under whom the Roman fortunes trembled in the balance and its greatness shook, was driven from Italy by a stone? *He* was crushed by a stone? A stone made *him* in trepidation flee and to be unlike himself? And as for the new rise to supreme power and to royal supremacy, was nothing accomplished by wisdom, by human strength? And in the return to the eminence of old was nothing contributed by the many generals outstanding in military science and practical experience?

Did the stone give power to some, to others weakness? Did it trip up some in the midst of success but extricate others from the despair of blasted fortune? And what man will believe that a stone taken from the earth, in no sense endowed with life, of sooty and black color, ⟨small⟩[162] physically, was the Mother of the Gods? Or who again would accept—for this remains the only alternative left—the belief that the power of any divinity dwelt in pieces of flint, like the potential fire hidden in its veins?[163]

"And how was the victory obtained if there was no divinity present in the stone from Pessinus?"

By the persistent efforts and the stout hearts of the combatants, we can say, by practice, time,[164] planning, reasoning; fate, too, and the vicissitudes of fortune are possible factors. But if by the aid of the stone the state of affairs was improved and a happy victory was obtained, where was the Phrygian Mother when by the decimation of so many great armies [165] the commonwealth lay prostrate and the danger of its fall was imminent? Why did she not counteract the menacing fate? Why did she not crush such blows delivered in the war and fend them off before these [166] frightful losses occurred by which all the blood was shed and life itself, with all its vitality spent, almost failed?

"She had not yet been brought over and she had not yet been asked to lend her favor."

Granted; yet a kindly helper never demands to be asked. He always brings his assistance of his own accord.

"She was not able to repel the enemy and put him to flight, because many lands and seas still separated her from Italy."

But to a god—if god he be—to whom the earth is a mere point and to whose nod all things are subject, nothing at all is far away.

51 [48]. But assume that the divinity, as you ask us to believe, were really present in that very stone: what mortal is there, however gullible he may be and however attuned his ears may be to any and all fictions, who would judge her to have been a goddess then or that she should be spoken of and named such today, a being who at one time requires this, at another demands that; who abandons and despises her own votaries, moves from the more lowly provinces and allies herself with the richer and more powerful peoples?

Again, let us grant her love for warfare and a penchant for being involved in the slaughter of battles, in death and bloodshed: if it is characteristic of gods—providing they are true gods and deserving to be identified by the meaning of that word and the import of that name—to do nothing with malice, nothing unjustly, to manifest themselves to all men with the same favor without any partiality—is there any man who ⟨would believe⟩ that she was of divine stock, or had any sense of fairness worthy of the gods, she who, meddling with the dissensions of men, broke the power of some, while offering and giving patronage to others; deprived some of their liberty, carried off others to the pinnacle of power; who subjugated the guiltless world [167] that a single state might become pre-eminent and its rise prove the perdition of humankind? [168]

NOTES

BOOK FOUR

Book Four continues the attack begun in Book Three on the ridiculous features of the pagan cults, centering its polemic at first upon the deifications of abstractions, the sinister gods, and multiple deities, and concluding with a vigorous onslaught upon the myths which impute lustful characters to both gods and goddesses and even to the great Jupiter himself.

On these myths as the pagans believed them, the reader will do well to consult the handbook on Greek mythology which has come down to us under the name of the *Bibliotheca* or 'Library' of Apollodorus, a writer of unknown date and identity. Arnobius shows no positive evidence that he knew the *Bibliotheca* (but cf. n. 176), which may be most conveniently consulted in the edition published in the Loeb Classical Library with very instructive notes by Sir James G. Frazer (2 vols., London-New York 1921).

Readers of the *Protrepticus* of Clement of Alexandria, which is also easily accessible in the same series with a translation by G. W. Butterworth (London-New York 1919), will be struck by the many passages in Arnobius which resemble others in the *Protrepticus*. The generally accepted opinion concerning these parallels, that Arnobius knew Clement's work and exploited it, is expounded most thoroughly in the Kiel dissertation of Alexander Röhricht, *De Clemente Alexandrino Arnobii in irridendo gentilium cultu auctore* (Hamburg 1892). A contrary opinion, however, is advanced in the Berlin dissertation of Friedrich Tullius, *Die Quellen des Arnobius im 4., 5. und 6. Buch seiner Schrift Adversus Nationes* (Bottrop i. W. 1934), but Tullius' work has recently been subjected to a strong and convincing counterattack by Emanuele Rapisarda, *Clemente fonte di Arnobio* (Turin 1939) who lists the many correspondences between the two authors on p. 67. See also Introd. 42 f.

[1] The Romans are mentioned specifically because the abstract deities he intends to name are all Roman. Cf. H. L. Axtell, *The Deification of Abstract Ideas in Roman Literature and Inscriptions* (diss. Chicago 1907) 85 f.; W. W. Hyde, *Paganism to Christianity in the Roman Empire* (Philadelphia 1946) 11 f. In a similar passage Lactantius (*Epit.* 21) lists Spes, Fides, Concordia, Pax, Pudicitia, and

Pietas. Rapisarda (*Arnob.* 139) cites also for *Adv. nat.* 4. 1: Augustine, *De civ. Dei* 3. 25, 4. 14 f., 4. 17 f., 4. 21, 4. 33.

[2] *Pietas*: a divinity embodying the abstract quality represented by the adjective *pius* which to the Romans connoted 'having the proper attitude towards the gods, the fatherland, and the family.' Aeneas was the typical incarnation of this quality (cf. Vergil's *pius Aeneas*). On the divinity, see Wissowa 331 f.; on the temple in Rome, Platner-Ashby 389 f. Cf. also 7. 9.—On Concordia, goddess of harmony, see Wissowa 328 f.; R. Peter, *LM* 1. 914-22; E. Pottier, *DA* 1. 1434; A. Aust, *RE* 4 (1901) 831. On the temple in Rome, see Platner-Ashby 138-40.—On Salus, goddess of safety and health, see Wissowa 131 f., 308 f.; *LM* 4. 295-301; J. A. Hild, *DA* 4. 1056-9; on the temple, Platner-Ashby 462.—For the god Honos, cf. Wissowa 149-51. At least three temples were erected to him in Rome; the earliest is mentioned by Cicero (*De leg.* 2. 58; cf. *CIL* 6. 3692 = 30913 = Dessau, *Inscr. lat. sel.* 3794); the second, set up in 234 B. C., was restored in 208 B. C. when another to Virtus was erected adjacent to it; while the third was built by C. Marius from the spoils taken from the Cimbri and Teutones (see Platner-Ashby 258 f., for evidence on all three). Cf. G. Wissowa, *LM* 1. 2707-9.—On Felicitas, cf. Wissowa 266 f.; H. Steuding, *LM* 1. 1473-5; J. A. Blanchet, *DA* 2. 1031-2; W. Otto, *RE* 6 (1909) 2163-6; on the temple, Platner-Ashby 207.

[3] The word *nomina*, occurring frequently in Arnobius in a similar sense, has often been changed by earlier editors to *numina*, but no one has felt it out of place here, because the deities mentioned are abstractions.

[4] Here the first person plural does not refer, as ordinarily, to the Christians as distinct from the pagans but to mankind in general.

[5] The MS reads *vestrorum de numinum delusione*: the error is doubtless due to dittography from *delusiones*.

[6] Both editors make this a question. Agahd (125) wants to make Cornelius Labeo the source, but even Kroll (70) joins Tullius (72) in denying that any source is needed. Cf. Cicero, *De nat. deor.* 2. 23. 61, 3. 24. 61, and Wissowa 83, 319.

[7] Marchesi would retain the MS *onerastis* ('burden') in place of Reifferscheid and Sabaeus' *honorastis* which seems better.—On Victoria, see Wissowa 139-41, 318, 340; K. Latte, *LM* 6. 294-302; H. Graillot, *DA* 5. 853 f. On the altar, see Platner-Ashby 569 f.; on the temple, *ibid.* 570.—On Pax, cf. Wissowa 329, 334 f.; Platner-Ashby 386-8.—On Aequitas, cf. Wissowa, 332; W. H. Roscher, *LM* 1. 86; E. Saglio, *DA* 1. 108 f.; A. Aust, *RE* 1 (1894) 604 f. No temple of Aequitas is known to have stood in Rome.

The Case against the Pagans: Book Four 545

[8] Though Lucretius (1. 422 f.) uses the same words, Arnobius does not intend the same special significance of the phrase which is discussed by H. J. Thomson, 'Communis Sensus,' *Class. Rev.* 34 (1920) 18-21. Cf. 2. 68, n. 420, and Waszink's note there cited.

[9] *Virtutem viri*, an almost untranslatable pun: the fundamental meaning of *virtus* is 'manliness.'

[10] The editors read *signatorum* (past part. of *signare* = 'to seal,' 'to stamp'). Earlier editors in general followed Gelenius' weaker *ignotorum*. Röhricht (*Seelenlehre* 34) thinks Labeo the source in this chapter and the next as well as in 4. 6-12.

[11] M. Terentius Varro. According to Tullius (73), Varro was not the only source.

[12] Arnobius seems to be the only authority for the feminine form. Faunus, in whose honor the feast of the Lupercalia was held and whose priests were called *Luperci*—the etymology apparently has to do with the keeping-away of wolves (cf. Wissowa 209)—was called Lupercus (Justinian 43. 1. 7). But, Lactantius (*Div. inst.* 1.20. 2) also refers to the divinization, as does Arnobius here, of the she-wolf, *lupa*, which nursed Romulus and Remus.

[13] Praestana, the goddess of excellence, from *praestare*, 'to excel.' Cf. Wissowa 273, who notes analogies with Jupiter Praestes. Here and later in this Book, the names of the divinities mentioned show traces of alphabeticity (Praestana, Pellonia, Panda), a fact noted by Gabarrou (*Oeuvre* 43) as possibly indicating that Arnobius had before him an alphabetical list.

[14] Quirinus, one of the *di indigetes*, afterwards identified with Romulus. Cf. Wissowa 153-6; LM 4. 10-18; J. A. Hild, DA 4. 807 f.; Hyde 17.

[15] According to the historians of early Rome (Livy 1. 11. 6; Dion. Hal., *Ant. rom.* 2.40), Titus Tatius bribed the girl Tarpeia to let the Sabines into the Capitol.

[16] *Pandere* = 'to open up.'

[17] Varro (quoted by A. Gellius 13.23. 4) mentions Panda Cela in company with Anna Perenna, Pales, and other divinities, and says (quoted by Nonius s.v. "pandere"): Hanc deam Aelius putat esse Cererem; sed quod in asylum qui confugisset, panis daretur, esse nomen factum a *pane dando*.

[18] The Palatine Hill (Palatium) was traditionally the site of the earliest Roman settlement. As a result of superiority in a javelin-throwing contest, Romulus became sole ruler of the new city which he and his brother Remus had just founded jointly.

[19] Reifferscheid reads *teli* which is certainly right. Marchesi's *tali* is clearly a misprint.

[20] See n. 15.

[21] Here Reifferscheid changed the MS *est* to *esset*—Marchesi omitted the word entirely but the indicative is probably what Arnobius wrote.

[22] No such point has previously been discussed but it may be that Bryce-Campbell are right in thinking the allusion really to 4. 8. This may provide some light on Arnobius' method of composition, i. e. he wrote sections out of order and failed to give his manuscript a thorough final revision.

[23] Her name is obviously derived from *pellere*, but she is apparently mentioned elsewhere only by Augustine (*De civ. Dei* 4. 21; cf. also *ibid.* 3. 17). Wissowa does not mention her. Gabarrou (*Oeuvre* 43) is sure the material on the *indigitamenta* in 4. 3-9 and 4. 12 comes from Cornelius Labeo's *Indigitamenta*.

[24] The remarkable balance of this sentence can hardly be rendered in English: *haec illi est pars hostis et illa huic hostilis*.

[25] Cf. 3. 23, n. 117.

[26] The Roman citizens.

[27] Originally this was so, but upon conquering other states, Rome regularly adopted the divinities of the conquered as a matter of public policy.

[28] An allusion to the famous defeat of the Romans by the Samnites in the Second Samnite War (321 B. C.) as described by Livy 9. 2. 6. The exact site of the *furculae Caudinae* has been much disputed but it was probably not far from the town of Caudium which lay on the Via Appia, 21 miles from Capua, 11 from Beneventum.

[29] The scene of a bloody battle near the town of Cortona in June, 217 B. C., when Hannibal defeated a Roman army under C. Flamininus who, with 15,000 of his men, was slain, according to Livy's account (22. 4-7).

[30] The region about Cannae, the site of another disastrous defeat of the Romans by Hannibal in 216 B. C. See Livy 22. 44-50, who in 25. 12. 5 calls the site *campus Diomedis*.

[31] *Vilia capita*, the allusion being to the lowest classes in the Roman census. Cf. the interesting parallel in 3 Kings 18. 27.

[32] The MS reads *dii laevi et laeva* which Marchesi changes to *dii laevi a laeva* and Reifferscheid to *dii laevi, deae laevae*. The gods on the left were unpropitious, of ill omen; though in the language of the augurs who exercised their office facing the south, thus having the

east, the propitious side, to their left, the *laeva*, the things on the left, were of good omen.

[33] Perhaps this sentence should be marked as a quotation of the *adversarius*.

[34] The words are bracketed more because in Latin they do not fit grammatically the framework of the sentence than because of their sense.

[35] For the unintelligible reading of the MS: *dextralia in nobis*, Marchesi reads *dextera, [alia in nobis]*.

[36] An otherwise unknown divinity also mentioned in 4. 11. Cf. R. Peter, "Indigitamenta," *LM* 2. 201; P. Kock, "Lateranus," *RE* 12 (1925) 904.

[37] *Laterculi*, small tiles or bricks.

[38] The epithet used here is not found in any other ancient author and is not mentioned by Wissowa. None of the examples cited by Orelli of the occurrence of arms in connection with Aphrodite seems much in point, but Lactantius (*Div. inst.* 1. 20. 32) refers to Venus Armata.

[39] *Perfica* is meant to be derived from *perficere*. Cf. Tertullian, *Ad. nat.* 2. 11 where Perfica is mentioned briefly. See also W. Ehlers, *RE* 19 (1937) 683.

[40] Tertullian (*Ad nat.* 2. 11) mentioned Pertunda in connection with Perfica and Tutunus and other gods. See also Augustine, *De civ. Dei* 6. 9.

[41] Tutunus, cuius immanibus pudendis horrentique fascino vestras inequitare matronas et auspicabile ducitis et optatis—also mentioned in 4. 11, appears in Tertullian, *Ad nat.* 2. 11. Cf. also Lactantius, *Div. inst.* 1. 20. 36.

[42] *Putationes* is cognate to 'amputation' in English, hence the name. *Peta* is presumably related to the verb *peto, petere*, 'to seek.'

[43] *Nemora*, from which Arnobius derives Nemestrinus.

[44] Both names are ostensibly derived from *patere*, 'to be exposed, evident.' Cf. Augustine, *De civ. Dei* 4. 8: Praefecerunt ergo . . . cum folliculi *patescunt*, ut spica exeat, deam *Patelanum*, where Welldon cites only Arnobius.

[45] Cf. Augustine, *loc. cit.*: Praefecerunt ergo . . . geniculis nodisque culmorum deum Nodutum. Welldon states that there is MS authority for *Nodotum*.

[46] That is, the tying of sheaves.

[47] Nothing is known of this goddess. Cf. R. Peter, "Indigitamenta," *LM* 2. 207 f.

[48] Here both editors indicate a corrupt passage; Gelenius reads *Vibilia*; Meursius, *Vehilia* or *Venilia*.

[49] Here again we are on doubtful ground. Tertullian (*Ad nat.* 2. 15) takes this goddess (he calls her *Orbana*) to be one who causes parents to be deprived of children rather than one who cares for those so deprived. Cicero, *De nat. deor.* 3. 25. 63 = Pliny, *Nat. hist.* 2. 16, do not help settle the question, nor does the brief mention in Wissowa 244.

[50] This goddess, whose name is spelled by Festus as *Naenia* (156 Lindsay) and *Nenia* (Paulus, *ibid.* 157), was worshipped in a shrine outside the Porta Viminalis at Rome. Cf. Augustine, *De civ. Dei* 6. 9.

[51] The MS *nam* (adversative!) is restored by Axelson for Marchesi's *iam*.

[52] This goddess is mentioned in the next chapter and also in 3. 30 (see n. 170). In the present instance the MS reads *Ossilago*, corrected by Canterus to *Ossipago*.

[53] Cf. also 4. 12; Augustine, *De civ. Dei* 4. 34, where the spelling is *Mellona*.

[54] *Exos*, a word also occurring in Lucretius (3. 721, cf. *exossato*, *ibid.* 4. 1271 and Bailey *ad loc.*).

[55] See above, n. 8.

[56] On the Lucrii, gods of gain—*lucrum*—see R. Peter, "Indigitamenta," *LM* 2. 203; C. Jullian, *DA* 2. 181; K. Latte, "Lucrii Dii," *RE* 13 (1927) 1695. Rapisarda (*Arnob.* 139) cites on this chapter: Augustine, *De civ. Dei.* 4. 8 f., 19 f., 24; 6. 6, 9.

[57] A fallacy—gain may be the result of being directly of service to others.

[58] The MS reads clearly *Libentinam* but this is apparently a confusion of Lubentia, a goddess of pleasure (cf. Plautus, *Asin.* 268; Augustine, *De civ. Dei* 4. 8; Venus Libitina or Lubentina in Varro, *De ling. lat.* 6. 47; Cicero, *De nat. deor.* 2. 23. 61; Servius, *Aen.* 1. 720; Wissowa 245) and the goddess of burial, Libitina, though the former is meant here.

[59] The MS reads *Burnum* which both editors mark with the obelus, since nothing is known of any Burnus and there are objections to each of the other suggestions: Gelenius *Liburnum*, Elmenhorst *Liburnam*, Meursius *Liberum*; Hildebrand *Prurium*, Kistner *Venerem*.

[60] Not mentioned by Wissowa, he appears as a god of the threshold (*limen*) in company with three other deities of similar nature: Forculus, Cardea, and Janus, in Tertullian, *De idol.* 15; *Scorp.* 10; and,

without Janus, in *Ad nat.* 2. 15, and Augustine, *De civ. Dei* 4. 8. All four also appear in Tertullian, *De cor. mil.* 13 except that two names are spelled *Forculus* and *Carnea*. See R. Peter, "Indigitamenta," *LM* 2. 202.

⁶¹ Stewechius, quoted by Orelli, quaintly remarks: "Dicam quod sentio. Limam deam, quae sit, ignoro; neque eam hic tolerandam puto." He goes on to suggest that Lima is merely a feminine counterpart for Limentinus, citing Robigus and Robigo, etc. Others suggest emendations, e. g. to Janus, etc.

⁶² The Limi are also unknown gods but *limus* = *obliquus* = 'slanting,' 'sloping.' See R. Peter, "Indigitamenta," *LM* 2. 202; W. Schur, "Limi Dii," *RE* 13 (1927) 671.

⁶³ Here Arnobius is right. The best modern experts identify Saturn as a god of sowing. Cf. Wissowa 204-8.

⁶⁴ Orelli prints a long note tending to show that mountains were regarded as sacred spots but of this Montinus nothing is known.

⁶⁵ On this goddess Murcia, see Wissowa 242, who connects her with Myrtea = Aphrodite-Venus, while other writers (Servius, *Aen.* 8. 636; Augustine, *De civ. Dei* 4.16) associate the name with *murcidus* = 'slothful.'

⁶⁶ Pecunia was not known as a goddess to Juvenal (1. 112-4):

Quandoquidem inter nos sanctissima divitiarum
Maiestas, etsi funesta pecunia templo
Nondum habitas, nullas nummorum ereximus aras.

But cf. Augustine, *De civ. Dei* 4. 21; 4. 24; 7. 3; R. Peter, "Indigitamenta," *LM* 2. 213; G. Mickwitz, "Pecunia," no. 2, *RE* 19 (1937) 16.

⁶⁷ The sign of equestrian or senatorial rank based on wealth and position. Cf. R. Cagnat, *DA* 2. 780; G. Humbert, *ibid.* 1. 296-9.

⁶⁸ New because in the preceding chapter the pagans are assumed to have assented to the suggestion that there is a god for each thing. Cf. n. 77. This sentence can hardly be attributed to the *adversarius* and refer to Christianity. Heraldus weakly changed *novarum* to *magnarum*.

⁶⁹ The gods in this chapter are all introduced in chapters 6-8. *Mutuno* is Gelenius' emendation of the MS *hoc ē uno*, restored by Sabaeus as *hoc est humi*.

⁷⁰ Mutunus is the feminine counterpart of Tutunus. Of these *indigitamenta*, only four (Mutunus, Tutunus, Pertunda, and Perfica) are mentioned by Tertullian, *Ad nat.* 2. 11.

⁷¹ That is, gods with a much better claim than those mentioned, yet still false. The sentence is sarcastic as usual.

⁷² The MS reads *esse falsum istos deos*; Oehler and Reifferscheid *falsum ⟨est⟩ istos*; Löfstedt *falsum est hos*. The word ⟨*est*⟩ seems necessary. Bryce-Campbell added *contendis* (from Gelenius).

⁷³ The remark certainly implies that Arnobius did not believe in the existence of *these* gods. See Introd. 30-3.

⁷⁴ The predictions. Cumont 278 n. 49 thinks this chapter *probably* indebted to Cornelius Labeo.

⁷⁵ *Fibris* here undoubtedly stands for the raw material used by the *haruspices* to which the opponent alludes in the last but one paragraph. The point is that Mellonia and Limentinus would be strange gods to expect to consult through liver inspection.

⁷⁶ *Antitheos*, a Greek word listed by Gabarrou (*Latin* 72-4). Lactantius, *Div. inst.* 2. 9. 13, uses it of the devil.

⁷⁷ In the light of the first sentence in 4. 11 this is apparently an inconsistency.

⁷⁸ Reading, with Wiman, *pro omnibus ⟨dis⟩, quos vocatis, patribusque se cunctis locorum divis ⟨reg⟩ionumque supponens*, etc.

⁷⁹ At this point Orelli inserts the sentence which in both the MS and the translation ends this Book.

⁸⁰ This is usually taken to be a reference to Cicero's *De natura deorum*, but since the word *theologi*, used below by Arnobius, is also employed by Cicero (*ibid.* 3. 21. 53), it is probable that Arnobius refers to other writers besides Cicero. Röhricht (*De Clemente* 4) says he here follows Cicero, *De nat. deor.* 3. 16. 42, 3. 21. 53, and in 4. 13, *ibid.* 3. 16. 42.

⁸¹ Usually thought to refer to Clement of Alexandria, *Protr.* 2. 27 ff.; but see the next note. Sextus Clodius is also cited by Lactantius, *Div. inst.* 1. 22. 11.

⁸² This word is found in the corresponding passage in Cicero (*De nat. deor.* 3. 21. 53). Those who think Arnobius is copying Cicero include Kettner 4; Kahl 720; Röhricht, *Seelenlehre* 4, 13; W. Michaelis, *De origine indicis deorum cognominum* (diss. Berlin 1898) The opposite view is maintained by V. Rose, *Aristoteles Pseudepigraphus* (Leipzig 1863) 617; W. Bobeth, *De indicibus deorum* (diss. Leipzig 1904) 15, and Tullius (61-7) who prefers to see in the *theologi*, of whom the Timotheus mentioned in 5. 5 and the Trebatius in 7. 31 are two, the real source of Arnobius. He also thinks M. Terentius Varro was another.

⁸³ There is close correspondence between Arnobius and Cicero, *De nat. deor.* 3. 21. 53, less striking between Arnobius and Clement of

Alexandria, *Protr.* 2. 28. 1. Cf. Lactantius, *Div. inst.* 1. 11. 48 (citing Cicero); Ampelius, *Lib. mem.* 9; Theophilus, *Ad Autol.* 1. 10, who names the following Zeuses: Olympius, Latiaris, Cassius, Tonans, Propator, Pannychius, Capitolinus, and Cretensis.

[84] Clement gives place of birth for all three. Cf. Cyprian, *Quod idola dii non sint* 2. On the tomb see Origen, *C. Cels.* 3. 43. On this Zeus, see A. J. Toynbee, *A Study of History* 1 (2nd ed. London 1935) 98.

[85] Cf. Cicero, *De nat. deor.* 3. 21. 54, which harmonizes completely with Arnobius—there is no corresponding passage in Clement.

[86] Cf. Cicero, *De nat. deor.* 3. 22. 56, again with no inconsistencies. Clement (*Protr.* 2. 29. 1) merely refers to the many Hermeses.

[87] Cf. 4. 22.

[88] It was on the island of Lemnos that Hephaestus fell when thrown from heaven by Zeus. Cf. *Iliad* 1. 590-4.

[89] Aeëtes, father of Jason's wife Medea.

[90] *Versipellis* is here undoubtedly an allusion to the changing of the shape of Odysseus' followers from men into swine, rather than the more usual sense of changer of her own shape.

[91] Hermes Argeiphontes.

[92] Cicero says also of laws.

[93] Arnobius here omits the name Theutis but gives it in 2. 69.

[94] Cf. Cicero, *De nat. deor.* 3. 23. 59 where we encounter for the first time some divergence between the accounts of Cicero and Arnobius: Cicero makes Minerva daughter of the second Jupiter, son of Caelus, whereas Arnobius says she was a descendant of Saturn, i. e. daughter of the third Jupiter, yet the correspondences are so striking that these inconsistencies probably are not to be unduly emphasized. Comparing Arnobius also with Clement (*Protr.* 2. 28. 2) we find two details in which Arnobius agrees with Clement and not with Cicero, and one in which he agrees with Cicero and not with Clement: Arnobius had either both sources before him or is following a different one altogether. We have seen above, however, that the correspondence between Arnobius and Cicero is too striking to be thought accidental. Röhricht (*De Clemente* 17 f.) cites this passage as the first of his parallels. Brakman (*Miscella tertia* 27) thinks Firmicus Maternus copied this passage of Arnobius.

[95] Athena was usually *parthenos*. Note also that Arnobius in 4. 22 follows the more usual tradition in making Latona the mother of Apollo. Clement makes the first Athena τὴν μὲν Ἡφαίστου which does *not* mean, as Butterworth and Stählin wrongly translate, the *daughter* of Hephaestus. On the use of the definite article with a

genitive to express other relationships than paternity, see Liddell-Scott-Jones 1195.

[96] According to Bobeth (18 f.) the data about the second, third, and fourth Minervas go back to Clement.

[97] Jupiter, according to Cicero.

[98] Cf. 4. 16 where he gives two derivations of this.

[99] Clement gives no hint of the reason for the murder but states the name of the mother, Titanis, daughter of Oceanus.

[100] Though despite his protestations Arnobius is a most prolix writer, in this chapter he really does summarize what Cicero gives in much greater detail.

[101] Not Cicero and Clement but their sources.

[102] So also Cicero, *De nat. deor.* 3. 22. 55. Clement, *Protr.* 2. 29. 1, merely implies that there were many.

[103] So also Cicero, *ibid.* 3. 23. 58—no corresponding passage in Clement.

[104] So also Cicero, *ibid.* 3. 22. 57. Cf. Edelstein-Edelstein, *Testim.* 380b.

[105] So also Cicero, *ibid.* 3. 23. 58—no corresponding passage in Clement.

[106] Neither Cicero nor Clement can be the source here. The following writers name only three: Herodotus 2. 43. f.; Arrian, *Alex.* 2. 16.

[107] So also Cicero, *ibid.* 3. 23. 59.

[108] So also Cicero, *ibid.* 3. 21. 53.

[109] So also Cicero, *ibid.* 3. 21. 54.

[110] So also Cicero, *ibid.* 3. 23. 60.

[111] Clement lists six and so also Cicero (*ibid.* 3. 23. 57).

[112] Bastgen is certainly right in changing *nominum* to *numinum*.

[113] In these two chapters Arnobius has exploited, though in a different order, all the information presented by Cicero in *De nat. deor.* 3. 21. 53 (beginning with *Principio Ioves*) to 3. 23. 60 (*Atque haec quidem . . .*). In one instance only does he appear to be following the *Protrepticus* of Clement of Alexandria rather than Cicero, but even in that instance there is evidence that he has had Cicero before his eyes, and since in another instance, that of the item concerning Hercules, he appears to have derived his statement neither from Cicero nor from Clement, we can safely conclude that he consulted some other writer or had at least remembered from some other source elements found in neither authors.

[114] Cf. Cicero, *ibid.* 3. 23. 60: . . . quibus (the stories about multiple gods) intellegis resistendum esse ne perturbentur religiones . . . .

The Case against the Pagans: Book Four   553

[115] Reading *et nullis* of the MS.
[116] Gabarrou (*Oeuvre* 44) thinks the source may be Cornelius Labeo.
[117] The two names are identical only in the nominative.
[118] See 4. 14 end; also n. 99. It is unnecessary to think that here Arnobius is following Clement's version of the murder as the fault of Minerva. Note how skillfully he makes the complaint fit the psychology of a jealous woman.
[119] Cf. Herodotus 4. 180.
[120] *Timaeus* 21e. Cf. Röhricht (*Seelenlehre* 23): Arnobius could have used other sources here for the name of the goddess Neith.
[121] The Greek root κορυφ- means 'head.'
[122] The third now turns away from the second and addresses the fourth.
[123] *Quis arbiter cervicibus tantis erit*, lit. "will have so stout a neck," i. e. will have the boldness, intrepidity, etc. Cf. Cicero's *Third Verrine*, 59. 135: qui *tantis* erunt *cervicibus* recuperatores? The allusion is doubtless to the Judgment of Paris.
[124] An evident allusion to persecution.
[125] Apollo.
[126] Pagan writers on the gods, as in 4. 14 f.
[127] *Sedit*. Cf. Vergil, *Aen*. 5. 418, 7. 611; Florus 2. 15. 4.
[128] The MS reads *ex hominum discripsit*, with *dis* marked as *de* in the hand known as P¹. Marchesi: *ex hominum [dei] scriptis*; Reifferscheid: *ex hominum scriptis*.
[129] Clearly a reference to Cicero's *De natura deorum*.
[130] Hagendahl *publicavisse* for *commentum esse* (Marchesi).
[131] Most difficult: *usque ad illos ipsos principali procreatione finita*.
[132] On birthplaces and burials of gods, see Tertullian, *Apol*. 10. 4.
[133] Here the three methods by which a bride entered the *manus*, legal power, of her husband—*usus, confarreatio* (Arnobius calls it merely *farreum*, 'the cake'), and *coemptio*—are strictly in accord with Roman law and practice. See C. Ferrini, "Die juristischen Kenntnisse des Arnobius und des Lactantius," *Zeitschr. d. Sav.-Stift. f. Rechtsgesch*. 15 (1894) 343-52, esp. 343-6, who points out the excellence of Arnobius' data on matters of law. *Usus*, the simplest method, which, as here, is always mentioned first, was one in which the woman was acquired by her husband like a piece of property for a year only, though she could break the *manus* by absenting herself for three nights each year. Cf. C. Lécrivain, "Manus," *DA* 3. 1586 f., and "Matrimonium," *ibid*. 3. 1657 f. *Confarreatio* was a patrician

ceremony involving a cake, and *coemptio* was a plebiean counterpart in which the father fictitiously sold the bride to the groom.

[134] *Speratas,* i. e. girls undergoing courtship without matrimony as yet having been agreed upon; *pactas,* engaged; *sponsas,* brides.

[135] *Audetis,* added by Marchesi; cf. 4. 27, 6. 27. Brakman suggested *oportet* which would give nearly the same sense. Castiglioni suggested *non erubescitis.*

[136] At this point the MS has *et quid* which both editors bracket as meaningless.

[137] Verses of a ribald character sung as part of wedding ceremonies. Cf. G. Wissowa, " Fescennini versus," *RE* 6 (1909) 2222 f.

[138] Obviously an allusion to the wedding of Peleus and Thetis to which the goddess of Discord (Eris) was not invited. In anger she threw into the palace the golden apple which, being inscribed " to the fairest," caused the dispute between Hera, Athena, and Aphrodite—the ultimate cause of the Judgment of Paris, the rape of Helen, and the Trojan War. Cf. Catullus 64; St. Augustine, *De civ. Dei* 3. 25.

[139] *Rector poli:* cf. Vergil, *Aen.* 9. 106, 10. 115.

[140] Cf. *Iliad* 1. 528; Vergil, *Aen.* 9. 106.

[141] Amalthea was according to variant traditions either the maiden who fed the infant Jupiter on goat's milk or the she-goat itself. Had Arnobius known the latter version, he would doubtless have used it with telling effect. Cf. H. W. Stoll, "Amaltheia," *LM* 1. 262-6; K. Wernicke, "Amaltheia" no. 1, *RE* 1 (1894) 1720-3; and the unsigned article in *DA* 1. 219 f. See also A .J. Toynbee, *A Study of History* 3 (2nd ed. London 1935) 260.

[142] For further castigations of this adulterous god, cf. Ps.-Clement of Rome, *Recogn.* 10. 20-23; Theophilus, *Ad Autol.* 1. 9; Lactantius, *Div. inst.* 1. 10-11; *Epit.* 10 f.

[143] But in 4. 14 the first Minerva is the mother of Apollo—here we have the more usual tradition.

[144] On the Dioscuri (Διὸς κοῦροι = sons of Zeus), cf. 1. 36 n. 164.

[145] Wife of Amphitryon. Cf. 2. 70.

[146] Cf. Ovid, *Met.* 4. 11; Diodorus Sic. 4. 5.

[147] Apollodorus (3. 4. 3) says that when Semele died, her sixth-month abortive child was caught up by Zeus and sewn into his thigh where the child remained the rest of the appointed time.

[148] *Adfabilium,* i. e. snakes which respond to words, hence tame, those wrapped round the *caduceus,* the wand borne by Mercury.

[149] An allusion to the epithet λευκώλενος (= 'white-armed') ap-

The Case Against the Pagans: Book Four 555

plied regularly to Hera by Homer (e. g. *Iliad* 1. 55) and Hesiod (e. g. 314). Perhaps the description of a well-known statue of Juno.

[150] F. J. Dölger, *Ant. u. Christ.* 3 (1932) 142 f., cites this passage as a proof that before Constantine violation of marriage was punishable by death.

[151] On Lynceus, son of Aphareus, see K. Seeliger, "Lynkeus," *LM* 2. 2206 f.; S. Eitrem, "Lynkeus," *RE* 13 (1927) 2469-71.

[152] In his affair with Leda. Reifferscheid deletes *cycnus*, probably on account of its position.

[153] In his escapade with Europa.

[154] A return to the affair with Leda.

[155] The Castors or the Dea Syria. Cf. 1. 36.

[156] Cf Hesiod, *Theog.* 188 ff.; Clement of Alexandria, *Protr.* 2. 14; Macrobius, *Sat.* 1. 8. 6. Cythera is the island off the southernmost point of the Peloponnesus (Cape Matapan). The rise of Venus from the sea is the subject of one of the most famous of Botticelli's paintings.

[157] Cf. Macrobius, *Sat.* 1. 8. 5.

[158] Cf. 3. 41; Lucretius 2. 630 ff.

[159] Cf. Apollodorus, *Bibl.* 1. 2. 1.

[160] Cf. Vergil, *Aen.* 8. 319-20; Minucius 21. 5-7; Tertullian, *Apol.* 10. 8; Cyprian, *Quod idola dii non sint* 2; Lactantius, *Div. inst.* 1. 13 f.; Augustine, *De civ. Dei* 7. 37, 18. 15.

[161] This derivation of *Latium* from *latere*, 'to hide,' goes back to Vergil, *Aen.* 8. 322; *Latiumque* vocari maluit quoniam *latuisset* tutus in *oris* (cf. Ovid, *Fasti* 1. 238), and was a long time dying. Cf. W. M. Lindsay-H. J. Thomson, *Ancient Lore in Medieval Latin Glossaries*, St. Andrews *Univ. Publ.* 13 (Oxford 1921) 99, on Vergil's *Aen.* 1. 6. It is not, however, approved by the modern etymologists: cf. A. Walde-J. B. Hofmann, *Lateinisches etymologisches Wörterbuch* (3rd ed. Heidelberg 1935) 770. Tertullian, *Apol.* 10, says Saturn gave his name to Italy, not to Latium. Lactantius, *Div. inst.* 1. 13. 9 quotes the derivation but omits it in 5. 5. 9. Cf. also Minucius 21. 6; Cyprian, *Quod idola dii non sint* 2: *Latium de latebra*.

[162] Juno. Cf. Tertullian, *Apol.* 14. 3; Firmicus Maternus, *De err. prof. rel.* 12. 4.

[163] Cf. Clement of Alexandria, *Protr.* 2. 36. 5, who says that Lycaon was an Arcadian and his son's name Nyctimus. Cf. Pausanias 8. 2. 3; Apollodorus, *Bibl.* 3. 8.1; Hyginus, *Fab.* 176; Ovid, *Met.* 1. 221; A. B. Cook, *Zeus* 1 (Cambridge 1914) 63.81. Clement also alludes to *Iliad* 1. 423, but Arnobius mentions this in 6. 4. This passage is

parallel no. 2 in Röhricht (*De Clemente* 12). Tullius (75) concludes that Arnobius did not read Clement.

[164] Pindar, *Pyth.* 3. 54-59, is quoted (in part) by Clement of Alexandria, *Protr.* 2. 30. 1, and by Tertullian, *Apol.* 14. 5, also in fuller form in *Ad nat.* 2. 14. From a comparison of these passages it seems clear that Arnobius is much closer to the last-named passage than to the others. Lactantius, *Div. inst.* 1. 10. 1, mentions the same story but says nothing of avarice.

[165] See Edelstein-Edelstein, *Testim.* 101a.

[166] This is obviously an allusion to the ambiguity of the oracle of Apollo at Delphi and perhaps a specific reference to the famous reply to Croesus, king of Lydia (cf. Herodotus 1. 53) which, misunderstood by Croesus, caused his downfall. Cf. also Clement of Alexandria, *Protr.* 3. 43. 4; Minucius 26. 6; Tertullian, *Apol.* 22. 10; Cicero, *De div.* 2. 115.

[167] Cf. Fulgentius, *Mythol.* 1.13; Suidas *s.v.* " Ἑρμῆς " and " Κερδῷος"; Lactantius, *Div. inst.* 1. 10. 7; Horace, *Carm.* 1. 10. 8; and N. O. Brown, *Hermes the Thief: the Evolution of a Myth* (Madison 1947).

[168] On Laverna, goddess of thieves, cf. 3. 26.

[169] Clement of Alexandria, *Protr.* 2. 31. 4, calls him Myrsilus of Lesbos. Little else is known of him except that he lived in the Alexandrian period and wrote a book on Lesbos. Clement states in greater detail that the Muses were Mysian handmaids purchased by Megaclo, daughter of Macar, king of Lesbos, and were taught by her mother to sing and play the lyre in order to soothe Macar's bad temper. Afterwards, Megaclo erected bronze statues in honor of the maidens and caused them to be worshipped in all the temples. Cf. also 3. 37 where the origin of the Muses is discussed in detail. Tullius (78) is sure of the independence of Arnobius from Clement, but Röhricht (*De Clemente* 13) lists this as parallel no. 4. Cf. R. Laqueur, "Myrsilos," no. 2, *RE* 16 (1935) 1148-50. For the fragments, see *Fragm. hist. gr.* 4. 455-60.

[170] For some reason this sentence is transferred by Orelli to the beginning of the next chapter.—Röhricht (*De Clemente* 19) compares Clement, *Protr.* 2. 13. 4, and lists this as parallel no. 5, but the parallelism does not seem very close. A closer resemblance may be cited in the *Sacra historia* of Euhemerus, lines 134-8, quoted by Lactantius, *Div. inst.* 1. 17. 9 = *Epit.* 9. 1, in E. H. Warmington's edition of the fragments of Ennius' translation of Euhemerus, *Remains of Old Latin* 1 (Cambridge, Mass.—London 1935) 430 f. This is the only extant passage of Euhemerus which seems to me close

enough to Arnobius to raise a question of interdependence. Arnobius also refers to Cinyras again in 5. 19 and 6. 6. Cf. Firmicus Maternus, *De err. prof. rel.* 10. 1.

[171] Palladia were idols of protective deities, known in the ancient Cretan religion. The armed goddess Athena especially was represented by them. Her most famous palladium was that of Troy. This was supposedly διοπετές, 'fallen from Zeus,' that is, 'heaven-sent.' According to the ancient myth, here repeated by Arnobius, it was made of the bones of Pelops. Varying accounts link it with the fates of the Trojan War and eventually transfer it to Italy and Rome. Cf. also Clement of Alexandria, *Protr.* 4. 47. 7; Firmicus Maternus, *De err. prof. rel.* 15. 1-5. Clement's account is so much fuller than that of Arnobius that the latter probably is not following him (so Tullius 78), but Röhricht (*De Clemente* 13) lists the passages as parallel no. 6.

Interestingly enough, the *Acts of the Apostles* (see 19. 35, Greek text), quoting an address by an official of the city of Ephesus, mentions a 'heaven-sent' image of the goddess Artemis (Diana), protectress of the Ephesians.

[172] Arnobius may be following Clement, *Protr.* 2. 29. 2, in this passage. As usual, Röhricht (*De Clemente* 14 f., 19 f.) lists this as a parallel (no. 7) and Tullius (79 f.) denies the dependence, preferring as a source a mythographic handbook unknown to us.

[173] Cf. 4. 36.

[174] Homer, *Iliad,* 5. 385-7, quoted by Clement, *loc. cit.* refers to the binding of Ares and his imprisonment for thirteen months by Otus and Ephialtes but there is no reference to Arcadia in Homer. Cf. also the notes in Frazer's edition of Apollodorus, *Bibl.* vol. 1, p. 59. Cf. also Tertullian, *Apol.* 14. 3; *Ad nat.* 1. 10.

[175] Arnobius is here obviously referring to Homer and mistranslates the epithet *Melesigénes* (cf. Pausanias 7. 5. 6; *Vita Hom.* 2; Statius, *Silv.* 3. 3. 60; 7. 33; Tibullus 4. 1. 200) applied to Homer as a result of a tradition that he composed the poems in a cave near the river Meles (not Mela) which flows by Smyrna. Cf. K. Scherling, "Meles" no. 2, *RE* 15 (1931) 492-4. The Mela (or Mella) is a small river in northern Italy.

[176] Clement of Alexandria, *Protr.* 2. 29. 4, is probably the source for he also ascribes these two statements to Apollodorus (*Fragm. gr. hist.* 244, fr. 126) as well as to Callimachus (frs. 187 f. Schneider).

[177] Clement of Alexandria, *Protr.* 2. 33. 7 and 9, alludes briefly to the story and quotes Homer, *Od.* 8. 324, but does not cite the poet by

name. The fact that three items, (1) the binding of Ares; (2) the sacrificing of dogs and asses, and (3) the adultery story, which appear in close order in Arnobius appear also in the same order in Clement, suggests strongly a causal relation, but when it is noted that both authors cite their authorities in the first two instances and not in the third, the parallelism is most striking.

[178] Here again we have to deal with a series of incidents in which Arnobius appears to be closely following Clement, *Protr.* 2. 35 f., though in different order. Tullius (81 f.) is convinced that Arnobius followed a very different list from that of Clement, while this passage is parallel no. 8 in Röhricht (*De Clemente* 20 f.) Cf. Minucius 23. 5; Cyprian, *Quod idola dii non sint* 2; and Lactantius, *Div. inst.* 1. 10. 3.

[179] Cf. Clement of Alexandria, *Protr.* 2. 35. 1, who says that Heracles was a slave of Omphale at Sardis. Cf. Lactantius, *Div. inst.* 1. 9. 7.

[180] The *locus classicus* of this story is the prologue to Euripides' *Alcestis*. Tertullian, *Apol.* 14. 4, tells the story but omits the servitude of Hercules. Cf. Cyprian, *Quod idola dii non sint* 2. Minucius 23. 5 resembles Arnobius' account, while Clement, *Protr.* 2. 35. 1, reverses the order.

[181] Poseidon who, with Apollo, built the walls of Troy for Laomedon. Cf. Clement, *loc. cit.* Poseidon was uncle to Apollo, son of Jupiter.

[182] In this sentence Arnobius appears to condense two statements of Clement, *Protr.* 2. 35. 2: in the first Clement speaks of Athena lighting the way for Odysseus (*Od.* 19. 34), while in the second he refers to Aphrodite's bringing a stool for Paris (*Il.* 3. 424).

[183] Cf. 3. 21. See Homer, *Iliad* 5. 855 ff., for the wounding of Aphrodite; 5. 343 for the wounding of Ares. Cf. Clement, *Protr.* 2. 36. 1; Tertullian, *Apol.* 14. 2; *Ad nat.* 1. 10. See Röhricht, *De Clemente* 15, 21, parallel no. 9. On the story, see Tullius 83.

[184] On Panyassis of Halicarnassus, fifth-century epic poet, see A. and M. Croiset, *Histoire de la littérature grecque* 3 (3rd ed. Paris 1929) 702-10. Clement (*Protr.* 2. 36. 2) says Panyassis (*Heracleia*, fr. 6, 20 Kinkel) related the wounding of Hera by Heracles, as says Arnobius, but he rightly cites Homer (*Il.* 5. 395-7) for the wounding of Hades by Heracles. We do not know whether Arnobius is right, for Panyassis' poem is lost.

[185] Polemon, a second-century historian; cf. fr. 24, *Fragm. hist. gr.* 3. 122. Cf. Clement of Alexandria, *Protr.* 2. 36. 2.

[186] Here the word probably has some sense of the masculine quali-

The Case against the Pagans: Book Four 559

ties of Pallas Athene, though in 5.24 and 5.37 (*ter*) it is used of Proserpina and has hardly more meaning than *virgo*. Ornytus was son of Sisyphus.

[187] Sosibius, a Spartan of the Alexandrian period, is also credited with this statement by Clement, *Protr.* 2.36.2. Cf. fr. 15, *Fragm. hist. gr.* 2.628. Both Apollodorus (2.7.3) and Hyginus (*Fab.* 31) say only that Heracles slew the sons of Hippocoon in Sparta and do not mention the wound.

[188] Clement, *Protr.* 2.37.4, credits Callimachus of Crete with this statement (cf. Callimachus, *Hymn to Zeus* 8 f.), which may have given rise to the traditional reputation of the Cretans as liars. Cf. Titus 1.12: Cretenses semper mendaces, malae bestiae, ventres pigri —alluded to by Tatian 27. On this reputation see A. J. Toynbee, *A Study of History* 2 (2nd ed. London 1935) 83; Geffcken 228. Cf. also Tullius 83 f. and Röhricht (*De Clemente* 13), parallel no. 10.

[189] Castor and Pollux were twins. Cf. Homer, *Iliad* 3.243 f., quoted by Clement, *Protr.* 2.30.4; Röhricht, *De Clemente* 16, 21, parallel no. 11.

[190] Clement (*Protr.* 2.30.4) attributes this view to Philochorus but since in the next sentence he cites Patrocles, it seems probable that Arnobius has misunderstood him.

[191] The MS here has *Hieronymus Plutarchus* which has been suspected by the editors. Reifferscheid reads *Hieronymus * * * Plutarchus* while Sabaeus changed *Hieronymus* to *Chaeroneus* and LeNourry changed *Plutarchus* to *Dicaearchus*. Clement (*Protr.* 2.30.7) cites "Hieronymus the philosopher" (a Peripatetic of the Alexandrine period) for certain details of Heracles' bodily appearance. He then cites Dicaearchus (another Peripatetic) for different details of the same type. Neither of these two men seems likely as a source for such details. He then says, "This Heracles, after a life of fifty-two years, ended his days, and his funeral was conducted on a pyre on Mount Oeta." (Cf. Sophocles, *Trach.*; Arnobius 1.36). It is not clear from a reading of Clement that he means to cite Hieronymus and Dicaearchus for the statement about the death; rather, it would seem more probable that they are meant to be the source only for the details about his appearance. From these considerations it might be possible safely to conclude that Arnobius read Clement hurriedly and wrote something like what Zink suggests: *Hieronymus aut* (or better still *et*) *Dicaearchus,* and that a copyist misread *Dicaearchus* as *Plutarchus*, were it not for the fact Plutarch did write a book on the life of Heracles, now lost. Cf. Minucius 22.7; Lactantius, *Div. inst.*

1. 9; Augustine, *De civ. Dei* 18. 4; Firmicus Maternus, *De err. prof. rel.* 7. 6; Hyginus, *Fab.* 36.

[192] *Morborum comitialium ruinas*, so F. J. Dölger, *Ant. u. Christ.* 4 (1934) 108.

[193] This chapter and the first two sentences of the next parallel a similar one in Clement, *Protr.* 2. 32 f. As usual, Röhricht (*De Clemente* 14, 21 f.) lists the present passage as among parallels to Clement (nos. 12-14) and Tullius (90-6) strongly denies any such relationship. Amphitrite was daughter of Nereus and Doris, Hippothoe, of Mestor and Lysidice, Amymone, of Danaus and Alcyone. Melanippe (or Menalippe) was an Amazon abducted by Heracles. Alcyone's parents were Atlas and Pleione. To these Clement adds Alope and Chione, as well as "countless others."

[194] Arsinoe was daughter of Leucippus, mother of Asclepias; Aethusa, daughter of Alcyone and Poseidon; Zeuxippe, aunt and wife of Poseidon; Marpessa, daughter of Evenus. While Apollodorus lists five Steropes, none is said to have been loved by Apollo, and the same is true also of Hypsipyle. Prothoe is not mentioned elsewhere, and Daphne, indeed, actually escaped from Apollo. Cf. Ovid, *Met.* 1. 452-503; Hyginus, *Fab.* 203. Clement has the same names.

[195] Cf. Junius Philargyrius on Vergil, *Georg.* 3. 93. The Centaur Chiron was born of this union (Apollodorus 1. 2. 4—see Frazer's n. 6, vol. 1, 12 f.).

[196] On Jupiter's progeny, see Apollodorus 1. 3. 1.

[197] The story of Jupiter's affair with Danae, who became as a result the mother of Perseus, was treated in plays by Sophocles (A. C. Pearson, *Fragments of Sophocles* 1 [Cambridge 1917] 38-46, 115-7) and Euripides (A. Nauck, *Trag. graec. fragm.* [2nd ed. Leipzig 1889] pp. 78-83, frs. 218-332). Cf. also Frazer's Apollodorus, vol. 1, p. 53, n. 3. Neither Clement nor Firmicus Maternus refers to Danae and the gold. The detail of Zeus as a satyr is lacking in both Apollodorus and Clement. The latter (*Protr.* 2. 37. 2) merely refers to Zeus as a δράκων while Apollodorus is silent on the point. The allusion to the bird refers to Leda (Apollodorus 3. 10. 6 f.) and Zeus as a swan, but Clement (*Protr.* 2. 37. 2-4) speaks of Zeus as an eagle also. This may be a corruption of the kidnapping of Ganymede who was carried to heaven by Zeus as or on an eagle. It was as a bull that Zeus appeared to Europa. The allusion to the ant is repeated in 5. 44. Different explanations of this appear in Clement, *Protr.* 2. 39. 6, and Apollodorus 3. 12. 6.

[198] On Alcmene Arnobius is clearly following Clement, *Protr.* 2. 33. 3. Hippolytus, *Ref.* 1. 23, speaks of a similar liaison between

THE CASE AGAINST THE PAGANS: BOOK FOUR

Zeus and Mnemosyne, mother of the nine Muses (cf. Hesiod, *Theog.* 567). The story was the subject of lost plays by Sophocles (Pearson, *op. cit.* 1.76 ff.) and Euripides (Nauck, *op. cit.* frs. 89-105). Archippus (fifth century) wrote two plays called *Alcmene* of which the fragments are collected in Meineke-Bothe, *Poet. com. gr.* (Paris 1855) 269 f. Cf. also Plautus' *Amphitruo*.

[199] Sequuntur: ille noctibus vix novem unam potuit prolem extundere concinnare conpingere, at Hercules sanctus deus gnatas quinquaginta de Thestio nocte una perdocuit et nomen virginitatis exponere et genetricum pondera sustinere. Cf. Clement, *Protr.* 2. 33. 4; Tatian 21. 3; Pausanias 9. 27. 6-8; etc.

[200] The 'some one' is Hercules (cf. Apollod. 1.9.19); Clement is likewise indefinite. Of Hyacinthus the lover was Apollo (Apollod. 1.3.3; Ovid, *Met.* 10.162 ff.). Pelops was loved by Poseidon: cf. Pindar, Ol. 1.38. On the case of Chrysippus both Clement and Arnobius overlook the fact that, at least as we have the story from pagan sources (e.g. Apollod. 2.5.5) it was a human, Laius, who was involved. This error was pointed out by Geffcken (287). Catamitus = Ganymede, the youth beloved by Zeus and carried off on the eagle to be his cupbearer. He is referred to again as Catamitus in 5.22 and as Ganymede in 5.44, 7.33. Cf. Firmicus Maternus, *De err. prof. rel.* 12.2.

[201] To the foregoing examples of divine pederasty, all of which Arnobius has copied from Clement, he himself adds a Roman. Cf. Festus 284 f. Lindsay; F. J. Dölger, *Ant. u. Christ.* 3 (1932) 208.

[202] Adapted from Clement, *Protr.* 2.33.7-9. Regarding Aurora and Tithonus, cf. Apollodorus 3.12.4; Luna and Endymion, *ibid.* 1.7.5; Nereis and Aeacus, *ibid.* 3.12.6; Thetis and Peleus, *ibid.* 3.13.5; Proserpina and Adonis, *ibid.* 3.14.4 (see also J. G. Frazer, *Adonis, Attis, Osiris* [3rd ed., London 1919]); Ceres and Iasion, *ibid.* 3.12.1 (also Homer, *Od.* 5.125-8, and Hesiod, *Theog.* 969-74). As to Venus, Vulcan was her husband; Phaethon, referred to in this connection only by Clement and Arnobius, should possibly read Phaon (so Potter, the eminent editor of Clement); Anchises is, of course, the character in Vergil's *Aeneid*.

[203] At least obstetrical (Juno), if not also medical (Aesculapius).

[204] *Terrenae fragilitatis*—cf. *a terrena fragilitate* in Firmicus Maternus, *De err. prof. rel.* 20.7.

[205] Perpetrated by Cronus upon his father Uranus (Hesiod, *Theog.* 164 ff.) There may also be an allusion to Attis, already met in 1.4, and who will be met again. In the following references to Cronus continue: fearing for his hegemony of the universe, Cronus swal-

lowed all his children—Hestia, Demeter, Hera, Pluto, and Poseidon—save Zeus, who escaped by a stratagem of his mother Rhea (*ibid.* 453 ff.). When Zeus had grown to manhood, he forced his father to disgorge his brothers and sisters. Cronus was deprived of his rule, a treatment he himself had visited upon his father Uranus, and was imprisoned in Tartarus (*ibid.* 666 ff.).

[206] Cronus = Saturn. Cf. 4. 24.

[207] E. g. the sons of Lycaon (Apollod. 3. 8. 1); Philemon and Baucis (Ovid, *Met.* 8. 631 ff.). The following allusions are to Aesculapius, Apollo, Hermes, etc.

[208] Euhemerus of Acragas in Sicily, a philosopher of the late fourth century B. C., whose works were translated into Latin by Ennius (mentioned in 3. 16, taught, as Cicero (*De nat. deor.* 1. 42. 119) says of him, the view that the gods had formerly been outstanding heroes or rulers and were after death deified. Arnobius may also have had before him a passage of Clement, *Protr.* 2. 24. 2, in which the learned Alexandrian mentions with respect Euhemerus, Nicanor (*sic*) of Cyprus, Diagoras and Hippo of Melos, and Theodorus of Cyrene. For the fragments of Ennius' Euhemerus, see E. H. Warmington, *Remains of Old Latin* 1 (Cambridge, Mass.—London 1935) 414-31. On Euhemerus, see Theophilus, *Ad Autol.* 3. 7; Minucius 21. 1; Lactantius, *Div. inst.* 1. 13-15; Epit. 13; Eusebius, *De praep. ev.* 2. 2. 55; Augustine, *De civ. Dei* 6. 7, 7. 26; Sextus Empiricus, *Adv. math.* 1. 17, 1. 51. Nicagoras was a disciple of Epicurus (Diog. Laert. 10. 20), and the only Nicanor known was a grammarian of the age of Hadrian. Leon of Pella wrote a book on Egypt, cited by Clement, *Strom.* 1. 106. 3; Tatian 27. 3; Tertullian, *De cor. mil.* 7. Theodorus of Cyrene (cf. Diog. Laert. 2. 86) and Diagoras of Melos (cf. Lactantius, *Div. inst.* 1. 2. 2) are mentioned by Cicero (*De nat. deor.* 1. 1. 2, 1. 23. 63, 1. 42. 117, Diagoras alone in 3. 37. 89). Röhricht (*De Clemente* 23 f.) lists this passage as parallel no. 15, but, as usual, Tullius (97 f.) is against the view that Arnobius knew Clement.

[209] Following Meursius' punctuation.

[210] Dionysus.

[211] Attis. Cf. 5. 13 where it is merely said that the Magna Mater loved Attis.

[212] Cf. 1. 36, 2. 73, 6. 23.

[213] This verb is plural (*existimetis*) but a little later Arnobius uses singulars (*putes* and *reperias*). For a similar case, cf. 2. 53.

[214] *Postilio* (also, like *postulatio*, from *postulo*): a demand by a

THE CASE AGAINST THE PAGANS: BOOK FOUR 563

god, made through some natural phenomena—e. g. certain thunderbolts—that some neglected or forgotten sacrifice be offered or the violation of certain ceremonial statutes, be expiated. Cf. Varro, *De ling. lat.* 5. 148; Cicero, *De har. resp.* 10. 20, 14. 31; Wissowa 545 n. 7.

215 Cf. Pliny, *Nat. hist.* 28. 2. 11; F. J. Dölger, *Ant. u. Christ.* 2 (1930) 242. For the flutist in the sacred rites of the Romans, see J. Quasten, *Musik und Gesang in den Kulten der heidn. Antike und christl. Frühzeit* (Münster 1930) 10-16.

216 *Patrimus*, i.e. one who has a father living. Because boys whose parents were both living (*patrimus et matrimus*) were required for certain sacrifices, Ursinus and Reifferscheid add ⟨*et matrimus*⟩. Cf. 7. 44.

217 The Ms reads *terram*, Meursius *aut tensam aut terram*. A *tensa* was the sacrificial car in which the images were borne, drawn by horses driven by the *puer patrimus et matrimus* who walked beside it. Cf. Wissowa 396, esp. n. 1.

218 Cf. Minucius 23. 1: Has fabulas et errores et ab inperitis parentibus discimus, et quod est gravius, ipsi studiis et disciplinis elaboramus, carminibus praecipue poetarum, qui plurimum quantum veritati ipsi sua auctoritate nocuerunt.

219 Here both editors and the text translated by Bryce-Campbell have *non*, which is omitted by Orelli. A *non* is needed, but in the next clause where the sense would otherwise be incomprehensible. See *Vigiliae Christianae* 3 (1949) 45.

220 Cf. Homer, *Il.* 1. 601-4.

221 *Chalcidicis aureis*—cf. 3. 10 and n. 38.

222 Arnobius returns to this theory that the stories are but allegorical accounts of natural phenomena in 5. 32. On allegory as applied to the gods, see Ps.-Clement, *Recogn.* 10. 29; Tatian 21. 6; Lactantius, *Epit.* 12; Origen, *C. Cels.* 4. 48, 8. 62.

223 Such *senatus-consulta* were among the most dread means of taking legal action against a danger. The passage implies that Republican forms were still being used even under Diocletian. Cf. C. Ferrini, "Die juristischen Kenntnisse des Arnobius und des Lactantius," *Zeitschr. d. Sav.-Stift. f. Rechtsgesch.* 15 (1894) 343-6.

224 Cf. Paulus, *Sent.* 5. 29 (*Lex Iulia* concerning treason).

225 An allusion to Tabula VIII of the Laws of the Twelve Tables (449 B. C.) which may be most conveniently consulted in E. H. Warmington, *Remains of Old Latin* 3 (London-Cambridge, Mass. 1938) 474 f. Cf. Cicero, *De rep.* 4. 12 (preserved in Augustine, *De civ. Dei* 2. 9, cf. 2. 12): Nostrae . . . XII Tabulae cum perpaucas

god, made through some natural phenomena—e. g. certain thunderbolts—that some neglected or forgotten sacrifice be offered or the violation of certain ceremonial statutes, be expiated. Cf. Varro, De ling. lat. 5.148; Cicero, De har. resp. 10.20, 14.31; Wissowa 545 n. 7.

[215] Cf. Pliny, Nat. hist. 28.2.11; F. J. Dölger, Ant. u. Christ. 2 (1930) 242. For the flutist in the sacred rites of the Romans, see J. Quasten, Musik und Gesang in den Kulten der heidn. Antike und christl. Frühzeit (Münster 1930) 10-16.

[216] Patrimus, i.e. one who has a father living. Because boys whose parents were both living (patrimus et matrimus) were required for certain sacrifices, Ursinus and Reifferscheid add ⟨et matrimus⟩. Cf. 7.44.

[217] The Ms reads terram, Meursius aut tensam aut terram. A tensa was the sacrificial car in which the images were borne, drawn by horses driven by the puer patrimus et matrimus who walked beside it. Cf. Wissowa 396, esp. n. 1.

[218] Cf. Minucius 23. 1: Has fabulas et errores et ab inperitis parentibus discimus, et quod est gravius, ipsi studiis et disciplinis elaboramus, carminibus praecipue poetarum, qui plurimum quantum veritati ipsi sua auctoritate nocuerunt.

[219] Here both editors and the text translated by Bryce-Campbell have non, which is omitted by Orelli. A non is needed, but in the next clause where the sense would otherwise be incomprehensible. See Vigiliae Christianae 3 (1949) 45.

[220] Cf. Homer, Il. 1.601-4.

[221] Chalcidicis aureis—cf. 3.10 and n. 38.

[222] Arnobius returns to this theory that the stories are but allegorical accounts of natural phenomena in 5. 32. On allegory as applied to the gods, see Ps.-Clement, Recogn. 10.29; Tatian 21.6; Lactantius, Epit. 12; Origen, C. Cels. 4.48, 8.62.

[223] Such senatus-consulta were among the most dread means of taking legal action against a danger. The passage implies that Republican forms were still being used even under Diocletian. Cf. C. Ferrini, "Die juristischen Kenntnisse des Arnobius und des Lactantius," Zeitschr. d. Sav.-Stift. f. Rechtsgesch. 15 (1894) 343-6.

[224] Cf. Paulus, Sent. 5.29 (Lex Iulia concerning treason).

[225] An allusion to Tabula VIII of the Laws of the Twelve Tables (449 B.C.) which may be most conveniently consulted in E. H. Warmington, Remains of Old Latin 3 (London-Cambridge, Mass. 1938) 474 f. Cf. Cicero, De rep. 4.12 (preserved in Augustine, De civ. Dei 2.9, cf. 2.12): Nostrae . . . XII Tabulae cum perpaucas

236 Referring to a celebrated passage in Eusebius, many writers take this and the following to be a clear allusion to the persecution of Diocletian, more specifically to his edict of 24 February 303 (see Bardenhewer 2. 521; Colombo 4; Monceaux 3. 248; Sihler 173, Heraldus, cited by Orelli; Oehler xii; Bryce-Campbell xii, but Le-Nourry [ML 5. 392 f.] thinks an earlier persecution possible). Eusebius, *Hist. eccl.* 8. 2. 4 (cf. also Lactantius, *De mort. pers.* 12 f.), states that this edict commanded "the churches to be levelled to the ground and the Scriptures to be blotted out by fire." The 'writings' (*scripta*) mentioned by Arnobius are, of course, the Holy Scriptures (Eusebius: τὰς γραφὰς); and to the ἐκκλησίαι, 'buildings for divine worship,' spoken of by Eusebius, correspond the *conventicula*, 'meeting-places' or 'worship-houses,' of Arnobius. For *conventiculum* as a word used often by early Christian writers to designate the building in which the Christians worshipped, cf. the passages listed by G. Koffmane, *Entstehung und Entwicklung des Kirchenlateins bis auf Augustinus-Hieronymus* (Breslau 1879-81) 80. Cf. the reference by the pagan writer Ammianus Marcellinus (27. 3. 13) to such a *conventiculum*: in basilica Sicinini, ubi *ritus christiani conventiculum*. In Latin Christian literature the first occurrence of the word *ecclesia* to designate a building, 'church,' seems to be in Lactantius, *De mort. per.* 12. 3, written probably in the year 314. On the early church buildings, see H. Leclercq, "Eglises," *DACL* 4. 2 (1921) 2292 ff.; H. Janssen, *Kultur und Sprache. Zur Geschichte der alten Kirche im Spiegel der Sprachentwicklung von Tertullian bis Cyprian* (Lat. christ. prim. 8, Nijmegen 1938) 24-37: "Kirchengebäude."

237 *Summus Deus*—the God of the Christians. The prayers to this God are said in common—*in quibus oratur*, that is in the *conventicula*; and it was precisely in these churches that the Christians were sometimes slaughtered en masse in time of persecution. See, e. g. Lactantius, *Div. inst.* 5. 11. 10: "Some were borne headlong into the business of slaying, as, for example, one in Phrygia who cremated an entire congregation along with the church (*conventiculo*) itself." Cf. H. Leclercq, "Persécutions," *DACL* 14. 1 (1939) esp. 571-82. The prayers "for all magistrates" have their early counterpart in the magnificent prayer for rulers found in Clement of Rome 60. 4— 61. 2; cf. J. A. Kleist, *ACW* 1 (1946) 47 and the literature cited 116 n. 175. For the cultic significance of the present and similar testimonies, cf. F. J. Dölger, *Ant. u. Christ.* 3 (1932) 120. Regarding the patristic testimony for commemoration of, and prayers for, the dead, see Leclercq, "Defunts," *DACL* 4. 1 (1920) 427-58; "Prière," *DACL* 14. 2 (1940) 1767-70; P. J. Toner, "Dead, Prayers for the,"

Cath. Encycl. 4 (1908) 653-8. Cf. especially an earlier witness, Tertullian, *De Monog.* 10.

[238] So also pagan testimony of Christians in Pliny's time: cf. *Ep. ad Trai.* 97. 7. Augustine, *De civ. Dei* 2. 28, speaks of pagan scoffers as being silenced on actually witnessing Christian worship.

[239] Marchesi keeps the MS *quos solidet* which is difficult. Long ago Wensky corrected to *quos sol videt,* approved by Meiser and Wiman. Coxe (*ANF* 6. 488) cites this sentence to show that Arnobius possessed knowledge made available only to those who had passed beyond the status of catechumen. I dissent.

[240] Here again the Epicurean concept of the gods is clearly followed. Cf. Micka, *passim.*

[241] Cf. 7. 39-44, which is anticipated by the present passage.

[242] The MS *comptu* is difficult and has been much emended but, as Marchesi says, *comptus = coniunctio* (= 'bond'). Cf. Lucretius 3. 845 f.; 258 f.; 4. 26 ff., and Reifferscheid, *Analecta* 9; Löfstedt, *Eranos* 10 (1910) 15.

[243] The bracketed words, first rejected by Salmasius, are agreed by most editors not to belong here. Orelli put them in 4. 13, as we have noted above. Bryce-Campbell are inclined to think they really belong here, saying that the gods "cannot possibly at once be incapable of feeling anger and yet at the same time be angry with Christians."

[244] The *explicit* and *incipit* are as follows: ARNOUII ORATORIS LIB. IIII. EXP. INCP. LIB. U. Note that the word *Orator* = *Rhetor* (cf. Introd. 6).

BOOK FIVE

With Book Five Arnobius turns the shafts of his keen invective against two famous myths which are told in detail and then criticized at great length, the story of the dealings of Numa Pompilius with Jupiter Elicius and the exotic legends involved in the Phrygian cults of Magna Mater and Attis. Having finished his polemic against these myths, he takes up the similarly wretched stories told about the founding of the various Greek mysteries, especially that established at Eleusis.

As will be seen from the individual notes, here again there are striking parallels with the *Protrepticus* of Clement of Alexandria, no fewer than seven of which are regarded by Röhricht (*De Clemente* 6 f.) as affording abundant proof of the indebtedness of our author to the great Alexandrian polyhistor. Tullius, however, is convinced (57 f.) that Arnobius owes nothing to Clement but posits rather as the sources of this book a *Liber de mysteriis* and another on the allegorical interpretation of the myths. On this point see the Introduction 42 f.

[1] Wiman's excellent suggestion of *suo* = *summo* by abbreviation, a passage which has caused many scholars to stumble.

[2] Valerius Antias was a Roman historian of the first century B.C. His work, probably bearing the title *Annales*, comprised at least 75 books. Little concerned about historical truth, he supplied, invented, and forged history to suit his literary and partisan purposes. Cf. Schanz-Hosius, *Geschichte der römischen Literatur* 1 (4th ed., Munich 1927) 318. The account given in the following constitutes fragment 6 of Valerius Antias in H. Peter, *Hist. rom. fragm.* p. 153 = *Hist. rom. rel.* pp. 239-41. For other versions of the same story, see Ovid, *Fasti* 3. 285-398, and Plutarch, *Numa* 15. 3-5; for a study of the incident related, see F. J. Dölger, ΙΧΘΥΣ 2 (1922) 299-302.

[3] Supposed founder of the ancient Roman religious observances, which Arnobius (2. 12) and Tertullian (*Apol.* 21. 29; *De praescr. haer.* 40) term *supersitiones*.

[4] Egeria was a fountain nymph and the wife and adviser of Numa. Cf. Livy 1. 21. 3; Ovid, *Met.* 15. 487; *Fasti* 3. 261 f.; G. Wissowa, *LM* 1. 1216-8.

[5] Cf. 1. 28 and n. 116.

[6] Cf. 2. 71 and n. 445.

[7] The Aventine, the largest and least important historically of the three isolated peaks standing near the Tiber.

[8] *Elici*—an allusion to Jupiter Elicius, honored by an altar on the Aventine. Cf. Ovid, *Fasti* 3. 327 f. and Frazer's note *ad loc.*, vol. 3. 90 f.; Wissowa, 121; *LM* 2. 656-61.

[9] *Dixe* is an archaic form of *dixisse*: cf. W. M. Lindsay, *The Latin Language* (Oxford 1894) 508.

[10] The meaning is by human sacrifice. Cf. Tertullian, *Apol.* 9. 2: *Infantes penes Africam Saturno immolabantur palam usque ad proconsulatum Tiberii.* In *Scorp.* 7, he speaks of human sacrifices to Jupiter in Latium (see F. Schwenn, *Die Menschenopfer bei den Griechen und Römern* [Religionsg. Vers. u. Vorarb. 15. 3, Giessen 1915] 180 f.).

[11] Jupiter had said that the expiation was to be made by the sacrifice of a head—*caput*. Now, *caput* was also the term for the bulb of an onion (*caepa, caepe, cepa, cepitius, cepitium*): cf. Walde-Hof-

mann, *Lateinisches etymologisches Wörterbuch* 1 (3rd ed., Heidelberg 1938) 201. Numa, determined to extenuate the severe sacrificial requirement, at once takes advantage of the double meaning of *caput* and suggests to Jupiter that he of course means an onion 'head.' The god then insists that he means a 'human head,' to which Numa promptly adds 'of hair.'

[12] Here the Latin of Marchesi's text (P has *animalia*; Sabaeus *animali*) means that Jupiter requires a living (*animali* = adjective) head, not an onion or the lifeless hair on a human head; but Numa at once pretends to take the word as a noun meaning an animal head and suggests the *maena*, a small sea fish. ⟨*Maena*⟩ is supplied, from below, by Heraldus.

[13] A *maena*, corresponding to Plutarch's (*Numa* 15.5) μαινίς = anchovy (Dölger) or sprat (Perrin, Loeb Class. Libr.).

[14] That is, the onion, hair, and fish. For the true place of these in the ancient sacrifical ritual, cf. Dölger, *op cit.* 300 f.

[15] Aposiopesis.

[16] Reifferscheid reads *fluenta isse* † *per fontium?* In his apparatus he conjectures *adisse propere?* Meiser has *petisse;* Löfstedt *adisse semper.*

[17] Marchesi and Thörnell rightly keep the MS *ad ipsum*: a preposterous question is asked—*reductio ad absurdum.* Sabaeus and Reifferscheid have *ab ipso.*

[18] Reading ⟨*vi*⟩ *evanescat* with Kroll. The passage has been much emended but with little change in sense.

[19] *In verrucula colli unius cum homunculo stantem.* The Aventine is *relatively* small.

[20] Cf. Book Seven, n. 81.

[21] Here the MS reads *Nisi homo praesumeret* which Marchesi prints [*Nisi*] *homo praesumens.*

[22] His real wish was to circumvent Jupiter; he pretended to want to know Jupiter's will and do it.

[23] Orelli states that no other ancient author mentions this Timotheus who is no. 15 in the list published by R. Laqueur, *RE* 2 R. 6 (1937) 1338. Cf. also *DBM* 3.1150 (no. 6); Cumont 223 n. 16. On the myth, see Ovid, *Fasti* 4.221 and Frazer's note *ad loc.* vol. 3, pp. 217-24; Cumont 43-68. On the cult of Cybele, see H. Graillot, *Le culte de Cybèle, mère des dieux, à Rome et dans l'empire romain* (Paris 1912) and the works cited in Cumont 220 f.

[24] The MS has *sita* but Bastgen *posita* and Castiglioni ⟨*expo*⟩*sita* which seems excellent.

THE CASE AGAINST THE PAGANS: BOOK FIVE   569

²⁵ Tullius (57) is right in maintaining that the following account of Attis owes nothing to the corresponding passage in Clement, *Protr.* 2.24. Cf. Catullus 63; W. W. Hyde, *Paganism to Christianity in the Roman Empire* (Philadelphia 1946) 46-9. The frequent use throughout this account of historical presents, a grammatical device not found elsewhere in Arnobius, may be a reflection of the particular source which our author is here following.

²⁶ On Themis, cf. Horace, *Carm.* 1.2; Pausanias 10.5.6; K. Latte, *RE* 2 R. 5 (1932) 1626-30; L. Weniger, *LM* 5.570-606; J. E. Harrison, *Themis* (Cambridge 1912) 480-535; R. Hirzel, *Themis, Dike und Verwandtes* (Leipzig 1907) 1 ff.

²⁷ The sole survivors in the Greek version of the Deluge. On the myth, see L. v. Sybel, *LM* 1.994-8; K. Tümpel, "Deukalion," *RE* 5 (1905) 261-76. Cf. *Vigiliae Christianae* 3 (1949) 45 f.

²⁸ Cf. F. Schwenn, *RE* 11 (1922) 2250-98; also Index, "Cybele."

²⁹ The MS and Marchesi: *Acdestis;* Reifferscheid: *Agdistis,* a difference in orthography preserved throughout the passage. On Agdestis (conceived, according to Arnobius: [Iuppiter] voluptatem in lapidem fudit victus. Hinc petra concepit), cf. A. B. Cook, *Zeus* 2 (Cambridge 1925) 1225; W. H. Roscher, "Agdistis," *LM* 1.100; G. Knaack, *RE* 1 (1894) 767 f.

³⁰ The god of wine, explaining the strategy employed in the following.

³¹ Sequuntur: ex setis scientissime conplicatis imum plantae inicit laqueum, parte altera proles cum ipsis genitalibus occupat. Exhalata ille vi meri corripit se impetu et adducente nexus planta suis ipse se viribus eo quo ⟨vir⟩ fuerat privat sexu. Cum discidio partium sanguis fluit immensus . . . .

³² On Nana, cf. Wagner, *LM* 3.4; F. Schwenn, *RE* 16 (1935) 1672; F. J. Dölger, ΙΧΘΥΣ 2 (1922) 336 f. (the pomegranate as symbolic of fruitfulness).—Sangarius was a king named for the river of Phrygia and Bithynia which flows into the Euxine. Cf. A. Nawrath, "Sangarius" no. 2, *RE* 2 R. 1 (1920) 2270: O. Höfer, *LM* 4.334. On the river, see L. Schmitz, *DG* 2.902. It is now the Turkish Ayala.

³³ Here the MS reads *formas* which Salmasius emends to *Phorbas* but no Phorbas is mentioned in other versions of the same story. Marchesi brackets [*formas*] and inserts ⟨*forma*⟩ before *scitulos,* comparing Plautus, *Rudens* 894. This Wiman approves. Heraldus reads *foret* and Kistner *foras.*

³⁴ So far as this phrase (*lacte hirquino*) goes, the sense is merely

'goat's milk,' but in 5.13 Arnobius pretends to believe that the adjective *hirquinus* (or *hircinus*) can refer only to a he-goat because this suits his purpose better. He is not completely fair to his opponents.

[35] I. e. the Lydians. Cf. *Etruria* = *Etrusci* in 2.62 (ter).

[36] Cf. Hesychius s. v. "'Αδαγνούς," who identifies him as a hermaphrodite god among the Phrygians.

[37] The principal town in west Galatia, central point for the Cybele cult. Cf. W. Ruge, *RE* 19 (1937) 1104-14.

[38] Cf. 2.73, 5.13. See also W. Drexler, "Midas," *LM* 2.2954-68; S. Eitrem, "Midas" no. 1, *RE* 15 (1932) 1526-36; L. Preller-C. Robert, *Griechische Mythologie* 1 (4th ed., Berlin 1894) 644 f.

[39] At the beginning of this sentence Reifferscheid places * * * indicating that he thinks there is a serious dislocation of the text.

[40] I have not been able to improve upon Brakman's suggestion *adora adora* (for the MS *adorandorum*) which is hardly satisfactory, as Wiman, *Eranos* 45 (1947) 147, says, but the same objection can be made to his *adorandorum ⟨insolito ardore⟩ deorum*, and to all other attempts to cure the passage.

[41] Marchesi reads: *mammas sibi demetit* † *Galli filia paelicis*, which Wiman, *Eranos* 45 (1947) 143, on the basis of 5.13 (see n. 74) expands as follows: *mammas sibi demetit Galli ⟨sese evirantis exemplo⟩ filia paelicis*.

[42] On Gallus, see W. Drexler, *LM* 1.1582 f. On this passage see Wiman, *Eranos* 45 (1947) 143.

[43] Lactantius, *Div. inst.* 1.7.7; *Epit.* 8, follows a divergent tradition.—Sequuntur in textu: (Attis) dicens: 'Tibi Acdesti haec habe, propter quae motus tantos furialium discriminum concitasti.' Evolat cum profluvio sanguinis vita, sed abscisa quae fuerant Magna legit et ⟨lavit⟩ Mater deum, inicit his terram, ⟨ut erant⟩ prius tecta atque involuta defuncti.

[44] What follows shows that at least a violet-colored flower is meant, but our violet does not climb. *Viola* is, however, sometimes translated as 'gillyflower,' a variety of which may be meant. See *Encyc. Brit.* 12 (11th ed., 1911) 24.

[45] A pine thus wrapped and garlanded, representing the dead Attis, was borne to the temple of Cybele on the Palatine by a confraternity known as *dendrophoroi* (= 'tree-carriers'); cf. Cumont 52.

[46] LeNourry, quoted by Orelli, wishes to identify this Valerius with Messalla (cf. A. Gellius 13.15; Macrobius, *Sat.* 1.9) but Messalla is described there as an augur, not a *pontifex*. Hildebrand

thinks this is Valerius Antias (Peter is silent on the point) who is cited in 5.1 but for quite a different story.

[47] Marchesi keeps the MS: *suffodit* † *etas*. Numerous conjectures have been made but none effects a cure of the corrupt passage.

[48] Either with her hands or, as Alleker seems to think, on the tree.

[49] My friend, F. L. Santee, M.D., writes that the phenomenon of growth of hair after death is so commonly met by physicians that it receives no attention in the standard medical books. Cf. Tertullian, *De an.* 51.2 and Waszink's note, p. 529; Aristotle, *Hist. animal.* 3.11 (518b).

[50] *Minimissimus*, repeated in 5.14—*superlativus e superlativo*. Cf. *extremissimus*: Tertullian, *Apol.* 19.4; *pessimissimus*, *De cultu fem.* 2.1.

[51] Reading *sacrorum antistitibus* for *sacerdotum* (*sacerdot⟨ior⟩um*: Reifferscheid) *antistitibus*, following the recommendation of Dr. Plumpe, "Some Critical Annotations to Arnobius," *Vigiliae Christianae* 3.4 (1949), who compares Cicero, *De domo sua* 104, and other passages. The 'annual rites' were performed during a cycle of feasts, 15-27 March, introduced by the emperor Claudius and honoring both Cybele and Attis. Cf. Wissowa 321 f.; Cumont 52-57.

[52] M. Terentius Varro. The information referred to him in the following appears as fragment 9 of Varro's *De gente populi Romani* in H. Peter, *Hist. rom. fragm.* p. 230 = *Hist. rom. rel.* 2, p. 14.

[53] A. Hirtius and C. Vibius Pansa were lieutenants of Caesar who lost their lives in April, 43 B.C., when, as consuls, they took the field against Antony. Thus, the Varronian calculations must have put the deluge somewhere about 2043 B.C. or a little later.

[54] If this sentence means anything, it must surely imply that Magna Mater no longer exists. Cf. Introd. 30-3.

[55] In a related sense, speaking of the obscene barbarities practiced in the cult of Cybele, the Mother of the Gods, St. Augustine, *De civ. Dei* 2.5, very effectively posits the case of Scipio Nasica, chosen in 204 B.C. for the honor of bringing the likeness of the Great Mother into Rome. He received the offer of having his mother deified by the Roman state. Surely, states Augustine, Nasica would wish that such honor be paid his mother. The same senator would revolt, however, at the very thought that his mother should be honored with the same disgraceful rites as are practiced in honor of the Mother of the Gods. In that case Nasica would much prefer 'that his mother lay stone dead.'—Cf. the previous chapter (2.4) where Augustine states: "There is something in the reverence that man has for his parents which not even profligacy can take away."

[56] Sequuntur: et quem pietas diiugare ab infando matris non valuit adpetitu, effusa libido diiunxit?

[57] Omisi: Et sane hoc loco frugalitatis magnae viri et circa res etiam flagitiosi operis parciores, ne sancta illa semina frustra videantur effusa, silex, inquit, ebibit Iovialis incontinentiae foeditatem.

[58] St. Augustine, *De civ. Dei* 7.26, remarks concerning the African type of the Galli, the unmanned priests of the Mother of the Gods venerated in Africa: "Up to very recently these effeminates were walking the streets and alleys of Carthage, their hair reeking with ointment, their face powdered white, with enervated bodies moving along like women, and even soliciting the man on the street for sustenance of their dissolute lives."

[59] *Cantheriorum* = 'geldings'; also used frequently of worn-out, decrepit animals—'nags,' 'dobbins,' 'jades.' Arnobius sarcastically implies that Liber was shrewd enough not to try to obtain the hair needed by tampering with the tails of more spirited horses, stallions, for example.

[60] *Sauciantem*, lit. = 'wounding'; cf. *Harper's Lat. Dict.*: *se sauciare* = to get 'shot.'

[61] The supplement of the lacuna is based on 5.6 by Wiman: *postquam ebrietas potu⟨m inde immoderatius Acdestim altissimo sopor⟩e mersit* for Marchesi's *postquam ebrietas potu emersit*. Sequuntur: inseruisse caute manus, contrectavisse virilia dormientis, atque ut omnia cingerent circumpositi laqueorum morsus, artificii i⟨ta⟩ tum rebus adhibuisse perituris.

[62] Here the MS reads *de divino aliquid ex corpore desecari* and Marchesi, following Salmasius, brackets [*de*].

[63] Ancient purple was cardinal.

[64] Hagendahl wishes to read ⟨f⟩*luminis* which seems less satisfactory.

[65] Zink adds *vino* which is the meaning even if Marchesi is right in omitting it.

[66] The people of Abdera in Thrace were proverbially stupid. Cicero, for example, writes to Atticus (4.16.6) when the senate to his mind had made a stupid decision: '*Hic abdera*,' 'here we are in Abdera.' Cf. O. Hirschfeld, *RE* 1 (1894) 22.f.

[67] The word (*patres*) has probably no more force than "sources."

[68] The Great Mother of the Gods, an appellative derived from Mt. Berecyntus, supposedly the original homestead of the ancient Cybele-venerating Phrygians. Cf. H. Steuding, *LM* 1.783; O. Jessen, "Berekyntia," *RE* 3 (1899) 280.

The Case against the Pagans: Book Five 573

[69] *Pignus* has here the meaning of 'child' instead of its more normal meaning of 'pledge.'

[70] Cf. 5. 6 and n. 34.

[71] The sort of *dilectio* characterized by Tertullian, *Apol.* 15. 2-5: Cybele pastorem suspirat fastidiosum ... non erubescentibus vobis.

[72] Reifferscheid makes this a question with telling effect.

[73] That is, the walls came with her as she lifted them up with her head. For sculptures showing these walls on Cybele's head, see S. Reinach, *Répertoire de la statuaire grecque et romaine* (Paris 1897-1924) 2. 269, 273; 3. 251; 4. 163; 5. 118.

[74] Pausanias (7. 17. 5) says that the father-in-law of Attis likewise mutilated himself; but he also says that Attis was the son of Calaus, a name which looks suspiciously like Gallus. Cf. also 5. 7. Gallus was the name of a river tributary to the Sangarius.—Sequuntur in textu: Tibi habe haec, inquit, propter quae res tantas animorum subversionibus concitasti. Nesciremus adhuc omnes, quid in adulti corpore furor desiderasset Acdestius, nisi puer abscisa insatietati obiecisset offensi.

[75] Sequuntur: Dicite o iterum, ergone deum mater genitalia illa desecta cum fluoribus ipsa per se maerens officiosa sedulitate collegit, ipsa sanctis manibus, ipsa divinis contrectavit ac sustulit flagitiosi operis instrumenta foedique, abscondenda etiam mandavit terrae, ac ne nuda in gremio diffluerent sic soli, priusquam veste velaret ac tegeret, lavit utique, balsamis atque unxit? Unde enim violae nasci potuissent odorae, nisi putorem membri unguentorum illa suffectio temperaret?

[76] This suggests 1 Tim 4. 7: *fabulas aniles,* but the phrase is too common in proverbs to show acquaintance with the Epistle.

[77] See n. 49.

[78] Cf. 1. 2 for the same idea, almost the same words.

[79] On these emasculated priests of the Phrygian cult, see Ovid, *Fasti* 4. 361-2; G. Lafaye, *DA* 2. 1455-9; F. Cumont, "Gallos" no. 5, *RE* 7 (1912) 674-82; also above, n. 57.

[80] Cf. n. 73.

[81] From *carere,* 'to be without,' therefore also 'to do without,' 'to abstain.' The neuter *castum* designated the period during which abstinence was practiced (Tertullian, *De ieun. adv. psych.* 16: *castum* Isidis et Cybeles). Abstention from bread was also enjoined on certain feast days of Ceres (cf. Wissowa 301). On *castus,* see G. Wissowa, "castus" no. 4, *RE* 3 (1899) 1780, and *ibid.* 2905; also F. J. Dölger's note on ἁγνεία: ΙΧΘΥΣ 2 (1922) 55 n. 3.

[82] The *Galli*.

[83] Cf. Cicero, De leg. 2. 14. 36; Livy 39. 8.

[84] A point of view which might have been followed more systematically to great advantage. The next sentence furnishes one example among others in Arnobius of the ancient rhetorical figure of omission—*praeteritio* (παράλειψις), really a rhetorical trick by which some incident or example, particularly an unpleasant one, is ostensibly passed over, but actually mentioned, and frequently in considerable detail. Cf. R. Volkmann, *Die Rhetorik der Griechen und Römer* (2nd ed., Leipzig 1885) 501.

[85] Cf. 1. 36. S. Brandt (*CSEL* 19. 1, pp. cii and 89) maintains that there is correspondence between this passage and Lactantius, *Div. inst.* 1. 22. 9 f. See Introd. 48-51.

[86] Sextus Clodius, a rhetor and known wit, was Mark Antony's teacher. When Antony had settled rich Sicilian lands on him, Cicero in the *Philippics* (3. 9. 22) punned that the teacher had become *ex oratore arator*. Cicero (*ibid.* 2. 17. 43) further taunted his archenemy by stating that he had learned little sense indeed, considering the tuition paid. Concerning this Clodius, cf. Schanz-Hosius, *Geschichte der römischen Literatur* 1 (4th ed., Munich 1927) 583.

[87] This Butas was probably a freedman of the younger Cato. Cf. Plutarch, *Romulus* 21. 6; G. Knaack, "Butas" no. 2, *RE* 3 (1899) 1080.

[88] Tullius (57) is convinced that the mention of the *Dii Conserentes* owes nothing to Clement. F. Dal Pane, "Sopra le fonti di un passo di Arnobio," *Studi ital. di filol. class.* 9 (1901) 30, cites Dion. Hal., *Ant. rom.* 4. 2; Pliny, *Nat. hist.* 36. 70. 204; Ovid, *Fasti* 6. 627-34, and maintains that the Conserentes = Lares. He thinks Arnobius is citing Granius Flaccus through Cornelius Labeo. So also Gabarrou (*Oeuvre* 41). Cf. Macrobius, *Sat.* 4. 6.

[89] Orelli identifies this Flaccus either with Granius Flaccus (cf. 3. 31) or with Verrius Flaccus the grammarian. The latter is much less likely.—Arnobius' text: Sed et deos Conserentis pari more ac dissimulatione taceamus, quos cum ceteris scribit Flaccus in humani penis similitudinem versos obruisse ⟨se⟩ cinere, qui sub ollula fuerat factus extorum: quem cum Tanaquil dimoveret Etruriae disciplinarum perita, subrexisse se deos et nervis obduruisse divinis. Corniculanae inde imperavisse captivae, ut intellegeret et agnosceret, quid sibi vellet; Ocrisiam prudentissimam feminam divos inseruisse genitali, explicuisse motus certos: tunc sancta ecferventia numina vim vomuisse Lucilii ac regem Servium natum esse Romanum.

[90] Cf. Livy 39. 8 f.; Firmicus Maternus, *De err. prof. rel.* 6; Clement of Alexandria, *Protr.* 2. 12. 2.

THE CASE AGAINST THE PAGANS: BOOK FIVE 575

[91] Omophagia is the Latin form of the Greek word ὠμοφαγία which means 'eating raw flesh.' Cf. Clement, loc. cit., in which Clement says that "the raving Dionysus is worshipped by Bacchants with orgies in which they celebrate their sacred frenzy with a banquet of raw flesh. Wreathed with snakes, they distribute portions of their victims, crying Εὑα, that Εὑα (Eve) through whom error entered the world; and a consecrated snake is the emblem of the Bacchic orgies" (Butterworth). He then goes on to state that according to correct Hebrew, the word *hevia* means a female snake. Aside from the rhetorical differences it is clear that Clement had a source which gave the Bacchic cry omitted by Arnobius. Röhricht (*De Clemente* 25, parallels nos. 16 f.) thinks that Clement is Arnobius' source, but Tullius (26) says that both are independent, the latter using a *liber de mysteriis* for his material.

[92] Cf. Cumont 201 and 319 n. 56.

[93] Cf. 4. 24, 6. 6; see Introd. 6 f.

[94] Cf. also 4. 24. Clement of Alexandria, *Protr.* 2. 13. 4, calls Cinyras a Cypriote and says he transferred the lascivious orgies of Aphrodite from night to day. Cf. also Firmicus Maternus, *De err. prof. rel.* 9. 3—10. 1.

[95] That is, those who undergo initiation.

[96] In the parallel passage (*Protr.* 2. 14) Clement is quite different. As Tullius (29 f.) says, Clement cannot be the source for Arnobius, which was probably a book on the mysteries. Cf. Firmicus Maternus, *De err. prof. rel.* 10. 26; F. J. Dölger, *Ant. u. Christ.* 3 (1932) 11.

[97] The parallel passage in Clement (*Protr.* 2. 19) is much fuller than that in Arnobius. Two of the Corybantes slew a third—their brother—shrouded the corpse's head with a purple cloak, wreathed and buried it, carrying it upon a bronze shield to the base of Mt. Olympus. The priests of these mysteries forbid wild celery to be placed on the table, for they believe the plant grew out of the blood of the murdered brother. Clement adds that a similar custom is observed by the women who celebrate the Thesmophoria: they are careful not to eat pomegranate seeds, because they believe that pomegranates spring from the blood of Dionysus. Again Tullius (32) maintains against Röhricht (*De Clemente* 26, parallel no. 18), that there is too much in Clement not in Arnobius to believe that Arnobius is here following Clement. Dr. Plumpe points out that Arnobius has expressly stated that he does not intend to use all the material at his disposal. Cf. Firmicus Maternus, *De err. prof. rel.* 12. 4; F. J. Dölger, ΙΧΘΥΣ 2 (1922) 432; Brakman, *Miscella tertia* 27.

⁹⁸ From Clement we learn that the murderers and murdered were Corybantes.

⁹⁹ Again the account of Clement (*Protr.* 2. 17 f.) is much fuller. Röhricht (*De Clemente* 26) lists this as parallel no. 19, but Tullius (33 f.) sees a different source than Clement.

¹⁰⁰ The mythical poet Orpheus, son of Oeagrus and the muse Calliope. Clement, *Protr.* 2. 17. 2, quotes two Orphic lines which mention some of the playthings of Liber, including the golden apples, here listed by Arnobius.

¹⁰¹ Chapters 20 ff. form a connected account of the mysteries known as Sabazian (Arnobius: Sebadian), which is paralleled by another in Clement (*Protr.* 2. 15 f.). The latter is considerably more concise but, on the other hand, gives details not found in Arnobius. Cf. Tullius' printing of the two accounts in parallel columns (35-7). Here again he (38-40) maintains, against Röhricht (*De Clemente* 10, 27 f.) that the sources of both apologists are different and that our author was following a Latin *Liber de mysteriis*.

¹⁰² That is, the 'grim or terrible one,' a name also given to Hecate (Artemis). Cf. Propertius 11. 16; Apoll. Rhod. 3. 861-2, 1211; Lycophron 1176; Hippolytus, *Ref.* 5. 3.

¹⁰³ Deinde: ad postremum filius vias satisfactionis inquirens comminiscitur remedium tale: arietem nobilem bene grandibus cum testiculis deligit, exsecat hos ipse et lanato exuit ex folliculi tegmine. Accedens maerens et summissus ad matrem et tamquam ipse sententia condemnavisset se sua, in gremium proicit [et iacit] has eius.

¹⁰⁴ Cf. also 5. 35; Wissowa 309-13.

¹⁰⁵ The goddess of the lower world.

¹⁰⁶ The issue, usually not described as a monster, was called Zagreus.

¹⁰⁷ Clement, who quotes a second line, speaks of an "idolatrous" or "symbolical poet." O. Crusius, *Rhein. Mus.* 45 (1890) 272, assigns this verse to the poet Rhinthon. Cf. also W. Kroll, *Rhein. Mus.* 72 (1917-8) 79 n. 2; Firmicus Maternus, *De err. prof. rel.* 26. 1.

¹⁰⁸ Clement calls them 'Sabazian.' Cf. Firmicus Maternus, *De err. prof. rel.* 10; Macrobius, *Sat.* 1. 18; Cumont 60-65, pl. 3, which shows the head and bust of Sabazios.

¹⁰⁹ The rest of the sentence—*et eximitur rursus ab inferioribus partibus atque imis*—has no counterpart in Clement.

¹¹⁰ Leda was the mother of the Castors.—Danae, daughter of Acrisius of Argos and Eurydice: cf. H. W. Stoll, *LM* 1. 946-9.—On Europa, daughter of Phoenix, cf. 5. 24 (*nondum mulier*) and see O. Crusius, *LM* 1. 14. 10-8; J. Escher, "Europe" no. 1, *RE* 6 (1912)

The Case Against the Pagans: Book Five 577

1287-98.—Regarding Alcmene, cf. Book Four, n. 198.—The Electra here mentioned was not the daughter of Agamemnon but the daughter of Atlas and Hesione, and mother of Dardanus. See Ovid, *Fasti* 4. 31 f.; Dion. Hal., *Ant. rom.* 1. 50, 1. 61; Vergil, *Aen.* 8. 134-7.— Latona was mother of Apollo and Diana, Laodamia, daughter of Bellerophon and mother of Sarpedon by Zeus (*Iliad* 6. 197). See H. W. Stoll, *LM* 2. 1826-9; M. Schmidt, *RE* 12 (1925) 698.

[111] Catamitus = Ganymede. Cf. 4. 26, 5. 44, 7. 33, and W. H. Roscher, *LM* 1. 856; E. Aust, *RE* 3 (1899) 1784.

[112] The MS reads *screnarum* for which Gelenius reads *scenarum* and Salmasius *sentinarum*.

[113] Cf. Minucius 31. 3: sic et deos colitis incestos, cum matre, cum filia, cum sorore coniunctos (cf. Vergil, *Aen.* 1. 46 f.). Cf. also Origen, *C. Cels.* 1. 17.

[114] Cf. Vergil, *Aen.* 10. 18.

[115] With *cohonestatum* the MS reads *esse*. Cf. Weyman 392.

[116] Here the word *censoria* suggests that, like a Roman censor, Jupiter examines all the rams to see which come up to specifications: . . . inspicientem testiculos arietinos, arripientem hos manu censoria illa atque divina.

[117] Here the MS has [*ferventi nullas*] which is meaningless in the text: tum deinde secreta rimantem [ferventi nullas] summotisque arbitris circumiectas prolibus diripientem membranulas.

[118] *Sub mundi hoc axe.* Both this sentence and the next lack main verbs.

[119] *Res omnes in antiquae speciem confunderet unitatis.*

[120] Arnobius has been unjustly charged (see the unusually excellent exegesis given by Bryce-Campbell 247 n. 6) with confusing the Eleusinian mysteries and the Thesmophoria, the two having much in common. Kettner (5), Röhricht (*De Clemente* 11), and Kroll (78) are among the critics at this point, but Bryce-Campbell's favorable attitude is strongly supported by Tullius (45) who is sure that this passage does not refer to the Eleusinia and that Arnobius is independent of Clement, a cardinal point in Tullius' thesis. Cf. P. Arbesmann, " Thesmophoria," *RE* 2. R. 6 (1936) 15-28; O. Höfer, " Thesmophoros," *LM* 5. 760-3; E. Cahen, *DA* 5. 239-42.

[121] *Pannychismi*, a Greek word meaning 'keeping vigils.' Cf. Cumont 54.

[122] For the story, cf. Ovid, *Fasti* 4. 393-620; Diodorus Sic. 4. 4; Apollodorus 1. 5; Hyginus, *Fab.* 146; Firmicus Maternus, *De err. prof. rel.* 7. 1-7, 8. 3.

[123] Sabaeus is probably right in changing *virago* to *virgo* here, but *virago* = *virgo* elsewhere in this MS.

[124] Cf. 5. 35.

[125] Clement begins his parallel story in *Protr.* 2. 17. 1, interrupts it with the account of the slaying of Dionysus and of the Corybantic orgies, and then continues the tale of Demeter (= Ceres) with her arrival at Eleusis, *ibid.* 2. 20. 1-21. 2. The fact that Clement places the swineherd Eubuleus on the scene of the abduction, eliminates the possibility that he is thinking of a Sicilian scene, as is Arnobius. Tullius (46) is convinced, as usual, that Arnobius owes nothing to Ovid's account but is following an epic treatment of the rape of Proserpina, unknown to us now but available to Arnobius in a prose form. Röhricht (*De Clemente* 3, 35) cites R. Foerster, *Der Raub und die Rückkehr der Persephone* (Stuttgart 1874) 282, for the view that 5. 24-6 owe much to Clement, and A. Ludwich, "Baubo und Demeter," *Neue Jahrb. f. Phil.* 141 (1890) 51 ff., for the opposite view.

[126] The Attic deme of Eleusis lay northwest of Athens, a short distance from the sea opposite the island of Salamis. In it was the great sanctuary of the Eleusinian mysteries of Demeter about which Pausanias (1. 38. 5-7) gives, as was to be expected, an unsatisfactorily brief statement. Pausanias learned nothing about the present tale of the origin of the mysteries, or, if he did, was silent. Cf. F. Lenormant, *DA* 2. 544-81; A. Schiff, "Eleusis," *RE* 5 (1905) 2336-8; P. Stengel, "Eleusinia," *ibid.* 2328-32.

[127] *Terrigenae* = 'earthborn,' 'autochthonous.' In Clement's list Dysaules comes second but the others are in the same order. Cf. Röhricht, *De Clemente* 10, 34-8, parallel no. 10.

[128] On Baubo, wife of Dysaules, see Schultz, *LM* 1. 752 f. (he believes Arnobius freely translates Clement); F. Lenormant, *DA* 1. 683; O. Kern, "Baubo" no. 1, *RE* 3 (1899) 150 f.; M. P. Nilsson, *Geschichte der griechischen Religion* (Munich 1941) 622-4. Cf. E. Rohde, *Psyche, the Cult of Souls and Belief in Immortality among the Greeks* (tr. by W. B. Hillis, New York 1925) 591. In modern times this sensual deity found a place in the Walpurgis Night of Goethe's *Faust*, part 1. 3962 ff.—Triptolemus was of royal Eleusinian descent, befriended by Demeter (= Ceres). Through her assistance he became the inventor of agriculture and civilization. She gave him a chariot with winged dragons and with these he rode through the world, acquainting it with wheat and the means of its production. Cf. Pausanias 1. 14. 2, 1. 38. 6; Hyginus, *Fab.* 147; Ovid, *Met.* 5. 638-

The Case Against the Pagans: Book Five

61; also above, 1. 38 and n. 181.—Eumolpus, a son of Poseidon, was the mythical founder of the Eleusinian mysteries. Cf. Pausanias 1. 38. 3.—Eubuleus, a brother of Triptolemus: cf. Pausanias 1. 14. 2.— Dysaules was the father of Triptolemus and Eubuleus: Pausanias 1. 14. 3, 2. 14. 2-4. Cf. H. W. Stoll, *LM* 1. 1208 f.

[129] The sacerdotal family at Eleusis. Cf. Preller-Robert, *Griechische Mythologie* 1: *Theogonie und Götter* (Berlin 1894) 787 f.

[130] The Athenians, whose city was said to have been founded by the first king of Attica, Cecrops. Cf. O. Immisch, *LM* 2. 1014-24.

[131] On the snakes on the *caduceus*, cf. 4. 22.

[132] As usual, Arnobius elaborates the details.

[133] *Cinnus*. Cf. Hesychius, s. v. κυκεών (wine, water, honey, barley, mixed).

[134] Note the anthropomorphism of the story.

[135] Clement says Baubo's feelings were hurt, a point not made by Arnobius.

[136] Sequuntur: partem illam corporis, per quam secus femineum et subolem prodere et nomen solet adquirere generi, tum longiore ab incuria liberat, facit sumere habitum puriorem et in speciem levigari nondum duri atque histriculi pusionis. Redit ad deam tristem et inter illa communia quibus moris est frangere ac temperare maerores retegit se ipsam atque omnia illa pudoris loca revelatis monstrat inguinibus. Atque pubi adfigit oculos diva et inauditi specie solaminis pascitur.

[137] Orpheus who is named by Clement.

[138] The verses, differing considerably from the parallel lines in Clement, *Protr.* 2. 21. 1, are:

> Sic effata simul vestem contraxit ab imo
> Obiecitque oculis formatas inguinibus res:
> Quas cava succutiens Baubo manu—nam puerilis
> Ollis vultus erat—plaudit, contrectat amice.
> Tum dea defigens augusti luminis orbes
> Tristitias animi paulum mollita reponit:
> Inde manu poclum sumit risuque sequenti
> Perducit totum cyceonis laeta liquorem.

[139] *Erechthidae*, that is, sons or descendants of Erechtheus, an Attic mythical hero—another appellative (cf. above, *Cecropidae*, n. 130) for the Athenians. See Ovid, *Met.* 7. 430.

[140] Athens is Athene's town.

[141] Note here the legal terms which appear to have escaped C. Ferrini, 'Die juristischen Kenntnisse des Arnobius und des Lactantius," *Zeitschr. d. Sav.-Stift. f. Rechtsgesch.* 15 (1894) 343-52.

[142] Both Reifferscheid and Marchesi mark this with a † but the lacuna is clearly supplied by the suggestion of Wiman, *Eranos* 45 (1947) 144: *Eleusiniorum vestrorum not⟨i hi versus in medium not⟩as et origines producunt*, etc. Kroll had suggested that *notas* be changed to *not⟨h⟩as*.

[143] On this religious password or liturgical formula of legitimation, see F. J. Dölger, *Ant. u. Christ.* 4 (1934) 145 n. 17. It should be noted that in the case of the abduction of Proserpina and the Baubo-Demeter episode which follows it, the source of Arnobius could not have been Clement, according to the view of Tullius (48-52), because of the too great differences between them, but was a work on mysteries unknown to us. See also another formula of the same type in Firmicus Maternus, *De err. prof. rel.* 18. 1 (cf. Cumont 65).

[144] *Sine honoribus praefatis.* Deinde sequuntur: quidquam quaeso spectaculi, quid in pudendis fuit rei verendisque Baubonis, quod feminei sexus deam et consimili formatam membro in admirationem converteret atque risum. . . .

[145] Reading *nos decentis* with Kroll and Wiman instead of the MS *noscentis* or *nos gentis* which is found in both editors.

[146] *Tricas conduplicare Tellenas.* Here the first and third words are difficult. Regarding the first, Nonius (1, p. 13 Lindsay) defines: *tricae sunt impedimenta et implicationes*, '*tricae* are hindrances and entanglements.' Further, Nonius (*ibid.*) quotes Varro: *putas eos non citius tricas Tellanas quam id extricaturos.* Here, too, a connotation of something involved, confusing, troublously puzzling, is evident. Again, the quotation from Varro also contains the word *Tellanas* = *Tellenas* (the latter spelling, also defended by Turnebus and Nettleship, may have escaped Lindsay in the present text of Arnobius). The Tellenii of Tellenae (Tellena?) are mentioned by Dionysius of Halicarnassus (5. 61; cf. also Pliny, *Nat. hist.* 3. 68) as having been members of the alliance of thirty Latin cities. The city was taken and destroyed under Ancus Martius and the inhabitants transplanted to Rome and given citizenship (Livy 1. 33). Cf. H. Philipp, "Tellenae," *RE* 2. R., 5 (1934) 405. What the Tellenii did to give their name to a difficult or 'inextricable' situation—the proverbial *tricae Tellenae*—is still a puzzle. Tullius (55) is, of course, quite right in laying emphasis on the point that whatever Arnobius' source here, it was not Clement.

[147] On the textual problems involved in this reference to the Halimuntian mysteries, see my note in *Vigiliae Christianae* 3 (1949) 46 f.

[148] For the contention that Arnobius is here indebted to Clement,

Protr. 2. 31. 2, cf. Kettner 5, Röhricht, *De Clemente* 17, and Kroll 78; for a denial of such dependence, see Tullius 54. Cf. W. Kolbe, "Halimus," *RE* 7 (1912) 2266 f.; L. Deubner, *Attische Feste* (Berlin 1932) 52, 80. See especially Röhricht, *De Clemente* 16 f., 28, parallel no. 22. Brakman, *Miscella tertia* 27, thinks Firmicus Maternus, *De err. prof. rel.* 12. 4, imitated the present passage.

[149] Cf. 4. 15. Cicero, *De nat. deor.* 3. 23. 58: the fifth Dionysus is the 'son of Nisus and Thyone and is believed to have established the Trieterides festival.' Bryce-Campbell are sure Arnobius had Cicero before him. Tullius (56) shows that the passage is not found in Clement. Cf. Diodorus Sic. 1. 15, 3. 59 f.

[150] An allusion to Semele, mother of Dionysus by Zeus.

[151] Cf. O. Höfer, *LM* 3. 3154 f.

[152] The word certainly is superfluous in: si sibi gereret [et] morem deus atque uxorias voluptates pateretur ex se carpi.

[153] The fabulous river at the boundary between the upper and lower worlds. Cf. O. Waser, *LM* 4. 1566-79.

[154] The three-headed dog with triple barking guarding the lower world (see Vergil, *Aen.* 6. 417-25; Ovid, *Met.* 4. 450 f.). Cf. O. Immisch, *LM* 2. 1119-35; S. Eitrem, *RE* 11 (1922) 271-84.

[155] Reading with Wiman: *index viae* in place of Marchesi's ⟨ex⟩*inde* for *inde*.

[156] Evius = Dionysus, Εὔιος. Cf. Cicero, *Pro Flacco* 25. 60; Lucretius 5. 742; etc. See also Jessen, "Euios" no. 1, *RE* 6 (1909) 992 f.

[157] For the parallel account by Clement, see *Protr.* 2. 34. 3-5. Arnobius continues: et ficorum ex arbore ramum validissimum praesecans dolat runcinat levigat et humani speciem fabricatur in penis, figit super aggerem tumuli et postica ex parte nudatus accedit subdit insidit. Lascivia deinde surientis adsumpta huc atque illuc clunes torquet et meditatur ab ligno pati quod iam dudum in veritate promiserat.

[158] Heraclitus fr. 127 Bywater, 15 Diels. This is also cited by Clement, *Protr.* 2. 34. 5.

[159] On the persecutions, see also 1. 26, 1. 65, 2. 5, 2. 77 f., 3. 36, 4. 36, 5. 29, and 6. 27.

[160] The disastrous effect of such mythological rot on the impressionable youth is also pointed out by Tatian 22; Minucius 23. 8.

[161] *Toga praetexta*, the garment worn by women and children and abandoned by boys upon assuming the *toga virilis*, had a colored border. Cf. Macrobius, *Sat.* 1. 6; F. W. Goethert, "toga" no. 2, *RE* 2. R., 6 (1937) 1651-60.

162 Arnobius is fond of compounding the felony by citing one example and then expanding it to a plural.

163 His sister-daughter Proserpina is meant.

164 Cf. Terence, *Eun.* 590 f.:

> At quem deum! qui templa caeli summa sonitu concutit
> Ego humuncio hoc non facerem? facerem ego illud vero itidem ac lubens.

Cf. also Augustine, *De civ. Dei* 2. 7.

165 The same four Latin words begin 5. 28.

166 See Book One, n. 132.

167 Here is a doubtful instance of *virtutes*, either 'virtues' or 'powers.' See Book One, n. 210.

168 *Caducus*, 'falling,' 'transitory,' 'destined to die' (cf. Vergil, *Aen.* 10. 622) is a favorite word with Arnobius.

169 Throughout the quotation, the pronoun 'you' is singular. In all ages city folk, arrogating to themselves the virtues of cultivation, have looked upon their country contemporaries as ignorant. Cf. the adjective 'urbane' (from Latin *urbanus*, 'citified') and 'boorish' (from Dutch-Afrikans Boer = 'farmer'). One would like also to derive 'astute' from ἄστυ ('city') and 'polite' from πόλις, but these derivations are false.

170 Cf. 4. 33; Pseudo-Clement of Rome, *Recogn.* 10. 163; Firmicus Maternus, *De err. prof. rel.* 17. 3.

171 Here the MS reads *viraginem* where one would expect *virginem*.

172 Here I adopt the suggestion of Wiman: *advocavere su⟨erant? an⟩ tum*, based on earlier suggestions of Reifferscheid and Castiglioni: ⟨*an*⟩ *tum*.

173 Wiman's earlier reading (*Textkritiska Studier till Arnobius* 47 f.): *interiore veritate coperta*, seems better than his later one (*Eranos* 45 [1947] 144 f.): *interver⟨tendae ver⟩ itati capta⟨s⟩ subdebant*, and much better than Marchesi's *inter veritate capta* which seems senseless.

174 The allusion is to the sacrifice of Iphigenia, daughter of Agamemnon, which was prepared to appease the gods so that they would send favorable winds for the expedition to Troy. The story of the sacrifice is presented in the *Iphigenia at Aulis*, an extant play of Euripides. In another extant play by the same, the *Iphigenia among the Taurians*, imitated by Goethe in his *Iphigenie auf Tauris*, the poet assumes that at the final moment at Aulis, Artemis substituted a stag for the body of Iphigenia which she then transported surreptitiously to one of her temples in the land of the Taurians, there to await the

THE CASE AGAINST THE PAGANS: BOOK FIVE 583

coming of Iphigenia's brother Orestes as told in the second play. Cf. Achilles Tatius, *Amor*. 6. 2; Ovid, *Met*. 12. 34; Hyginus, *Fab*. 98. This story of substitutionary human sacrifice has its Hebrew counterpart in the story of Abraham and Isaac as told in Genesis 22.

[175] Proserpina.

[176] Hic omissa: quid exsecti arietis proles, quid satisfactio his facta.

[177] *Quid novatio et revelatio pudendorum.*

[178] Here the word 'to' (*in*) has been transposed from where it appears in the MS (*singula in singulis*) to this point. Cf. Wiman, *Eranos* 45 (1947) 132 f.

[179] Cf. 5. 24 where he is the King of the Shades but is not named Summanus, as he is in 3. 44, where cf. n. 272. Note the new detail here about the four-horse chariot. Cf. also F. J. Dölger, IXΘYΣ 2 (1922) 302.

[180] Reading leg⟨e r⟩em allegorica[m] video, with Wiman, *Eranos* 45 (1947) 145. Cf. Thörnell, *Patr*. 14.

[181] The Trojan War, dated by the ancients in the year now called 1184 B.C., is doubtless chosen as a typical event known to every one. The trial of Socrates occurred in 399 B.C.—Arnobius alludes elsewhere (4.4) and by another name to the disastrous defeat of the Romans at Cannae in 216 B.C. The proscription of L. Cornelius Sulla (82 B.C.) was the earliest occasion on which was published a list of Romans who might be put to death with impunity.

[182] In one of his earliest addresses as pleader in criminal court, Cicero, *Pro Rosc. Amer*. 32. 89, sarcastically compares the legalized murders of Sulla's proscriptions with the slaughter of Romans at the disastrous battles of Cannae and Lake Trasimenus.

[183] Coxe (*ANF* 6. 542, elucid. 5) maintains that the bronze pine cone which now gives its name to the *Giardino della Pigna* in the Vatican was originally used in the ceremonials of the Magna Mater, but the best evidence goes to show that the cone was intended to be a fountain. See W. Helbig, with W. Amelung, E. Reisch, and F. Weege, *Führer durch die öffentlichen Sammlungen klassischer Altertümer in Rom*, 1 (3rd ed. Leipzig 1912) 71-3, no. 120; W. Amelung-H. Holtsinger, *The Museums and Ruins of Rome* 1 (New York 1906) 58.

[184] The MS says 'mother goddess.' Meursius, Orelli, and Reifferscheid, change 'goddess' to 'of the gods' (*deum*), as elsewhere in this Book. Cf. 5. 7, 5. 16.

[185] Arnobius here evidently confuses the family of the Nebridae on the island of Cos, which claimed to be descendants of Aesculapius,

with the *nebrizontes*, wearers of the fawnskin (*nebris*) in the Dionysiac cult. See Preller-Robert, *Griechische Mythologie* 1: *Theogonie und Götter* (Berlin 1894) 695 n. 1, 715; E. Wüst, *RE* 16 (1935) 2156.

[186] Cf. the opening words of 5. 34.

[187] Bryce-Campbell wrongly make this sentence declarative and assigns it to the adversary.

[188] Cf. Tertullian, *Apol.* 6. 2.

[189] See above, 5. 6 and n. 36.

[190] The best-known account of the Phaethon myth—of the privilege rashly asked of his father to drive the chariot of the sun for one day, and his tragic undoing—is by Ovid, *Met.* 1. 747-2. 332. The myth was dramatized by Aeschylus and Euripides. Cf. G. Türk, *RE* 19 (1938) 1508-15.

[191] Quid enim subiciemus pro illis fluctibus, quos super aggerem tumuli Semeleiae subolis urigo contorsit?

[192] Cf. 4. 26, 5. 22, 7. 33.

[193] Cf. 4. 26 and n. 197.

[194] The allusion is to the Leda story.

[195] An affair with Antiope, a Maenad, daughter of Nycteus. Cf. A. B. Cook, *Zeus* 1 (Cambridge 1914) 735-9, who points out that only Roman authors represent Zeus in this instance as appearing in the form of a satyr.

[196] Alluding to the Danae story.

[197] *Addidistis garo gerem*: an epigrammatic phrase, in which *garum* or *garon* designates a rich, pungent sauce prepared of certain tiny fish, especially Spanish mackerel (cf. Pliny, *Nat. hist.* 31. 93; Horace, *Serm.* 2. 8. 46), and *ger(r)es*, a cheap salted fish (cf. Pliny, *Nat. hist.* 32. 148). Hence, the addition of the latter could only deteriorate the former—an excellent thing is cheapened or spoiled by contamination with a worthless thing.

BOOK SIX

In Book Six Arnobius begins by defending the Christians from the specific charge of showing disrespect to the pagan gods in building to them no shrines, erecting no images or altars, and presenting no offerings of blood sacrifice, incense, salted meal, and libations of wine. The defense, which seems to Rapisarda (*Clemente* 12) suggestive of Justin Martyr and Minucius Felix, is that true gods would scorn such symbols of worship. The argument then launches into an attack upon two of these features of worship, the temples and images, while the polemic against the ceremonials is reserved until Book Seven.

Once again Book Six, like the three preceding, contains parallels with the *Protrepticus* of Clement of Alexandria. These are discussed in the notes and are listed by Röhricht (*De Clemente* 6 f.) as his parallels nos. 23-30. Tullius, however, again takes the negative view. His theory (1-24) is that the divergences between the two authors are too great to permit us to believe that Arnobius is following Clement. He once more carries his attempt to see divergences to such an extreme that he does not allow sufficiently for personal idiosyncrasy, for artistic style, for temperament, etc. Particularly weak is his pretense of seeing significance in differences of order. But he has pointed out, as indicated below, too many passages in which the parallels differ to make it sure that here Arnobius is following Clement.

In Book Six, he concludes, Arnobius used two sources, one a Christian apologist unknown to us who wrote in Latin on the general theme of *de templis et simulacris*, a source posterior in date to Sammonicus (middle of the third century), the latest author cited. Since Clement lived too early to have read such a book, he concludes that the unknown had rather read Clement and incorporated into his work the parallel passages noted, together with much additional material. This theory is certainly a tortuous one.

Even less easy is it to agree with his contention that in the introductory sentences in 6.9, 6.17, and 6.24, Arnobius is actually quoting a pagan work, rather than positing a pagan opponent quite imaginary.

On Tullius' views as a whole, see the Introd. pp. 39-41, and the introductory notes to Books Three, Four, and Five.

[1] Cf. Minucius 10.2: cur nullas aras habent (Christiani), templa nulla, nulla nota simulacra, numquam palam loqui, numquam libere congregari, nisi illud, quod colunt et interprimunt, aut puniendum est aut pudendum. Cf. also *ibid.* 32.1.

[2] Probably further proof of ignorance of the Old Testament.

[3] On incense, cf. 7.26.

[4] Micka (71 n. 30) cites Kahl (720 f.) for the belief that in passages brought forth to support statements of this kind, the source is Cornelius Labeo.

[5] Here *virtutum* appears to have its more usual meaning. Cf. Book One, n. 210.

⁶ Epicurean ἀταραξία.

⁷ Note that here Arnobius perhaps implies that the pagan gods exist in a form other than as gods, but see the Introd. pp. 30-33.

⁸ Gabarrou (*Oeuvre* 65) points out that in this passage and in 7. 1 and 7. 26-8 Arnobius appears to know nothing of Christian ritual; but cf. 4. 36 and notes *ad loc.*

⁹ Note carefully that here Arnobius is talking in terms of pagan shrines and temples, not of Christian structures. In the period before the end of the persecution, Christian meeting places were perforce unostentatious and unmarked by architectural elegance and could in no way be confused with pagan temples and shrines. Cf. the extremely informative study by F. J. Dölger, "Kirche als Name für den christlichen Kultbau. Sprach- und Kulturgeschichtliches zu den Bezeichnungen Κυριακόν, οἶκος, κυριακός, *dominicum, basilica,*" *Ant. u. Christ.* 6 (1941) 161-95.

¹⁰ The meaning is that it is made to believe in anthropomorphic deities.

¹¹ Cf. Minucius 32. 1: et cum homo latius maneam, intra unam aediculam vim tantae maiestatis includam?

¹² Clement (*Protr.* 3. 44. 1) speaks of Phoroneus, or Merops, or some other person who set up temples and altars to the daemons and are said in legend to have been the first to offer sacrifices. See Röhricht, *De Clemente* 29; also Kroll, *Rhein. Mus.* 72 (1917) 83, who expresses the view that Arnobius used Clement for these details but borrowed the citation to the *Admiranda* of Varro from another author. This is Röhricht's parallel no. 23. Cf. Lactantius, *Div. inst.* 2. 2.

¹³ Scholars usually equate this Merops with the Egyptian king mentioned by Ovid (*Met.* 1. 263, 1. 763, 2. 184; *Trist.* 2. 4. 30), but Tullius (4) maintains that *Aegyptius* cannot be taken with Merops, still less with Phoroneus, and he cites a *scholium* to Clement (1. 310. 11 Stählin) which says that Phoroneus was an Argive, Merops a Coan. He therefore concludes that a word has dropped out of the text and that we have Arnobius citing four, rather than three: (1) Phoroneus, (2) the unnamed Egyptian, (3) Merops, and (4) Aeacus. But some have thought the reference to Merops a corruption rather of Cecrops (cf. Rapisarda, *Clemente* 14).

¹⁴This was one of the *Logistoricon libri LXXVI*, and bore the title of *Gallus Fundanius de miris seu de mirandis.* This series of works consisted of discussions of philosophical (and chiefly ethical) questions with plentiful additions of historical material, partly derived

from mythology, resembling, possibly, the works of Heraclides Ponticus and certainly the *De senectute* and *De amicitia* of Cicero. Cf. Schanz-Hosius, *Geschichte der römischen Literatur* (4th ed., Munich 1927) 560 f.

[15] Aeacus was the mythical king of the island of Oenopia (= Aegina), son of Zeus and Aegina, daughter of the river-god Asopus. He is associated with Minos and Rhadamanthus in judging the shades of the departed. Cf. Hyginus, *Fab.* 52, 155.

[16] Cf. Lucretius 2. 27 f.; Horace, *Carm.* 2. 18. 1-8; Ovid, *Fasti* 1. 203 f., 1. 223 f.; Suetonius, *Aug.* 30; Lactantius, *Div. inst.* 5. 8. 4.

[17] Cyprian, *Quod idola dii non sint* 9, comments on the ridiculousness of shutting up the majesty of the gods in a temple.

[18] Reading with Wiman *pruinas* for *pluvias*, which seems repetitious after *imbres*.

[19] Cf. Seneca, *Ep.* 41. 1; Lucian, *Demonax* 27.

[20] As Rapisarda (*Clemente* 15) points out, Arnobius' rejoinder has been anticipated by Justin, *Dialog. c. Tryph.* 127.2, and Theophilus, *Ad Autol.* 2. 3.

[21] Not a perfect conception of astronomy.

[22] Reading with Axelson ⟨ae⟩que for ⟨quo⟩que.

[23] Cf. *Iliad* 1. 423-5.

[24] The 'blessed isles' of the ancients. Cf. C. T. Fischer, *RE* 7 (1912) 42 f.

[25] Cf. Vergil, *Georg.* 1. 30: tibi serviat ultima Thule; Tacitus, *Agr.* 10. Thule was the northernmost part of the inhabitable world as known to the Greeks and Romans, perhaps identical with Mainland, the largest of the Shetland Islands.

[26] Cf. 2. 12, n. 76.

[27] The great nation inhabiting the eastern part of the Sahara Desert. Cf. H. Dessau, "Garamantes," *RE* 7 (1912) 751 f.

[28] *Quadrini cardines.*

[29] The transition seems abrupt.

[30] The list of examples of graves within sanctuaries which appears in this chapter corresponds rather closely, down to and including that of Cinyras, with another which appears in Clement (*Protr.* 3. 44. 4–45. 4). The divergences between the two lists, which will be mentioned in subsequent notes, greatly impress Tullius and, coupled with the fact that Arnobius' list is longer (Apis, and Olus in 6. 7), make Tullius (8-18) feel that Arnobius and Clement are both following a common source, inferior in precision to Clement and copied blindly by Arnobius. What is certain, however, is that if Clement is the

source as far as he goes, there was another also, and at least as late as Sammonicus (third century) who is mentioned in 6. 7 as one of those who give the story of Olus.

[31] *Busta*, that is, places where bodies were burned.

[32] Antiochus of Syracuse, a Greek historian (fl. 420 B.C.). Cf. Clement of Alexandria, *Protr.* 3. 45. 1.

[33] Arnobius says *in Minervio*, i.e. the area sacred to Athena on the Acropolis. This is slightly different from Clement who merely says ἐν ἀκροπόλει. I cannot agree with Tullius (7) that such a divergence implies that Arnobius was following a source more detailed than Clement. It is to his purpose to show that the area was defiled by the tomb.

[34] That is, the acropolis at Argos. Cf. W. Geiger, "Larisa" no. 1, *RE* 12 (1925) 840.

[35] Acrisius of Argos was father of Danae and thus grandfather of Perseus. Cf. W. H. Roscher, "Akrisios" no. 1, *LM* 1. 213 f.; J. Toepffer, *RE* 1 (1894)1196 f.

[36] That is, Athena Polias. Cf. Pausanias 1. 27. 1-3, 2. 30. 6, 7. 5. 9, 8. 31. 9. Cf. O. Höfer, *LM* 3. 2608-14.

[37] Erichthonius, in earlier times identified with Erechtheus, was in the later version (Pindar, Euripides) made the son of Hephaestus and Atthis or Athena. Athena handed him over (in a box) to the daughters of Cecrops who were enjoined not to open the box. Two of them disobeyed and when they saw the child, in the form of a snake, went mad and either were killed by the snake or jumped from the Acropolis. Athena then cared for the child who, upon reaching maturity, drove out Amphictyon, took possession of the kingdom, and established the worship of Athena, building an Erechtheum. Cf. Lactantius, *Div. inst.* 1. 17. 11; *Epit.* 9. 2; Origen, *C. Cels.* 8. 61; R. Engelmann, *LM* 1. 1303-8; K. Escher, *RE* 6 (1909) 439-46.

[38] In Clement's version of the story (*Protr.* 3. 45. 1) this name appears in such a way that the normal interpretation would be that Daeira was the mother of Eumolpus' son Immardus, not his brother. Tullius (7) states his disbelief in the possibility that a man of Arnobius' competence could misunderstand Clement, though he cites C. Wachsmuth, " Bausteine zur Topographie von Athen," *Rhein. Mus.* 23 (1868) 58 f., for the opposite view.

[39] P reads *Inmarachus*; P² *Inmarnachus*; Sabaeus *Immarnachus*; Salmasius *Immarus*; the MSS of Clement Ἴμμαρος changed by Stählin to Ἰμμάραδος, doubtless on the strength of Pausanias 1. 5. 2, 1. 27. 4, 1. 38. 3, where see Frazer's useful note. Cf. also Apollodorus 3. 15. 4.

⁴⁰ That is, the celebrated Athenian shrine at the base of the Acropolis, a parallel institution to that in which the Eleusinian goddesses, Demeter (= Ceres) and Core (= Persephone = Proserpina) were venerated at Eleusis. Arnobius states that the Athenian *Eleusinium* was located 'below the city,' *civitati,* for which we should expect *arci subiectum,* 'below the citadel' (cf. Clement, *Protr.* 3.45.1). In Greek, however, we find the same—τὸ Ἐλευσίνιον τὸ ὑπὸ τῇ πόλει; cf. C. Wachsmuth, "Eleusinion," RE 5 (1905) 2333. The sanctuary is referred to by Thucydides 2.17; Andocides 1.110-32; Pausanias 1.14.3; etc.

⁴¹ Cf. Clement, *loc. cit.;* Homeric *Hymn to Demeter* 105 ff.; Pausanias 1.38.3 (where the number and names of the daughters differ from the account in the Homeric hymn); see O. Kern, "Keleos" no. 1, RE 11 (1921) 138-42.

⁴² Cf. Clement, *loc. cit.*

⁴³ Clement (*Protr.* 3.45.2) says the same thing in different words: "Why recount to you the Hyperborean women? They are called Hyperoche and Laodice, and they lie in the Artemisium at Delos; this is in the temple precincts of Delian Apollo" (Butterworth). I cannot agree with Tullius (8) who sees much more precise information in Clement's account. This is paring things too closely: he does not allow for the variations of a different writer. On the shrine, see V. von Schoeffer, "Delos" no. 1, RE 4 (1901) 2459-502..

⁴⁴ A fabled people living far to the north, wondrously righteous and happy. Regarding these and also Hyperoche and Laodice, cf. especially Herodotus 4.32-35.

⁴⁵ Cf. Clement (*loc. cit.*); Diogenes Laertius 1.28; E. Bux, "Leandros" no. 2, RE 12 (1925) 1047. For the fragments, see *Fragm. hist. gr.* 2.334-8.

⁴⁶ On the temple of Zeus and Apollo at Didyma near Miletus, cf. L. Bürchner, "Didyma" no. 2, RE 5 (1905) 437-41.

⁴⁷ The MSS of Clement (*loc. cit.*) Κλέαρχον but Stählin changes to Κλέοχον on the strength of Apollodorus 3.1.2 and of Arnobius.

⁴⁸ Zeno of the Carian town of Myndus, mentioned also by Clement (*Protr.* 3.45.3), is named by Diogenes Laertius (7.35) as a grammarian. Cf. also Eusebius, *Praep. ev.* 2.6.

⁴⁹ On this priestess of Artemis, see Pausanias 1.26.4, who says the Magnesians worshipped the Leucophryenian Artemis; Schirmer, "Leukophrye," LM 2.2000.

⁵⁰ For Magnesia on the Maeander river, see W. Ruge, RE 14 (1930) 459-73.

[51] There were two towns called Telmessus, one in western Lycia, the other in Caria (see Pape-Benseler, *Wörterbuch d. griech. Eigennamen* [Braunschweig 1884] s.v. Here again Tullius (8) points out that Clement (*loc. cit.*) is more precise in stating that the altar is reported to be a monument to Telmessus, but I do not read Clement to mean that there was both an altar and a monument: the altar was the monument because the body was buried beneath it. Cf. Cicero, *De div.* 1. 41; E. Honigmann, *RE* 5 (1934) 409-15.

[52] Ptolemaeus of Megalopolis, who lived at the court of Ptolemy Philopator (d. 205 or 204 B.C.) and wrote his history; cf. the fragments in *Fragm. hist. rom.* 3, p. 66. He also is cited by Clement, *Protr.* 3. 45. 4, and, for other facts, by Athenaeus 6. 48. 246, 10. 27. 425. At this point Clement leaves off his list of graves within sanctuaries, and Tullius (8) with somewhat surer reasoning makes the point that Arnobius' list goes on and that this implies at least more sources than Clement.

[53] Cf. 4. 24 and n. 170; 5. 19 and n. 94.

[54] That is, between the reappearances or reincarnations of Apis, the sacred bull which was inhabited by the god Osiris. Cf. Augustine, *De civ. Dei* 18. 5; E. Meyer, "Apis" no. 1, *LM* 1. 419-21; R. Pietschmann, "Apis" no. 4, *RE* 1 (1894) 2807-9.

[55] W. Kroll (*Rhein. Mus.* 72 [1917] 84) interprets this as "die langen Götterlisten Varros," etc., but as Tullius (9) points out, Arnobius is not listing gods but sanctuaries in which human remains lie buried. Cf. also Lactantius, *Epit.* 67. 7: Tunc fiet terrae motus et scindentur montes et subsident valles in altitudinem profundam et congerentur in eam corpora mortuorum et vocabitur nomen eius Polyandrium. That is, a *polyandrium* is a sort of cemetery.

[56] The MS reads *in populi Capitolium*; Marchesi [*in*] *Capitolium*; Reifferscheid *in Capitolio*.

[57] *Regnatoris populi*, Rome itself.

[58] Dionysius of Halicarnassus, *Ant. rom.* 4. 59-61, relates the remarkable tale here adumbrated. The younger Tarquinius, surnamed Superbus, set about building temples to Jupiter, Juno, and Minerva, as had been vowed by his grandfather. In the course of excavations on the Tarpeian Hill, the head of a man recently slain was found in the digging. Tarquinius took this to be an extraordinary omen. When the native soothsayers were unable to interpret it, a group of leading citizens was sent to Etruria to place the omen before its ablest soothsayer. The Etruscan at once recognized the significance for the future of the country that could claim the prodigy as its own and tried to jockey the Romans into transferring the prodigy to his own

THE CASE AGAINST THE PAGANS: BOOK SIX 591

country. He indicated that he needed fuller information and proceeded to outline the Tarpeian Rock on the ground. He then pointed to various parts of the sketch, asking whether it was there that the head had been found. But the visitors, forewarned of such captious questions, refused to agree that it was any such spot pointed out—that is, in the mind of the soothsayer, a spot on Etruscan soil!—and always answered that it was on the Tarpeian Hill at Rome that the discovery was made. When the Etruscan finally realized that it was useless to endeavor to secure the omen for his own country, he interpreted it to mean that the place in which the head was found was destined by fate to become the head of all Italy. Dionysius adds that since that time the Tarpeian Hill was called the Capitoline (from *caput* = 'head') Hill. Livy, 1.55 (cf. also 5.54), gives fewer details and mentions only one temple, that of Jupiter. Servius, commenting on Vergil, *Aen.* 8.345, also gives the story and identifies the head with that of Olus. See also Pliny, *Nat. hist.* 28.2.15; Plutarch, *Camill.* 31. Cf. W. Drexler, "Olus," *LM* 3.835; G. Türk, "Olus" no. 1, *RE* 17 (1937) 2504.

[59] Q. Serenus Sammonicus was a scholar under Septimius Severus and is supposed to have owned a library of 62,000 volumes. Cf. Macrobius, *Sat.* 3.9. See G. Funaioli, *RE* 2.R., 1 (1920) 2129-31; Röhricht, *De Clemente* 17, 29, parallel no. 24.

[60] Cf. 3.31 and n. 172.

[61] The MS here reads *Valerianus*, whom LeNourry thinks is the Cornelius Valerianus mentioned by Pliny, *Nat. hist.* 3.12.108, 14.1.11, 10.2.5, but Ursinus changed to *Valerius Antias*, a reading not, however, accepted by Reifferscheid and Marchesi. Cf. H. Peter, *Hist. rom. fragm.* (Leipzig 1883) fr. 13* = *Hist. rom. rel.* 1 (Leipzig 1914) pp. 244 f., fr. 1e*.

[62] Fr. 12 in *Hist. rom. fr.* pp. 22-23 = *Hist. rom. rel.* 1, pp. 23-5. On Q. Fabius Pictor, see *ibid.* pp. lxix-c. Cf. also Pliny, *Nat. hist.* 28.15; Servius, Vergil, *Aen.* 8.345; Cassius Dio, Epit. of Zonaras 7.11, p. 38 Boissonade, and other passages cited by Peter.

[63] That is, the Olus mentioned. These references to the fate of Aulus or Olus evidently show that Arnobius identifies or confuses the owner of the unearthed head with the son of the Etruscan soothsayer, who as is indicated by Dionysius and Servius, had forewarned and instructed the Roman delegation concerning the captious questioning they would be subjected to by his father (see above, n. 58). Servius (*loc. cit.*) tells the sequel: When the soothsayer saw that the Romans could not be outwitted, he asked them whether someone had

put them on their guard. They readily admitted that such was the case, that a youth whom they had met had prewarned them. The soothsayer—he is called Olenus Calenus by Pliny (*loc. cit.*)—mounted his horse, followed the youth, who was his son Argus, and slew him where Rome later stood.

[64] That is, *Capitolium* from *caput* + *Olus* = Olus' head.

[65] Criticism of the pagan cult of statues and images was a favorite theme of the apologists: see Justin, *Apol.* 1. 9; Tatian 33 f.; the writer *Ad Diogn.* 2; Theophilus, *Ad Autol.* 2. 2; Minucius 23. 9-13; Firmicus Maternus 28. 2-6; also Tertullian, *Apol.* 12; the *Martyrium Apollonii* 14, etc.

[66] Tullius (23 f.) maintains that this sentence and the opening sentences of 6. 17 and 6. 24 reflect a definite *written* source which Arnobius is following and refuting. I dissent.

[67] The allusion is to the devotion to the gods of but certain parts of the sacrificed victim and the customary use by human beings of the remainder. See Book Two, n. 450.

[68] Cf. A. Otto, *Die Sprichwörter und sprichwörtlichen Redensarten der Römer* (Leipzig 1890) 128; for the second saying, 41.

[69] For representations of the Sun (Helios) as a human being, see S. Reinach, *Répertoire de la statuaire grecque et romaine* (Paris 1897-1924) 1. 169, 2. 110 f., 3. 30, 3. 147, 4. 61, 5. 42.

[70] Cf. Lucretius 5. 731-50; Reinach 2. 319, 3.255, 4. 192.

[71] Evidently a subtle allusion to the proverbial fickleness of feminine moods and fashions.

[72] *Intestinis et domesticis flatibus.*

[73] Reinach has no representation of Frugiferius but see the list of lions in 5. 593 f. (index). Cf. G. Wissowa, "Frugifer," *RE* 7 (1912) 121 f. Cf. also Minucius 28. 7: de capro etiam et homine mixtos deos et leonum et canum vultibus deos dedicatis. Cumont, p. 28, pl. 1, shows a figure of a lion-headed man, found in the Mithraeum at Ostia, but this is a Mithraic representation of the god Kronos or time regarded as an all-consuming deity.

[74] The translation here is based on Wiman's emendation (*Eranos* 45 [1947] 145 f.): *atque ut olim felicones linguam ore de patulo pue⟨rili fa⟩tuitate*, which seems certain. Marchesi's reading (*patulo † puetitate*), besides being senseless, fails to account for the space in the MS between *pue* and *tuitate*. Marchesi and most other editors also have *fessi canes* for *felicones* ('urchins') which seems hardly appropriate in view of the phrase *puerile fatuitate*, but it may be right.

⁷⁵ In the corresponding passage (*Protr.* 4. 46) Clement mentions in order: the Scythians' sabre, the Arabs' stone, the Persians' river; earlier peoples who worshipped wooden poles (*xoana*); the statue of Artemis in Icarus; the Cithaeronian Hera in Thespiae; the Samian Hera, which, as Aethlius states, was first a beam but afterwards under Procles was made into human form. Then follows the comment that when these began to be shaped in human likeness, they received the name of βρέτη from βροτοί (mortals). Then he mentions that Varro the prose-writer (= M. Terentius Varro) said that the object representing Ares was a spear at a time when the artist's skill had not yet brought corruption. Tullius (11 f.) maintains with considerable probability that the divergences between Clement and Arnobius in this instance are significant of a different source (see following notes), but consider Röhricht (*De Clemente* 29 f., parallel no. 25).

⁷⁶ Clement makes this singular, a difference found elsewhere in the following.

⁷⁷ *Memorialia scripta*, probably the writings mentioned in 5. 5, 7. 49. For the term *memoriales* (*libri*), cf. A. Gellius, *praef.* 8; see also Tertullian, *passim*. The jurist Masurius Sabinus wrote a work entitled *Memorialia*.

⁷⁸ Compare the Kaaba at Mecca. Cf. H. Lammens, *Le culte des Bétyles et les processions religieuses chez les Arabes Préislamites* (Cairo 1919). See also Maximus of Tyre 38.8; Suidas *s.v.* θεὸς Ἄρης.

⁷⁹ Cf. Herodotus 4. 62; Ammianus Marcellinus 31. 2. 23.

⁸⁰ Clement says that they worshipped the Cithaeronian Hera, not a branch. Röhricht (*De Clemente* 30) thinks this detail goes back to Labeo. Cf. Tullius 11 f. Regarding Cinxia, cf. 3. 25 and n. 123, also 3. 30.

⁸¹ So Clement. Icaros or Icaria is an island or peninsula west of Samos.

⁸² The black stone. Cf. 2. 73, 5. 5, 7. 49, and Book Two, n. 460. This item is not in Clement.

⁸³ Evidently an allusion to the identification of Mars with Quirinus (*quiris* = 'spear'): cf. 1. 41.

⁸⁴ The phrase *Varronis Musae* probably means no more than 'Varro the poet.' Cf. *Musa Lucretia* in 3. 10 which has a similar meaning.

⁸⁵ Aethlius of Samos, fr. 1, *Fragm. hist. gr.* 4. 287. So also Clement. Athenaeus cites the same writer for other statements (14. 63, 14. 68).

⁸⁶ On this statue of wood, see K. Mras, "Die in den neuen ΔΙΗΓΗ-ΣΕΙΣ zu Kallimachos' Aitia erwähnten Kultbilder der samischen Hera," *Rhein, Mus.* 87 (1938) 277-84.

[87] F. J. Dölger, *Ant. u. Christ.* 5 (1936) 126 f., maintains that the reference to the worship of small images here (and in 6.13 and 6.18) stems from Tertullian's spirit (cf. *De orat.* 16).

[88] Aposiopesis.

[89] Cf. 3.13.

[90] On the persecutions, see 1.26, 1.65, 2.5, 2.77 f., 3.36, 4.36, 5.29, 6.27.

[91] In the following Röhricht (*De Clemente* 30: parallel no. 26) sees a parallel with Clement, *Protr.* 460 f.

[92] The god Ammon of the Egyptian city of Thebes. The Greeks identified him with Zeus, the Romans with Jupiter (= Iuppiter Hammon). He was represented as a ram or as a man with a ram's head, hence called *corniger, tortis cornibus* Hammon; cf. Cicero, *De nat. deor.* 1.29.82; Ovid, *Met.* 5.328; Lucan 9.514; etc. See Minucius 22.6; for illustrations, see Reinach 2.12, 3.7 (both with horns); 1.195, 1.608 (both without horns).

[93] Cf. G. Wissowa, *LM* 4.426-44; J. A. Hild, *DA* 4.1083-90, fig. 6124, showing the sickle clearly.

[94] Mercury = Hermes whose brimmed travelling hat was the *petasus*. Cf. Plautus, *Amphitr.* 143 ff; Reinach, 2.149-68, 170, 171, 174, 175; 4.41-53; 4.78-96; 5.64-76.

[95] Cf. Tertullian, *De spect.* 10. There is a long list of representations of Liber = Bacchus = Dionysus in Reinach's index, 5.565 f.

[96] For Aphrodite = Venus, see Reinach 2.340-4, 346-356, 359-65; etc.

[97] For Vulcan with cap and hammer, see Reinach 1.368; 2.39 f.; 3.13; 4.26; and 1.71 (with forge?). It is generally the right hand which holds the hammer.

[98] Apollo. See Reinach 2.92-5; 4.56; 5.35.

[99] For representations of Poseidon = Neptune with trident preserved, see Reinach 1.65, 1.428, 1.434, 1.435; 2.27-30; 3.228; and without trident preserved, 3.10; 4.19 f., 5.12 f.

[100] The sun-god Apollo was the tutelary deity of the door or entrance, of departure and return, and hence called προστήριος, θυραῖος (cf. Sophocles, *Electra* 673; Tertullian, *De idol.* 15). Regarding conical columns erected in his honor near doors and vestibules, cf. Preller-Robert, *Griechische Mythologie* 1: *Theogonie und Götter* (Berlin 1894) 276.

[101] For representations of Mars in armor see Reinach 1.346 f.; 2.179-92; 3.57-60; 4.102-15; 5.263-77.

[102] On Arnobius' list, cf. Clement, *Protr.* 4.53.4-6, which has the

The Case Against the Pagans: Book Six 595

following order: (a) Phidias and Pantarces; (b) Praxiteles and Cratina; (c) Phryne; and (d) the Hermae modelled on Alcibiades. So far as the order goes, the only difference is that the first and fourth examples have exchanged places.

[103] *Hermae* (herms) were busts attached to rectangular shafts. Cf. J. J. Bernoulli, *Griechische Ikonographie* 1 (Munich 1901) 205-8 (on Alcibiades); P. Paris, *DA* 3. 130-4; S. Eitrem, *RE* 8 (1913) 696-708; Reinach, 1. 176, 364; 2. 522; 3. 269; 4. 330-3; 5. 262.

[104] The brilliant but erratic Athenian statesman, ward of Pericles and in the army with Socrates, lived from about 450 to 404 B.C. Cf. Clement, *Protr.* 4. 53. 6; the biographies by Plutarch and Nepos; J. Toepffer, "Alkibiades" no. 2, *RE* 1 (1894) 1516-33.

[105] Cf. also 6. 22, n. 155.

[106] The MS reads *Posidippi* (gen.) which requires an accusative noun thereafter.

[107] One of the most celebrated artists of antiquity, an Athenian flourishing in the first half of the fourth century B.C. He was a finished master of marble sculpture, as can be gathered from the originals surviving: a Hermes which stood in Olympia (Pausanias 5. 17. 3) and is now preserved in the museum there, and a number of reliefs found in Mantinea on the Peloponnesus. Cf. O. Antonsson, *The Praxiteles Marble Group in Olympia* (Stockholm 1937).

[108] Only copies of the Cnidian Venus survive; see *LM* 1. 416. For the counterpart of the text in Clement, *Protr.* 4. 53. 5.

[109] On Phryne, cf. Pausanias 1. 20. 1, 9. 27. 3-5, 10. 15. 1; Cicero, *Verr.* 4. 2. 4. Arnobius is here much more detailed than is Clement, *Protr.* 4. 53. 6.

[110] Tullius (14) is, I think, clearly right in thinking this point derived from a source other than Clement who has no corresponding words, but Röhricht (*De Clemente* 30) thinks Arnobius is here "poetizing," in lieu of genuine sources.

[111] That is, images of Venus.

[112] Heralded by antiquity itself as its greatest sculptor, Phidias was an Athenian, born *ca.* 500 and died, probably in prison (cf. Plutarch, *Pericles* 31), in *ca.* 432. He was the master of bronze sculpture and numerous monumental works. Cf. H. Lechat, *Phidias et la sculpture grecque au Ve siècle* (Paris 1924); G. Lippold, "Pheidias" no. 2, *RE* 19 (1938) 1919-36.

[113] Again Arnobius is much more detailed than Clement, *Protr.* 4. 53. 4.

[114] The celebrated cult statue in the temple at Olympia, one of

antiquity's Seven Wonders (cf. Hyginus, *Fab*. 223), to have seen which was accounted by the Greeks as the sum total of happiness. Pausanias (5.11) gives a detailed description of it. The enthroned god, raised to a height of about forty feet and located in the center of the temple, was done in ivory and gold. It was still in place in the year 363 A.D., and seems to have been destroyed by fire, either in 426 when Theodosius II decreed the destruction of the temple, or in a conflagration in Constantinople in 476. Cf. Lippold, *art. cit.* 1920-4.

[115] Pantarces means 'all-powerful.' Pausanias (5.11.3) states that the youth, a victor in the Olympian games, was represented in a contest scene appearing on a panel of the richly decorated throne.

[116] Tullius (15) is right in objecting to Kroll's contention (*Rhein. Mus.* 72 [1917] 86) that Arnobius must have misunderstood Clement, if he is following him. There is no divergence at this point.

[117] That is, bones of elephants (ivory).

[118] The rest of this chapter shows considerable parallelism with Minucius 23.9-13, and with many other Christian writers cited by J. H. Waszink, *Tertulliani De an.* (Amsterdam 1947) 578.

[119] Here and in the following Arnobius very evidently speaks of jewelry and other precious articles contributed by the ordinary citizenry when a statue or some other image to a deity was to be commissioned and made. Frequently, too, such statues were vowed in time of war and then executed from the spoils taken from the enemy. Thus at Delphi there was an Apollo and a Victory offered by the Tegeans from the spoils of the Lacedaemonians (Pausanias 10.9.5). The celebrated colossal bronze statue of Athena Promachus at Athens was a work of Phidias and wrought out of the spoils taken from the Persians defeated at Marathon (Pausanias 1.28.2).

[120] The elephant.

[121] Minucius (23.13) asks: Quando igitur hic (deus) nascitur? Ecce funditur fabricatur sculpitur: nondum deus est; ecce plumbatur, construitur, erigitur: nec adhuc deus est; ecce ornatur, consecratur, oratur: tunc postremo deus est, cum homo illum voluit et dedicavit. Rapisarda (*Clemente* 28) cites also Theophilus, *Ad Autol.* 2.1 on this passage of Arnobius.

[122] *Insensilia*, perhaps a Lucretian echo. Cf. Lucretius 2.865, 887.

[123] *Foris*, lit., outside the human representation.

[124] The singular is used: *rationale animal.*

[125] Marchesi makes this a question.

[126] Dr. Plumpe remarks that the soles of the feet were obviously not

The Case against the Pagans: Book Six   597

rendered in realistic fashion but were made flat so as to hold the statue more firmly to the plinth or a similar base.

[127] *Spirantia signa*, which recalls Vergil's celebrated line, *Aen.* 6. 847: Excudent alii *spirantia* mollius aera.

[128] Correspondence between this passage and Minucius 24. 1 has been rightly seen by Orelli, R. Heinze, "Tertullians Apologeticum," *Ber. d. Kgl. Sächs. Gesellsch. d. Wiss., philol.-hist. Kl.* 62 (1910), 355, and Kroll (86), but is denied by Tullius (17). The words of Minucius are as follows: Quanto verius de diis vestris animalia muta naturaliter iudicant! Mures hirundines milvi non sentire eos sciunt: rodunt inculcant insident, ac, nisi abigatis, in ipso dei vestri ore nidificant; araneae vero faciem eius intexunt et de ipso capite sua fila suspendunt. Vos tergetis mundatis eraditis et illos quos facitis, protegitis et timetis . . . . Cf. also Tertullian, *Apol.* 12. 7.

[129] Cf. Vergil, *Georg.* 4. 242 f. The cock in Lucian, *Somnium* (*galli*) 24, remarks in relating his dream (trans. by H. W. and F. G. Fowler): "I was like those colossal statues, the work of Phidias, Myron, or Praxiteles; they too look extremely well from outside; 'tis Posidon with his trident, Zeus with his thunderbolt, all ivory and gold; but take a peep inside, and what have we? One tangle of bars, bolts, nails, planks, wedges, with pitch and mortar and everything that is unsightly; not to mention a possible colony of rats or mice. There you have royalty!"

[130] There is some resemblance between this passage and one in Clement (*Protr.* 4. 52. 4) who mentions swallows and other birds as unconcernedly defiling statues. Arnobius' point is that they are powerless to resist or object. In addition, he does not cite the specific examples found in Clement: the Olympian Zeus, the Epidaurian Asclepius, the Athena Polias, or the Egyptian Sarapis, and he is much more rhetorical throughout the passage. The differences between the two writers are, as usual, emphasized by Tullius (16), but see Röhricht, *De Clemente* 14. For the motif in other authors, see Geffcken xxi.

[131] Tullius (15) who wishes to add here 'the statues . . . already,' ⟨*statuas*⟩ stercoris ⟨*iam*⟩ plenas, but this is unnecessary. Wiman and Brakman read ⟨*pilas*⟩ iacularier stercoris plenas.

[132] Bryce-Campbell translate as if they took the second sentence of the quotation to be part of Arnobius' rejoinder.

[133] At this point there appears in the MS a sentence which Reifferscheid brackets. What is involved, however, is a transposition caused by the repetition of the word *anteponant*. The words "But . . .

stars" appear in P in the next chapter immediately after "bases." The correction should be credited to Thörnell and Wiman. On this chapter, cf. Tertullian, *De an.* 32. 6 and Waszink's note, p. 390.

[134] As actually the statues were held by hooks and poured-lead clamps.

[135] The words of the supplement to the lacuna are really the MS reading of part of the last sentence of the preceding chapter. See Wiman, *Eranos* 45 (1947) 148.

[136] *Maximitas*, an archaism, according to Freppel (88).

[137] The reader, aware of the Christian doctrine of the all-pervading presence of God, mentioned by Arnobius in 6. 4, may hastily think our author not quite fair to his pagan opponents in making such a point, but the pagans themselves possessed no such conception of their divinities. These were strictly limited to one locality: they dwelt on Mt. Olympus, on Mt. Ida, on the Capitol, etc., and when they went elsewhere, they were absent from home. See the extremely illuminating example of this fact mentioned below in n. 164 and Arnobius' own words in 6. 4 above.

[138] That is, uncompounded.

[139] See also the argument by Theophilus, *Ad Autol.* 2. 3.

[140] The meaning of this difficult sentence very probably is that even if it is possible for a single divinity to reside in all the images at different times, it becomes absurd to believe that he is everywhere at any one time.

[141] Cf. Cyprian, *Ad Demetr.* 14; Lactantius, *Div. inst.* 2. 4; Tertullian, *Apol.* 29. 3.

[142] The *aeditui* were the custodians or caretakers of the sacred edifices. Cf. P. Habel, "Aedituus," *RE* 1 (1894) 465 f.

[143] Cicero states in one of his earliest speeches (*Rosc. Amer.* 20. 56) that "the state lets contracts for the feeding of geese and also has dogs kept on the Capitol that they may give warning of approaching thieves." Livy (5. 47) tells the celebrated story of the geese saving the Capitol from capture by the Gauls, while the watchmen and dogs had failed to observe the imminent peril. In Plutarch's account of the incident (*De fortuna Rom.* 12) it is stated that even in his time the Romans commemorated the watchfulness of the geese and the sleepiness of the dogs by carrying in solemn procession a goose perched high on a magnificent couch and parading a crucified dog. St. Augustine (*De civ. Dei* 2. 22) also mentions the incident, sarcastically remarking on a third party of sleepers—the immortal gods! Cf. also Lucretius 4. 680-3; Vegetius, *De re mil.* 4. 26; Plutarch, *Cam.* 27; etc. See also Wissowa 190 n. 10.

144 *Momine* (Ursinus, Marchesi), *nomine* (P and many editors) but Weyman: *conamine*.

145 Here Arnobius gives three examples of *sacrilegium*, ἱεροσυλία (temple-robbing, on which subject see K. Pfaff, "Sacrilegium," *RE* 2 R., 1 (1920) 1678-81; T. Thalheim, "Ἱεροσυλίας γραφή," *RE* 8 [1913] 1589 f.). Röhricht (*De Clemente* 30 f., parallel no. 28) maintains that he took the story of Antiochus of Cyzicus from Clement (*Protr.* 4. 52. 3) and the two stories about Dionysius from Cicero (*De nat. deor.* 3. 34. 83). Kroll (87) and W. Michaelis, *De origine indicis deorum cognominum* (diss. Berlin 1898) 15, think only the second story can have been taken from Cicero. Tullius (18-20) goes still further in maintaining emphatically that none of the three examples can have come from either Clement or Cicero, since he sees significant divergences. Lactantius, *Div. inst.* 2. 4. 16-20, gives the same story in much the same terms.

146 Antiochus IX Philopator, king of Syria (116-95), one of the Seleucid dynasty. Cf. O. Rossbach, "Antiochos" no. 32, *RE* 1 (1894) 2483 f.

147 Clement has fifteen and Tullius makes much of this divergence.

148 Cf. Cicero, *De nat. deor.* 3. 33. 83, who states that a cloak placed on a statue of Jupiter by the tyrant Gelon was stolen, and specifies the time and attendant circumstances, details which Arnobius omits. Cf. Lactantius, *loc. cit.*; Aelian, *Var. hist.* 1. 20.

149 Cf. Cicero, *De nat. deor.* 3. 33. 83 f., who mentions also the theft of silver tables, statues of Victory, and the sale of the stolen objects by auction, none of which corresponds to anything in Arnobius. Cf. Valerius Maximus 1. 1. 3; Minucius 22. 5. See also Edelstein-Edelstein, *Testim.* 683c, vol. 2, p. 220.

150 Long and thick like the proverbial philosopher's. Cf. Tatian 25; Juvenal, *Sat.* 14. 12 (*barbatos magistros*); Prudentius, *Apoth.* 200 (*barbati Platonis*); A. Gellius 9. 2. 4: 'Video,' inquit Herodes (Atticus), 'barbam et pallium, philosophum nondum video.'

151 Marchesi makes this sentence a question.

152 Philostephanus, with Apollonius of Rhodes, Aristophanes of Byzantium, and Eratosthenes, a pupil of Callimachus in the fourth century B.C. For the fragments of his work on Cyprus and other geographical works, cf. *Fragm, hist. graec.* 3. 28. 34. The Pygmalion story, lacking the detail that he was king, is also given by Clement, *Protr.* 4. 57. 3. Cf. also Ovid, *Met.* 10. 243 ff., for whom Pygmalion is an artist who becomes enamored of his own masterpiece. Cf. M. Türk, "Pygmalion," *LM* 3. 3317-9; also Röhricht, *De Clemente* 32, parallel no. 29.

[153] Textus est: sublevato in lectulum numine copularier amplexibus atque ore resque alias agere libidinis vacuae imaginatione frustrabiles.

[154] Posidippus, fr. 1, *Fragm. hist. gr.* 4. 482. Cf Arnobius 6. 13; also Clement, *loc. cit.* Both Röhricht and Kroll think that Clement is Arnobius' source but this is, as usual, denied by Tullius (22) on the grounds of divergences. Here the discrepancies seem rather insignificant.

[155] Omisi: genialibus usum toris et voluptatum consequentium finibus.

[156] Though but a single goddess has been mentioned, the plural may be either the result of thinking of two statues of her (cf. above 'the one Venus and the other') or it may be Arnobius' usual habit of intensifying the charge by expanding a single instance into more.

[157] In the corresponding passage (*Protr.* 4. 53. 2 f.) Clement lists the location of fires as follows: Argos, Ephesus, Rome (many fires), Alexandria, Athens, and Delphi. Here also Röhricht (*De Clemente* 32 f., parallel no. 30) and Kroll think Clement Arnobius' source, but Tullius (24) disagrees with them entirely.

[158] Fires took place in the Capitoline temple in Rome in 83 B. C., 69 A. D., and again in 80 A. D., and lightning frequently did much damage—see Platner-Ashby 229 f. for the evidence. Clement merely refers to the frequency of the fires.

[159] That is, the cult statue. A curious problem, evidently overlooked by Arnobius, is posited by Lucretius (6. 417-20): why it is that Jupiter strikes and destroys his own temples and statues. Earlier, Aristophanes states the same problem: *Nubes* 398-402. It was a source of argument which Lactantius did not leave unexploited: *Div. inst.* 3. 17. 12 f.

[160] Juno and Minerva, the other members of the Capitoline triad.

[161] Ruins of the Argive Heraeum, one of the earliest excavations of the American School in Athens, are still to be seen on the eastern slope of the hills surrounding the Argive plain, some distance from the city. (The distance from Argos forms a principal feature of the well-known story of Cleobis and Biton, as told by Herodotus 1. 31.) Thucydides (4. 133) says the fire was caused by Chrysis' carelessness, though she escaped. Cf. Pausanias 2. 16. 2—17. 1.

[162] All Clement says is that the temple of Sarapis in Alexandria was burnt.

[163] Clement calls him Dionysus Eleuthereus and Butterworth's note appears to imply that the temple meant is one at Eleutherae, a town in Attica from which the worship of Dionysus was brought to

The Case against the Pagans: Book Six 601

Athens (cf. Pausanias 1.2.5, 1.38.8): but there were two temples of Dionysus at Athens (cf. Pausanias 1.20.3 and Frazer's note) and since both Clement and Arnobius expressly state that the temple was at Athens, it must be one of these that is meant, as Frazer recognizes.

[164] Arnobius does not date the fire, but Clement says it was after the time of the Amazons, a fact which implies that he was not thinking of the fire in 356 B.C. which was set by Herostratus and is said to have occurred while Artemis was absent to attend Olympias at the birth of Alexander the Great. Cf. Cicero, *De nat. deor.* 2.27.69.

[165] An example omitted by Clement. On the *robbing* of this temple, see Dio Cassius, Bk. 30, fr. 101.2 Boissonade = vol. 2, pp. 469-71 Cary.

[166] Clement (*Protr.* 4.53.3) refers to the temple at Delphi, but does not make it a victim of brigandage, but says that it was once levelled by a storm, and again utterly by fire. Arnobius may here have in mind, as Oehler states, one of the several temples of Apollo plundered and gutted by fire during Rome's war with the pirates (67 B.C.) in which Varro of Reate, here Arnobius' authority, served under Pompey. Temples of Apollo attacked and sacked by the pirates were those at Claros, Didyma, Actium, and Leucas. Cf. Plutarch, *Pomp.* 24.

[167] Fr. xii (3) of A. Riese's edition (Leipzig 1865), p. 240, of the Menippean satires of M. Terentius Varro. Cf. 6.11.

[168] *Scripulum*, less common form of *scrupulum*, was originally a very small stone but came to mean 1/24 of an *uncia* (= slightly more than a gram or grain), which is the meaning here.

[169] That is, the swallows who commonly built their nests under the eaves of temples and shrines (see above, 6.16), found this temple razed to the ground.

[170] The observant reader is astonished to note that Arnobius passes over completely the example of one of the most notorious temple-robbers in history—an example recorded in Latin over many pages and one occurring much more recently than the examples given— the case of C. Verres as reported in Cicero's Fourth Verrine Oration (*De signis*). This *cause célèbre* was not ignored by Lactantius: *Div. inst.* 2.4.27-37.

[171] A very obscure passage which Reifferscheid and Marchesi both mark desperate: † *remedorum obscuritate* †. Wiman suggests changing to *remediorum*. See the discussion by Dr. Plumpe, *Vigiliae Christianae* 3.4 (1949).

[172] The MS and both editors read *Canacheni* which appears to be meaningless. Heraldus suggested *Saraceni*, Zink *Commageni*, and

Vahlen, with some hesitation, *cacomechani*. P. Cassel, however, in an article which seems to have escaped the notice of Arnobian critics, "Die älteste historische Erwähnung der Zigeuner," *Jahrh. f. Gesellschafts- und Staatswiss.* 8 (1867) 317-22, argued convincingly that the form should be *Caracheni* and that gypsies are meant. Cf. McCracken, *Vigiliae Christianae* 3 (1949) 45. Wiman has recently (*Eranos* 45 [1947] 148 f.) put forth the suggestion of c⟨h⟩arac[h]eni and thinks Persian sorcerers are involved.

[173] Cf. Cicero, *De leg.* 2.11.26; *De nat. deor.* 1.42.118; Polybius 6.54.6-15.

[174] Pascal would bracket 'or guiltless,' but the point is that where no one has been guilty, there can be no conception of guiltlessness.

[175] For coins showing Saturn with the sickle, cf. E. Babelon, *Description historique et chronologique des monnaies de la République romaine* (Paris 1885-86) 1, nos. 288, 399; 2, nos. 188, 214, 216, 254.

[176] Cf. Ovid, *Fasti* 1.99; Macrobius, *Sat.* 1.9.7, states that Janus "is represented with a key and staff as the guard of all doors and guide of all roads."

[177] That is, with the *ricinium*, a small woolen cloth worn in two folds over the head. Cf. Varro, *De ling. lat.* 5.132.

[178] The MS reads *caestus*, which was a leather strap studded with pieces of lead or iron and wrapped by boxers around their hands and arms—the counterpart of the modern brass knuckles. The *cestus* was an ornate belt or girdle, associated as a love-arousing article especially with Venus. Walde-Hofmann, *Lat. etym. Wörterb.* 1 (3rd ed. Heidelberg 1938) s.v. 'caestus,' state that the two words must not be confused. Arnobius, intending sarcasm, may have confused them intentionally. At any rate, Homer, *Il.* 14.181, describes the goddess as putting on a girdle adorned with a hundred tassels.

[179] Undoubtedly an allusion to Athena and not to some statue of Juno with a maiden associated in some way not clear.

[180] Cf. Reinach 2.269, fig. 3; 2.270, fig. 1. J. Quasten, *Musik und Gesang in den Kulten der heidn. Antike u. christl. Frühzeit* (Münster 1930) 54–58 and Tafel 18; 21, 1.

[181] An ancient stringed instrument resembling the zither, mentioned numerous times in the Old Testament: 1 Par. 13.8; 16.5; Ps. 32.2; 56.9; Dan. 3.5, etc. The Muses Terpsichore and Erato were represented with string instruments.

[182] The MS reads *pinnatus angyforonites* which is commonly emended to *argiphontes*, a reference to Hermes as the slayer of a monster, Argus. This is certainly right but Marchesi's text, following Wiman, reads *anguifero nitens* and refers it to Aesculapius, to

which we may object that the same idea is implied in what immediately follows, *baculum*, mentioned as an attribute for Aesculapius (cf. n. 183).

[183] Aesculapius was usually represented with a staff encircled by a snake. Cf. Edelstein-Edelstein, *Testim.* 689a.

[184] Vulcan.

[185] For representations of Anubis, see Reinach 1. 607, 2. 423, 3. 260, 4. 256, 5. 226 f. Anubis was an Egyptian god with the head of a jackal, erroneously thought by the Greeks and Romans to be that of a dog. With Thoth he conducted the dead to their judgment. Hence he was often equated with Hermes (Mercury) whose task it was also to conduct the departed souls into the underworld. Cf. F. Robiou, *DA* 1. 392 f.; R. Pietschmann, *RE* 1 (1894) 2645-9. See Vergil, *Aen.* 8. 698 (quoted by St. Augustine, *Conf.* 8. 2. 3); Firmicus Maternus, *De err. prof. rel.* 2. 2; Athanasius, *C. gent.* 22.—For Priapus, described in the following as *genitalibus propriis inferior*, god of shepherds and sailors, cf. Reinach 2. 73-5, 3. 21, 4. 40, 5. 26 f.

[186] Gabarrou (*Latin* 72-4) lists this word *caliandria* as the equivalent of the Greek καλλύντριον: a lady's cap resembling a *fontange*.

[187] It will be noted that this chapter forms a sort of introduction to Book Seven and, indeed, in the American reprint of Bryce-Campbell (*ANF* 6. 518), it is actually printed there. But the allusion to the persecution, a characteristic of the conclusions of Books One, Two, and Four, leads me to retain it here.

[188] Cf. 1. 26, 1. 65, 2. 5, 2. 77 f., 3. 26, 4. 36, and 5. 29.

BOOK SEVEN

Book Seven continues the argument begun in Book Six where the attack on the pagans centered in their temples and images. Here the polemic is directed against the ceremonials. Various possible motives for the rituals are discussed in turn and each rejected. They are not intended to nourish the gods nor please them nor appease their wrath, still less to win favors from them, nor even to do the gods honor. As usual, the apologist employs with telling effect the *reductio ad absurdum* which reaches its high peak in the remarkable address to Jupiter by an ox about to be slaughtered. This animal complains of the injustice in washing away human sin through the blood of an innocent animal.

Following the attack against animal sacrifices, the apologist discusses various other types of offerings including a series of eccentric foods, and the more customary offerings of incense and wine, and finally discusses the ridiculousness of religious games. This gives him an opportunity to recount the classic story of the pestilence brought upon Rome through the pollution of the games by the punishment of a slave in the circus. The thought of the pestilence leads naturally to Aesculapius, the god of healing, and his introduction into Rome, from which it is another easy step to the similar discussion of the importation of Magna Mater from Phrygia in the time of the Second Punic War. With a critique of her cult the book ends rather abruptly. Indeed, Orelli has attempted to mend the conclusion by placing at the end chapters 35-37 which seemed to him to offer a more satisfactory finale.

It should be noted also that this Book shows more evidence of incompleteness than any other. In chapter 44 there is a repetitious passage which doubtless was a variant version preserved by the author with his notes and included, probably through error, when he or some literary executor, otherwise completely unknown, came to put the pages together.

Gabarrou (*Oeuvre* 45) is sure that this Book owes much to Cornelius Labeo, but, as we have seen, the dependence of Arnobius upon this shadowy figure is very doubtful. See Introd. pp. 38-40, and the introductory notes to Books Three-Five. The last chapters of Book Six constitutes the prefatory paragraph for Book Seven; see n. 187 to Book Six.

[1] M. Terentius Varro, as the next chapter shows.
[2] *Dominus rerum . . . atque omnipotens ipse.*
[3] Cf. Tertullian, *Ad Scap.* 2: Non enim eget deus, conditor universitatis, odoris aut sanguinis alicuius. Tatian (4. 5) says that we must not importune God with gifts; He who needs nothing would only be put in an unfavorable light by such giving.
[4] Here there is a pleonastic *quod* (and no need to mark a *lacuna*, as does Reifferscheid): cf. E. Löfstedt, *Philologischer Kommentar zur Peregrinatio Aetheriae* (Uppsala 1911) 303.
[5] I take this to balance the reference to incense, which is an inanimate object not used for food by human beings, but Bryce-Campbell translate "or the life only of the victim is offered to the gods" on the basis of the statement of Macrobius, *Sat.* 3. 5. 1, in which Trebatius is made to distinguish between victims slaughtered for purposes of divination and others simply slaughtered as sacrifice. Cf. also Servius, *Aen.* 3. 231.

THE CASE AGAINST THE PAGANS: BOOK SEVEN 605

[6] Here the Greek word used (*cnisae*) is employed in a form not generally found in Greek authors, i.e. in the plural, but cf. Porphyry, *De abstin.* 2.42. The κνῖσα (epic κνίση) was the steam and odor of fat rising from roasting meat (cf. Homer, Il. 1.317) or the pieces of fat in which the sacrificial victim was wrapped (Il. 1.460). See also Gabarrou (*Latin* 72-4) where the word is listed as a borrowing from Greek. The writers of comedies often compounded the term with other words to designate parasites who frequented kitchens and pantries: Knisodioktes, Knisokolax, Knisoteretes, etc. For 'previous victims' in the following, cf. Dr. Plumpe, *Vigiliae Christianae* 3.4 (1949).

[7] That the gods feed upon sacrifices.

[8] *Animique ut dicitur causa*: there is no good English equivalent for this connotation of *animus*; compare the German *Stimmung*.

[9] The Epicurean view.

[10] How disagreeable to the senses the odor of burning flesh of many sacrificed animals must have been throughout a wide area surrounding the temples is hardly within the comprehension of ordinary modern experience. A slaughterhouse can hardly reproduce the sensation: only those who have participated in modern combat can have any complete conception of this. For a description of the butchery at an animal sacrifice, cf. Lucian, *De sacrif.* 12 f.

[11] Note the vegetarianism.

[12] That is, the fact that man and the brutes are both animals.

[13] An imitation of a phrase of Lucretius (6.1223).

[14] Rapisarda (*Arnob.* 177) cites on this phrase the Epicurean χειμών, lit. 'winter,' 'stormy weather' = mental agitation.

[15] Cf. 1.18.

[16] On this sentence Rapisarda (*Arnob.* 173) calls attention to Lucretius 2.646-51, but does not think it the only source.

[17] Greek theology lacked any counterpart to the divine law given to Moses.

[18] Arnobius is not quite fair to his pagan opponents at this point for there are countless examples in pagan literature to show that in the view of the pagans themselves the gods did appear in early times to men. Moreover, the argument is a two-edged sword: cf. John 1.18: *Deum nemo vidit umquam*.

[19] *Panes* = pieces of bread, a common device for pacifying childish tantrums, rather than statuettes of Pan, as Bryce-Campbell appear to think ('puppets').

[20] *Multiformium morum varietatibus lubricum*.

[21] The word *praesul* (cf. also 4.37) means a head dancer in re-

ligious rites. This is an allusion, in anticipation, to a story told in 7. 39 ff. where *praesul* has an ironic meaning (see below, n. 130), from which fact may be deduced the conclusion that Arnobius had already composed his version of the classic account, or at least decided to use it, before he wrote the present chapter.

[22] An allusion to the temple-robbing in 6. 21.

[23] The defilement of sacred ground, the clearing of sacred groves on the Alban Hills to make room for private buildings, was a crime with which Cicero charged Publius Clodius Pulcher: *Pro Milone* 31. 85.

[24] Micka (153 f.) compares this passage with one in Lactantius (*De ira Dei* 7. 2 f.), "clearly directed against Arnobius' idea of man as a miserable creature, differing but slightly, if at all, from animals" : Nec omnino quisquam, qui modo vel leviter sapiens videri vellet, rationale animal cum mutis et inrationalibus coaequavit, etc.; but the resemblance is not conclusive.

[25] Cf. Juvenal 15. 165 f.

[26] Cf. Ovid, *Met.* 1. 144. 9.

[27] The *annales* were chronicles in which events were recorded year by year.

[28] Here Colombo (109) maintains that the fatalist argument is adduced by Arnobius in this chapter merely for polemical reasons; but Micka (58 n. 67) rightly points out that 1. 47 contains the same idea; though there Arnobius plainly states that Christ's power broke that of inexorable fate.

[29] The learned men—determinist philosophers, such as the Stoics.

[30] Lucian, *Jupiter trag.* 25, 32 makes Zeus admit before the assembled gods that in the affairs of men "only the Fates are competent, and we cannot interfere." The early apologists vigorously denied the rule of an improvident fate: cf. Justin Martyr, *Apol.* 1. 43 f.; 2. 6; Tatian 8-11; Athenagoras, *Leg.* 25; Minucius 36.

[31] Again, the learned ones.

[32] K. Ziegler notes this in his edition of the *De err. prof. rel.* of Firmicus Maternus (2) as a possible parallel.

[33] One thinks, of course, of the widow and her mites (Mark 12. 41-4; Luke 21. 1-4) but the passage is no proof that Arnobius was also thinking of that Christian teaching.

[34] Many good people are in modern times disturbed by the apparent dilemma which prayers uttered by both sides in time of war seem to put upon God. They forget, however, that God is not forced, according to the Christian view, to grant every prayer. Hence,

there is no dilemma, God in His Providence being free to grant either or neither.

[35] The MS reading is here followed where the editors insert an unnecessary *ut*.

[36] This archaic word (*averruncare*) is also used in 1. 32 and 3. 43.

[37] *Potentioribus imperiis*. Bryce-Campbell thinks this a reference to Christ's teaching but reject the suggestion of Orelli (in his appendix) that Mark 10. 42 f. is meant. They themselves propose 1 Peter 2. 17.

[38] Here, out of place, the MS has [*primum*] which most editors, including Marchesi and Wiman, transpose to the beginning of the next sentence.

[39] The gods cannot be anthropomorphic; but cf. Genesis 1. 27: *Et creavit Deus hominem ad imaginem suam*, and 1 Cor. 11. 8, etc., which texts imply that man is theomorphic.

[40] *Ustrinae, rogi, busticeta* have practically the same meaning: places for burning the dead.

[41] Cf. Tibullus 2. 1. 13 f.; Justin Martyr, *Apol.* 1. 62; Lactantius, *Div. inst.* 5. 20. 3.

[42] Reading *fetidius* (Meursius) for *infelicius* (P and Marchesi) which does not seem to fit.

[43] See above, n. 10.

[44] Asses were sacrificed to Priapus, so Ovid states, *Fasti* 1. 391 f. That such were sacrificed by the Scythians, Arnobius himself has remarked earlier (4. 25). Curiously, Juvenal (12. 102-14) says that some extravagant sacrificers do *not* sacrifice elephants only because they cannot get them in Latium!

[45] Arnobius of course speaks of animals normally offered or not offered in sacrifice. Orelli adduces testimony for dogs offered to Hecate in Samothrace (Cf. M. P. Nilsson, *Geschichte der griechischen Religion* [Munich 1941] 686), fattened camels sacrificed by the Arabs, etc. Julius Capitolinus, *De Maxim. et Balb.* 11. 5, tells of the emperor Balbinus offering a hecatomb of lions.

[46] *Sollertia*. The point is skill in effecting results.

[47] Arnobius can hardly have been familiar with Matthew 23. 23 when he wrote this sentence.

[48] An ordinary example would not be sufficient—the *reductio ad absurdum* must be used.

[49] Human in that they wanted to worship a divinity.

[50] Cf. the trite saying that a dog looks upon his master as a god!

[51] Bryce-Campbell wrongly insert "[you reply]" and make this a

statement of the opponent which it cannot be, since the Christians did not sacrifice bulls.

[52] Reading *cernetis* with Gelenius and Wiman, in preference to *cernitis* (P and Marchesi).

[53] *Morbidis*, in a Lucretian sense (cf. 6.955, 1092, 1097, 1152, 1224).

[54] Reading *cariem vestram in [v]aletudinem vertere* with Wiman in *Eranos* 45 (1947) 150, correcting his earlier suggestion of *incuriam* for *cariem* and Marchesi's *curam*.

[55] The MS here has *novis* ('new'), Reifferscheid reads *vestris* ('your'). Marchesi's reading (*nothis*) has been adopted with hesitation, since there seems to be some justification for thinking that the foods are not counterfeit but familiar, i. e. *notis* may be right.

[56] The bracketed word [*minus*] is thus treated by Wiman.

[57] Cf. 3. 8 where this point is discussed.

[58] From the way the Latin reads here (*his albas, illis atris*) one might infer that the white victims were for male divinities, the black for female, but the next sentence makes clear that the demonstratives do not refer to any stated antecedent but to new hypothetical ones.

[59] Cf. 4. 5, 7. 23.

[60] The color black—black spots and stripes—also was a capital consideration in the choice of fish to be sacrificed to the nether deities: cf. F. J. Dölger, "Melanurus und Erythrinus," ΙΧΘΥΣ 2 (1922) 353 f.

[61] Cf. Juvenal 2. 107-110:

Esse aliquos manes et subterranea regna,

* * * * * * *

Nec pueri credunt, nisi qui nondum aere lavantur.

[62] Cf. Ovid, *Fasti* 2. 538, and Frazer, vol. 2, p. 435.

[63] So Wiman: *horrorem* for *honorem*.

[64] Minerva (Pallas Athena).

[65] See Edelstein-Edelstein, *Testim.* 290e.

[66] In the view of W. Kahl, "Cornelius Labeo, ein Beitrag zur spätrömischen Literaturgeschichte," *Philologus* Suppl. 5 (1894) 717-807, esp. 720-7, the distinction between the good and bad gods which Arnobius makes in this chapter goes back to Cornelius Labeo. Kahl's evidence is contained in a passage of Augustine, *De civ. Dei* 2. 11: Cum praesertim Labeo, quem huiuscemodi rerum peritissimum praedicant, numina bona a numinibus malis ista etiam cultus diversitate distinguat, ut malos deos propitiari caedibus et tristibus sup-

plicationibus adserat, bonos autem obsequiis laetis atque iucundis, qualia sunt, ut ipse ait, ludi, convivia, lectisternia. See Introd. pp. 38-40.

[67] Rapisarda (*Arnob.* 175) compares on this sentence Lucretius 2. 651.

[68] Röhricht (*Seelenlehre* 33) thinks Labeo the source for 7. 24-34.

[69] Cf. the note on *apexabo* and *longavo* in J. D. Vehling, *Apicius, Cookery and Dining in Imperial Rome* (Chicago 1936) 289 f. The TLL is uncertain as to whether *apexao* or *apexabo* is the correct spelling. Cf. Varro, *De ling. lat.* 5. 111 and Kent's note. I had already prepared the above when it was my good fortune to listen to an address by Mr. Vehling himself which was afterwards printed in *Class. Journ.* 44 (1948) 195-200. Mr. Vehling kindly prepared for me a series of notes on the curious foods which Arnobius mentions in this chapter. The note on *apexabo* (or *apexao*) identifies it as a "black pudding, blood sausage of a 'round' shape, a forcemeat in a sausage."—*Hirciae* = forcemeat, also identical with *ircei*, a sort of sacrificial sausage; cf. Walde-Hofmann, *Lateinisches etymologisches Wörterbuch* 1 (3rd ed., Heidelberg 1938) 650.—*Silicernium*, quoting Vehling: "Evidently a blood sausage thickened with wheat flour, which is being prepared today. Perhaps from *siligo*, winter wheat, or *sil* (or *seselis*), hardwort, a kind of cumin, also used today for flavoring sausage." *Silicernia* were also funeral repasts: cf. F. J. Dölger, *Ant. u. Christ.* 2 (1930) 86.—"*Longavi* are probably long sausages made with the straight gut" (Vehling).

[70] The bridge carrying from *taedae* in the present meaning to the original meaning = pine wood, pine torch, is not clear. So, too, *neniae* as here used, is quite as unintelligible with respect to its normal meaning (= funeral songs, dirges), as Arnobius states at the end of this chapter. The *offae penitae* (*offa* = a bite or ball or lump of meal or ground meat) are, as Vehling says, a favorite modern dish.

[71] Regarding *polimina*, cf. Festus 266 Lindsay.—Vehling derives *omen* from *omenta*, since this part of the body was used in sacrifices for predictions. This derivation is not known to Walde, *Lat. etym. Wörterbuch* (2nd ed. 1910) 539.—*Palasea* is identified by Vehling with buttock of beef, modern round of beef. Like *offa penita*, it was dusted with wheat flour before broiling or roasting.

[72] Here Marchesi has a misprint: *vatem* for *autem* (Reifferscheid).

[73] Little can be said regarding most of these terms beyond what Arnobius states in the following. Several of the items are mentioned by Arnobius alone: cf. *TLL s. vv.*

[74] Festus 410 f. Lindsay says that *strebula* is Umbrian. Vehling: "Modern round of beef. Cf. *palasea* and *augmina*."

[75] Reading *prunis* with Reifferscheid and Wiman, rather than *prius* (P and Marchesi).

[76] All three terms designate intestines, entrails.

[77] *Rumen* (*rumare*, *ruminare* = to chew), in modern physiology is the first part of the four-chambered stomach of typical ruminants. Whether this is referred to by Arnobius (*rumen*, *ruma*, *rumis* really = 'gullet,' 'esophagus') when he describes the *rumae* as *prima in gurgulionibus capita*, is not clear.

[78] On *magmenta* and *augmina* as additions of bits of meat to "augment" the offered *exta* (heart, liver, lungs, gall, caul), cf. Wissowa 418. See in the following note, *prosiciae*.

[79] The *praesiciae* or *prosiciae* (*partes*) were pieces of meat or fat cut from the intestines or other parts. It is a collective term for *magmenta* and *augmenta*. Cf. Wissowa, *loc. cit.*

[80] The *offa penita*, mentioned above.

[81] Cf. Tertullian, *Apol.* 30. 6, where wine, incense, and blood, the three elements of pagan offerings, are sharply attacked. Festugière (123) points out in another connection that Hermetism opposed the use of incense (he cites *Asclepias* 41 and J. Kroll, *Die Lehren des Hermes Trismegistos* [1913] 328 f.). Thus, it is possible to attribute Arnobius' antagonism to a Hermetic source, but since other early Christian writers besides Tertullian (e. g. Justin Martyr, *Apol.* 1. 13; 2. 4; Athenagoras, *Leg.* 13; Clement of Alexandria, *Strom.* 7. 6. 32. 5; Lactantius, *Div. inst.* 6. 25) are of the same mind as Arnobius, it is quite probable that he had observed this striking divergence from pagan custom while he was still a pagan. The early Christian abhorrence of incense in worship became especially apparent and was severely tried in the time of persecution. The sprinkling of a few grains of incense on a pagan altar was one of the ways in which Christians could satisfy the Roman government. Those among the lapsed (*lapsi*) Christians who abjured their Christian allegiance in this manner were known as *thurificati*. The *De lapsis* and many letters of St. Cyprian illustrate the problems posited by such weak Christians when they asked to be reinstated after the end of the Decian persecution. On the history of incense, cf. E. G. C. F. Atchley, *A History of the Use of Incense in Divine Worship* (London 1909); S. Eitrem, *Opferritus und Voropfer der Griechen u. Römer* (Christiania 1914) 228-76; J. A. MacCulloch, "Incense," *Hastings Encyc.* 7 (1915) 201-5; K. Hofmann, "Weihrauch," *LTK*

10 (1938) 783-5; E. Fehrenbach, "Encens," *DACL* 5. 1 (1922) 2-21. The latter states (6) that there is no positive proof of the use of incense in Christian worship (it was used in Christian everyday life!) before the second half of the fourth century. Even St. Augustine still writes, *Enarr. in Ps.* 49. 21: Non imus in Arabiam thus quaerere . . . : sacrificium laudis quaerit a nobis Deus.

⁸² The late introduction of incense in Rome is also referred to by Ovid, *Fasti* 1. 340 f.

⁸³ Cf. Cicero, *De div.* 1. 2. 3: *De harusp. resp.* 9. 18: Tertullian, *De spect.* 4.

⁸⁴ *Pium far* = *mola salsa*, spelt meal mixed with salt. Cf. Vergil, *Aen.* 5. 745; Horace, *Carm.* 3. 23. 20; Tibullus 3. 4. 10.

⁸⁵ Cf. Seneca, *Oed.* 305.

⁸⁶ Cf. Tertullian, *Apol.* 30. 6.

⁸⁷ Panchaia, a fabled island in the Erythraean Sea, east of Arabia, home of precious stones, incense, and myrrh: cf. Vergil, *Georg.* 2. 139; Tibullus 3. 2. 23; Ovid, *Met.* 10. 478.

⁸⁸ Rendering the stilted Latin: *et reciprocos halitus auris commeabilibus ducit.*

⁸⁹ See above, 7. 3.

⁹⁰ *Masculum tus*, considered the best for sacrificing: cf. Vergil, *Ecl.* 8. 66; Pliny, *Nat. hist.* 12. 14. 61.

⁹¹ Cf. Lucretius 1. 304, quoted twice (*De an.* 5. 6, where see Waszink's note, p. 130, and *Adv. Marc.* 4. 8) by Tertullian.

⁹² Cf. Ovid. *Trist.* 5. 5. 11 f.; Horace, *Carm.* 1. 19. 13-15 (see Rapisarda, *Arnob.* 242). The offering of incense and wine was the initial act in a solemn sacrifice: see Wissowa 417.

⁹³ Retaining the MS *tauris* in place of the editors' *lautis* suggested first by Zink.

⁹⁴ Juppiter Optimus Maximus, often abbreviated 'Iuppiter O. M.,' was the official title of the Capitoline Jupiter (Wissowa 125-9) —note the devastating sarcasm in the use of the title!

⁹⁵ As usual, Arnobius cites a single example and then uses the plural for effect.

⁹⁶ Cf. Valerius Maximus 2. 1. 5: Vini usus olim Romanis feminis ignotus fuit, ne scilicet in aliquod dedecus prolaberentur, qui proximus a Libero patre intemperantiae gradus ad inconcessam venerem esse consuevit.

⁹⁷ The formula: MACTUS HOC VINO INFERIO ESTO. The word *inferius* occurs also in 4. 16: *inferia vina defundi.*

⁹⁸ C. Trebatius Testa was a friend of Cicero, who dedicated his *Topica* to him (cf. also his letters to him—*Ad fam.* 7. 6-22). He be-

came an adviser of Augustus, and wrote *De religionibus* and *De civili iure*. Antistius Labeo was his pupil.

⁹⁹ These instruments were used in the cults of the oriental deities Cybele, Isis, Dionysus. See the chapter " Die Musik in den Mysterienkulten," in: J. Quasten, *Musik und Gesang in den Kulten der heidnischen Antike u. christl. Frühzeit* (Münster 1930) 45-68 and Plates 12-21. The symphoniae are mentioned repeatedly in Ch. 3 of Daniel as one of the instruments at the sound of which all were to adore a statue of gold dedicated by Nabuchodonosor of Babylon.

¹⁰⁰ For this passage see J. Quasten, *ibid.* 5, 40 f., 83. *Excitationes,* lit. ' wakenings ' or ' rousings,' were ceremonial salutations performed in the early morning especially in honor of Isis and Serapis when the priests opened their temples and shrines. Similarly, the *dormitiones,* mentioned in the following, were songs addressed to Isis, bidding her to sleep well for the night.

¹⁰¹ On this *lavatio* of the goddess, which was directed by the Quindecimvirs and took place annually on 27 March, see Ammianus Marcellinus 23. 3; Ovid, *Fasti* 4. 136 and Frazer's note, vol. 3, pp. 191-3; Wissowa 319, 321; Hyde 48; Cumont 225 n. 42. The sacred stone or statue of the goddess was taken down to the brook Almo and there, with the sacred utensils, was washed. St. Augustine, *De civ. Dei* 2. 4, mentions having witnessed, as a young man, the ceremonies on the feast of the *lavatio*. Regarding the obscenities uttered by the players and curious onlookers, he remarks: " If this is *purification, what is pollution?* "

¹⁰² The *epulum Iovis* was a magnificent banquet offered Jupiter in the course of the *ludi Romani,* on the anniversary of the founding of the Capitoline temple, 13 September, and during the *ludi plebei,* 13 November. Cf. Wissowa 126-8, 423, 453 f.

¹⁰³ Not having eaten since the last annual festival!

¹⁰⁴ The MS here reads *Esculapi* which Marchesi prints in his text as † [*Esculapii*]. The passage is certainly corrupt. Various suggestions have been made: Meiser *ieiunus escae Liberi;* Wiman *His cal. Priapi;* Castiglioni either *Euii patris* or *Ecce Euhii.* What is clear is that no other reference to a connection between Aesculapius and vintages can be found: Liber must be meant. Cf. Edelstein-Edelstein, *Testim.* 574, p. 184.

¹⁰⁵ The *lectisternia* (*lectus* + *sternere* = arranging of a bed) were an importation from the East. In these ceremonial acts magnificent couches (*pulvinaria*) were set up for the gods in their temples. Puppets of the divinities were placed on the couches and splendid repasts set out on a table nearby. In times of national crises or disasters com-

mon *lectisternia* for six or more gods were decreed (cf. e. g. Livy 22. 10. 97). Wissowa 421-3; *RE* (1925) 1108-15.

[106] On 13 December: cf. Wissowa 301, 422 n. 2.

[107] The feast of the Fordicidia, 15 April: cf. Wissowa 192. The present passage has sometimes been cited as evidence that Arnobius was unaware of any observance of the feast of Christmas. Others will not admit the evidence. See especially, G. Brunner, "Arnobius eine Zeuge gegen das Weihnachtsfest?" *Jahrb. f. Liturgiew.* 13 (1935) 172-81).

[108] The question whether a Christian might attend the pagan games and shows occasioned a special treatise by Tertullian, *De spectaculis.* A pseudo-Cyprianic work bears the same title. Cf. also Cyprian, *Ad Don.* 7 f.—It is probably significant that the *ludi Florenses,* observed 28 April to 3 May in honor of the goddess Flora, are mentioned by way of example: these were of especially lascivious character. Cf. Wissowa 197 f. See Lactantius, *Inst. div.* 1. 20. 6 (for a criticism of his euhemeristic version of Flora: Wissowa 198); Minucius 25. 8. Augustine, *De cons. evang.* 1. 33. 51, states: In quibus ludis tanta exhiberi turpitudo consuevit, ut in eorum comparatione ceteri honesti sint.—The *ludi Megalenses* were celebrated 4-10 April in honor of the Great Mother, Cybele—cf. Wissowa 318. Cf. Cicero, *De har. resp.* 10. 22 ff.; Festus 112 Lindsay.

[109] The *Amphitruo* of Plautus deals with the love of Jupiter for Alcmene, mother of Hercules. On Alcmene, cf. 2. 70 (n. 431), 4. 22, 4. 26 (n. 198), 5. 22. On Europa, cf. 5. 22 (n. 110). On Leda, daughter of Thestius and Eurythemis, cf. 2. 70 (n. 436), 4. 22, 5. 22; on Ganymede, son of Tros and Callirhoe, see 4. 26, 5. 44, and 5. 222; W. Drexler, *LM* 1. 1595-603; P. Perdrizet, *DA* 3. 707 f.; P. Friedlaender, *RE* 7. 737-49; on Danae, cf. 5. 22 (n. 110).

[110] On Adonis, cf. W. H. Roscher, *LM* 1. 69-77; E. Saglio, *DA* 1. 72-5; F. Dümmler, "Adonis" no. 2, *RE* 1 (1894) 385-95.

[111] Hercules.

[112] The *Hercules Furens.*

[113] However fanatically the Romans of the late Republic and of imperial times were given to exhibitions and shows of every kind, it was part of their ancient tradition, of the *mos maiorum,* that music, dancing, and histrionics of any sort—especially if engaged in for pay —were not reconcilable with the virtue and dignity of a Roman citizen. Actors had no place in the citizens' army nor voice in the citizens' council. There are numerous instances in Cicero's orations in which he with biting sarcasm taunts prominent Romans—Verres, Clodius, Piso, Gabinius, Antony—for having saltatory or histrionic

proclivities or for associating with the scum practicing such arts. The players on the stage or in the circus were non-Romans, slaves, freedmen, or foreigners. Parallel with this attitude is the exclusion of Romans from the ritual or even the professions in honor of adventitious deities, e.g. of the Magna Mater Idaea on the feast of the Megalensia (cf. the very interesting observations by Dionysius of Halicarnassus, *Ant. rom.* 2.19.3-5). On the subject of infamy attaching to stage performers, cf. Valerius Maximus 2.9; Tertullian, *De spect.* 22; Augustine, *De civ. Dei* 2.13 (quoting Cicero, *De rep.* 4.10). See also K. Pfaff, "Infamia," *RE* 18 (1916) 1537-40.

[114] The *stupidus*, 'blockhead,' 'lout,' probably a regular character in Roman comedy: cf. Juvenal 5.171; Julius Capitolinus, *Anton. Phil.* 29.2.

[115] That is, the slap which one character gives to another in comedy. The text here reads: *salappitarum sonitu atque plausu, factis et dictis turpibus, fascinorum ingentium rubore.*

[116] Men on the stage acting the part of women and pantomiming unnatural vices—cf. Clement of Alexandria, *Paed.* 2.113.2; Cyprian, *Ad Don.* 6; Lucian, *De salt., passim.*

[117] The pugilist's "boxing gloves" consisted of straps loaded with leaden or iron balls wound around his hands and arms; cf. above, n. 178 to Book Six.

[118] Reading with Wiman: *notisque inmani[b]us concrepare*, in place of Marchesi's *vocibusque inmanibus concrepare.*

[119] The *fabula Atellana* was a form of comedy or farce, a hybrid of Oscan-Greek elements originating in the Campanian town of Atella. Four masked characters—Maccus (the blockhead), Bucco (the glutton), Pappus (the old man), Dossennus (the hunchback)—played in it and depicted the life of the Atellan people. Pomponius (70 titles preserved, one of them by Arnobius 2.6, see n. 31) and Novius (44 titles) popularized the farce at Rome in the eighties of the first century B.C. Cf. Schanz-Hosius, *Geschichte der römischen Literatur* (4th ed., Munich 1927) 245-53.

[120] If the opponents retort with Arnobius' usual weapon, the *reductio ad absurdum*, the implication of this argument is that the gods enjoy being dirty!

[121] The MS here reads *gruenearum* and Marchesi changes this to *gricenearum* on the basis of Festus 88 (Lindsay) who identifies *gricenea* as *funis crassus*, without other explanation. Sabaeus and Reifferscheid both read, however, *herniarum.*

[122] The conclusive nature of chapters 35-7 led Orelli, following in this respect an unnamed French scholar, to transpose them to the

THE CASE AGAINST THE PAGANS: BOOK SEVEN 615

end of Book Seven where they appear as chapters 49-51. Because they show evidence of the hasty composition of Book Seven, I have, however, left them where they appear in the MS, but for the convenience of the reader who may have access to Orelli's edition or its reprint in *ML* 5, I have added his chapter numbers in brackets from this point on.

[123] *Dei summi.* Cf. Firmicus Maternus, *De err. prof. rel.* 4. 4, 7. 9, 16. 4.

[124] Brunner (*art. cit.* 173) maintains that if 7.32 is evidence against the existence of a Christmas festival in Africa in Arnobius' time, then the present statement is also applicable to Christ. But, adds Brunner, it is easy to demonstrate that Arnobius was neither a Docetist, nor an Ebionite, nor an Artemonian.

[125] The MS here has a genitive *discordiarum* where an accusative is needed or some noun on which the genitive can depend. Bryce-Campbell regard this error, as well as the lacuna (⟨things of this kind⟩) below, as attributable to Arnobius and not to a copyist, and maintain that these are signs of Arnobius' haste in writing the conclusion. They are probably right.

[126] The *Parentalia* were a period of eight days, 13-21 February, devoted to commemorating the dead, when all magistrates put off the toga praetexta, temples were closed, no marriages were permitted, and every attention given to the resting-places of the *di parentum*—the shades of the forbears. Included was a sacrifice to the dead, an invitation to the departed to partake of the repast placed at their tombs. The ceremony was termed *parentare.* Cf. Wissowa 232 f.; J. A. Hild, *DA* 4. 333 f.

[127] E. g. Cybele, Aesculapius (see n. 132).

[128] Statues on columns are certainly meant in Cicero's description of what happened to much of the statuary on the Capitoline Hill in the year 65 B. C.: *Cat.* 3. 18. 19 f. Columns were erected in Rome for the following emperors: Augustus (Platner-Ashby 134); Trajan (*ibid.* 243 f.); Antoninus Pius (*ibid.* 131), and M. Aurelius (*ibid.* 132), of which those of Trajan and M. Aurelius are still standing. Since all of these emperors were deified after their death, these columns fit the requirements of a divinity on a column but they are not foreign divinities. It is a curious fact that Arnobius does not attack the cult of the emperors. Note that here the pagan is speaking.

[129] Cf. Lucretius 6. 50-5.

[130] This famous story is found with variations in the following extant writers: Cicero, *De div.* 1. 26. 55; Livy 2. 36; Dion. Hal. 7. 68 f.; Plutarch, *Coriolanus* 24. 2; Valerius Maximus 1. 7. 4; Lactantius,

Div. inst. 2.8.20 f.; Augustine, *De civ. Dei* 4.26; Macrobius, *Sat.* 1.11.2-5; there is also a brief allusion to it in Minucius 7.3 and 27.4. Cicero tells us that it also appeared in the works of Q. Fabius Pictor (fr. 15, H. Peter, *Hist. rom. rel.* 1 [Leipzig 1914] 26-8 and note, see also pp. cciv-v), Cn. Gellius (fr. 21, Peter, *ibid.* 1.154), and L. Coelius Antipater (fr. 49, Peter, *ibid.* 1.174). See also P. v. Rohden, *RE* 2 (1896) 2105; F. Münzer, *ibid.* 12 (1925) 925; T. Mommsen, *Römische Forschungen* 2 (Berlin 1879) 113 ff., 123 ff. The event is dated by Cicero, who does not identify the persons, in the period of the Latin War (338-336 B.C.) at a point when the games were stopped because the citizenry were aroused by an attack. Livy's date for the occurrence, however, is 491 B.C. and he gives the farmer's name at T. Latinius, while Dionysius of Halicarnassus puts it in the consulship of Q. Sulpicius Camerinus and Spurius Larcius Flavus = 490 B.C. Plutarch's account, which is by far the longest, gives the name as T. Latinus, and appears to have been derived from that of Dionysius. Valerius Maximus fails to mention the date but gives the name as T. Latinius. Lactantius, or his immediate source, has mistaken the name as Tiberius Atinius, the initial letter of the *cognomen* having combined with the *praenomen* (possibly 'Ti.'). It should be noted that Lactantius' version is relatively short. Augustine's account can hardly have been derived from Lactantius for he also has the name as T. Latinius. Macrobius dates the event in 474 a.u.c. = 279 B.C. (if Varro's chronology is the one used). Lactantius calls the *paterfamilias* Antonius Maximus, while Macrobius has it as Autronius Maximus and his form of the name of the farmer is Annius, without a *praenomen*. The brief allusions in Minucius cannot have been Arnobius' source. He probably had Cicero's account before him, for neither Cicero nor Arnobius names either the *pater familias* or the *rusticus,* and there are other significant correspondences as well.

[131] *Praesul* is to be taken in a cryptic sense, such as was common in oracles. Cf. 4.37 and 7.9 where the story is foreshadowed. Cf. also Artemidorus, *Oneirocrit.* 1.78.

[132] In the present section Arnobius unites two cases of the importation of foreign gods in times of great national crises. The first refers to the introduction of the Epidaurian god of health and healing, Aesculapius. The occasion was a severe plague which struck Rome and the territory around it in the year 293 B.C. A consultation of the Sibylline books had suggested the importation. Cf. 3.21 and n. 99; Livy 10.47.6 f.; Wissowa 306 f. The second case was the intro-

The Case against the Pagans: Book Seven

duction of the cult of the Phrygian goddess Cybele, Magna Mater, when her "sacred stone" was brought to Rome during the final years of the Hannibalic war. Cf. 2. 73 and nn. 458, 460.

[133] It is abundantly clear that this refers, not to the great cult statue of Jupiter within the Capitoline temple, but to another, set upon a pillar outside the temple, since the statue within was both protected from lightning by the roof and could hardly be reoriented on the occasion of the restoration, as is indicated a little further on, without making it face the east wall of the *cella*. The same event is also described by Cicero (*Cat.* 3. 8. 19 ff.) in a passage which contains so many striking verbal resemblances to Arnobius that the latter must have been following Cicero.

[134] Cf. Otto, *Sprichwörter* 147, who also mentions Jerome, *Ep.* 133. 5. 1.

[135] Platner-Ashby (118) give the length of the arena of the Circus Maximus as 568 meters. Assuming that a lap is roughly twice that distance (1136 m.), seven laps would have come to something less than 8,000 meters, depending on how much space was needed for turning, or about four and one-half English miles. The seven laps are also referred to by Ovid, *Hal.* 68; Lactantius, *Div. inst.* 7. 27. 1.

[136] Castiglioni would insert *servus* which is in any case necessary to the sense.

[137] *Caput* here has the sense of a person worthy only to be counted as a head.

[138] The public games were in charge of the aediles. The spectators paid no admission fees of any kind. The state appropriated a certain lump sum toward the expenses and the aediles who aimed at the higher offices of praetor and consul and, consequently, needed a pleased and satisfied public, paid the rest. These contributions (and sums borrowed!) sometimes were recklessly high. Cf. Wissowa 451; W. W. Fowler, *Social Life at Rome* (New York 1909) 294-9.

[139] Cf. Livy 34. 2. 11.

[140] Cf. 1. 51 and nn. 253-4.

[141] Jupiter.

[142] *Pestilitas*, a Lucretian word (cf. 6. 1098, 1125). The borrowing is not noted by Bailey.

[143] That is, had the rustic been made willing, had he been forced to co-operate by punitive action taken *ab initio* on his own person. As it was, the first measure taken by Jupiter, of doing away with the sons, proved entirely futile, serving only to show the god's lack of foresight or his utter brutality. The elliptic language of the present

passage indicates again Arnobius' failure to subject this section of his work to a final revision.

¹⁴⁴ The bracketed paragraphs contain many statements which are to be found in adjacent chapters and have therefore been generally rejected as spurious by most editors. Thus, Ursinus and Marchesi bracket them, while Gelenius, Canterus, Salmasius, and Orelli omit them entirely, and are followed by the German translators, von Besnard and Alleker. Stewechius, followed by the English translators, Bryce-Campbell, relegates them to an appendix. Cf. Reifferscheid, p. xiv. It is, as Marchesi says, possible that Arnobius wrote them but intended to revise them at a later date.

¹⁴⁵ *Puer matrimus*: lit. a boy whose mother was still living. See 4.31: *puer patrimus*, and n. 216.

¹⁴⁶ The occasion of the importation of the god Aesculapius to Rome has been referred to above, n. 132. Ovid (*Met*. 15.622 ff.) graphically relates the legend that the holy serpent of its own accord left its ancient sanctuary at Epidaurus, crawled through the town and down to the shore to board the ship that was to bring it to Rome; and that on its arrival it proceeded to the islet in the Tiber, indicating that here was to be its sanctuary, the new Asclepieum. There the temple vowed to the god was consecrated on 1 January 291 B.C. Cf. Livy 10.47 and *epit*. to Book 11; Valerius Maximus 1.8.2; Plutarch, *Qu. Rom*. 94.286; Pliny, *Nat. hist*. 29.72; Augustine, *De civ. Dei* 3.17; Lactantius, *Div. inst*. 1.17.15, 2.7.13., etc. See E. Schmidt, *Kultübertragungen* (Religionsg. Vers. u. Vorarb. 8.2, Giessen 1909) 31-46; Wissowa 307 f.; R. Herzog, *Die Wunderheilungen von Epidaurus* (Leipzig 1931); J. Quasten, *Theol. Revue* 30 (1931) 538-41.

¹⁴⁷ Mother of Aesculapius.

¹⁴⁸ *Magni agminis*: lit., great train; cf. Vergil, *Georg*. 3.423.

¹⁴⁹ Marchesi: *quo mentiri se posse⟨t nec possent⟩ quisnam esset aut qualis homines intueri*, certainly the best emendation of the many thus far proposed.

¹⁵⁰ The MS here has [*debuit*] which has given much trouble, since it makes a rather senseless apodosis. Orelli deletes the clause but it does make sense if we assume, with Zink and Marchesi, that this word is a repetition of the *debuit* above.

¹⁵¹ *Colubra, anguis, serpens*: a *coluber* (fem. *colubra*) was a common, small variety—a house snake. *Anguis* is a term applied to the snake as something that writhes and coils itself about objects. It is used especially to designate snakes of great size and fright-inspiring appearance. *Serpens* is the creeping, crawling thing. The word is

THE CASE AGAINST THE PAGANS: BOOK SEVEN 619

used also for several constellations. This gradation of terms from the more common to the more imposing, this dwelling here and in the following, on the low physical traits of the serpent god, is, of course, calculated to emphasize the absurdity of the pagan worship of Aesculapius.

[152] In the Second Punic War near the river Bagradas in Africa. The serpent was supposedly 120 feet long and subdued only after many soldiers had perished and the regular siege machinery for taking cities had been employed against it. Cf. Livy, *Epit.* Bk. 18; Valerius Maximus 1.8.19; Pliny, *Nat. hist.* 8.14.36 f.; A. Gellius 7.3; Florus 2.2.20.

[153] An almost exact repetition, thus far, of the second sentence in this chapter.

[154] *Libris fatalibus* (cf. Livy 5.14.4), that is, the Sibylline books.

[155] See the illuminating comments on this and other explanations of the cures given by H. J. Rose, *Class. Rev.* 71 (1947) 52.

[156] On chapters 49-51 see K. Hidén, "Die Erzählung von der grossen Göttermutter bei Arnobius (Adversus Nationes VII 49-51)" in his *De Arnobii Adversus nationes libris VII commentationes*, no. 1, extract from *Annales Academiae Scientiarum Fennicae*, ser. B, 15, no. 7 (Helsingfors 1921). The arguments for believing that the importation was from Pergamum and not from Pessinus are given by Frazer on Ovid, *Fasti*, vol. 3, pp. 227-30. See also E. Schmidt, *Kultübertragungen* 1-30.

[157] Hannibal. Cf. 7.50.

[158] Especially the battle of Zama (202 B.C.).

[159] *Angellis prominentibus.* Cf. Lucretius 2.428: angellis paulum prostantibus.

[160] Frazer (on Ovid, *Fasti*, vol. 3, pp. 227-30) thinks this evidence that the stone was still visible in 300 A.D.

[161] Et quem omnes hodie ipso illo videmus in signo oris loco positum: this difficult passage along with a passage in the poet Prudentius (*Perist.* 10.157) figure in the controversy whether or not the sacred stone was encased in a head or mask of silver; cf. Meiser (14-18): "Das Steinbild der Magna Mater"; Wissowa 319 n. 5.

[162] There is a lacuna in the text, which both editors leave unfilled. Hildebrand adds ⟨parvi⟩ on the basis of *lapsis . . . non magnus* in 7.49.

[163] Cf. Vergil, *Aen.* 6.6 f.; *Georg.* 1.135.

[164] Doubtless an allusion to the length of the Second Punic War (218-202 B.C.).

[165] Allusions to the battles of the Trebia, Lake Trasimenus, and Cannae, when Roman armies were completely destroyed.

[166] Reading *hac,* lit. 'here,' for *ac* (Souter).

[167] Here Arnobius is an African patriot.

[168] The *explicit* of Book Seven (ARNOUII LIBER UII EXPLI) is followed by: INCIPIT LIBER UIII FELICITER which refers, not to a Book Eight of the *Adversus nationes* but to the *Octavius* of Minucius Felix, likewise preserved solely by the *Codex Parisinus* 1661. The confusion of *Liber Octavii* with Liber octavus appears in several early editions (see the bibliography, pp. 232 f.). The *Octavius* was first printed separately by F. Balduinus (Heidelberg 1560, reprinted Frankfurt 1610).

INDEX

INDEX

[Pages 1 to 372 are in Volume One;
Pages 373 to 620 are in Volume Two.]

Abdera, 422, 572
Abdias, 311
abiogenesis, 306
aborigines, 433
Abraham, 243, 583
abstinence, 180
abstract qualities, 375, 544
Academics, 309, 331
Acantho, 385
Accius, 363
Acdestis, 414-7, 421, 423-6, 569, 573
Achaea, 125
Achelois, 368
Acheron, 127, 436
Acherontic books, 173
Achilles, 357, 398
Achilles Tatius, 583
Acrisius, 457, 576, 588
Acropolis, 288, 588 f.
Acta Pilati, 281 f.
Actaeon, 219, 366
Actium, 601
actors, 405, 564, 613 f.
Acts, 3. 1-10: 293; 5. 38: 303; 8. 17 ff.: 313; 11.26: 244; 14. 8-10: 293; 15. 29: 345; 17. 28: 270; 19. 35: 557.
Acts of Thomas, 311 f.
Adeimantus, 336
adfectus, 277
Admetus, 396
Adonis, 398, 516, 561, 613
adoption of divinities, 546
adversary, 45, 344, 547, 549
adversus, meaning of, 48
Adversus gentes, 2, 5, 240 f., 262, 264
Adversus nationes, 3-6, 9-11, 15, 18 f., 26 f., 34, 41, 48, 52, 262, 348; composition of, 22; date, 345
Aeacus, 398, 455, 561, 587
aediles, 617
aeditui, 598

Aeetes, 551
Aegina, 587
Aegistheus, 299
Aelian, 272, 325, 599
Aelius Stilo Praeconinus, L., 35, 222, 368, 272, 545
Aeneas, 184, 222, 285, 369, 398, 544
aenigmata, 354
aeons, 303, 321
Aequitas, 544
aer, 363
Aeschylus, 298, 361, 584
Aesculapius, 36, 47, 80, 84, 86, 89, 96, 177, 187, 210, 222, 284, 292, 356 f., 364, 395, 474, 478, 503, 515, 531 f., 534 f., 561 f., 583, 602-4, 615 f., 618 f.; the three gods so called, 386
aetas legitima, 341
aether, 274
Aether, 385
Aethlius of Samos, 34, 462, 593
Aethusa, 397, 560
aetiology, 36, 38, 40
Afranius, 365
Africa, 264, 312, 572; Christianity in, 301; patriotism in, 241
africia, 505
Agahd, R., 260, 358, 360, 544
Agamemnon, 299, 577, 582
Agdus, 414
Agesarchus, 458
agnosticism, 27, 167, 438 f.
Aius Locutius, 77, 280
air, 163, 216, 274, 333
Alamanni, 70
Alba, 184, 508
Alcestis, play by Euripides, 558
Alceus, 516
alchemy, 269, 337
Alcibiades, 306, 338, 464, 595
Alcmaeon of Croton, 367

623

624 INDEX

Alcmene, 182, 285, 302, 344, 393, 398, 431, 560 f., 577, 613
Alcyone, 397, 560
Alexamenos, 355
Alexander (Paris), 273
Alexander of Aphrodisias, 308
Alexander Severus, 272, 564
Alexander the Great, 64, 273, 601
Alexandria, 600
Algeria, 6
allegory, 40, 440 f., 443-9, 451, 563
Alleker, J., 57, 333, 343, 571
Almeloveen, T. J., 266
Almighty Father, 156
Almighty God, 149, 156, 164 f., 173, 185, 188 f.
Almighty King, 158
Almighty Ruler, 177
Almo, 612
aloofness, of God, 28, 277, 330, 333; of gods, 75
Alope, 560
Altaner, B., 245, 256
altars, 110, 189, 211, 375, 452, 483, 490 f., 495 f., 506, 509, 521, 544, 584, 590
Alzog, J., 253
Amalthea, 554
Amann, E., 313
Amatucci, 17, 42
Amazons, 560, 601
Ambrose, St., *De fide*, 1.9.60, 1.11.73: 283
ambrosia, 277, 354
Ambrosiaster, 265
Amelung, W., 583
amens, 246
Ammianus Marcellinus, 272, 366, 565, 593, 612
Ammon, 594
Ampelius, L., 551
Amphilochus, 280
ampitheaters, 153
Amphitrite, 397, 560
Amphitruo, play of Plautus, 516
Amphitryon, 285, 344
Amphictyon, 588
amulets, 325
Amyclae, 272

Ammone, 397, 560
anacolouthon, 339
Anaphe, 272
Anaximenes, 307
ancestral traditions, 61, 125
Anchises, 84, 285, 398, 561
Ancus Marcius, 580
Andocides, 589
Andres, F., 326
Andronicus of Rhodes, 308
angels, 147, 264, 290, 303, 326; names of, 290
anger, 453; of God, 28, 47, 246, 254 f., 274, 276 f., 314; of gods, 38, 70 f., 407, 424 f., 485 f., 520, 566
anima, 306, 327. See *animus*
animal sacrifice, 152, 189, 211, 310, 314, 337, 345, 497, 505, 603, 607
animal worship, 78, 203, 281
animus, 306. See *anima*
Anna Perenna, 545
annales, 35, 258, 521, 531, 606
Annales Maximi, 244
annihilation, 127, 302
annihilationism, 254
Annius, 616
anointings, 212; of stone, 87
anthropomorphism, 21, 192, 196, 201, 204 f., 340, 348, 517 f., 579, 586, 607
Antias, Valerius, 409
Antioch, 9
Antiochus of Syracuse, 34, 457, 588
Antiochus of Cyzicus, 473, 599
Antiochus IX Philopator, 599
Antiope, 357, 584
Antistius Labeo, 612
antitheos, 550
Antoninus Pius, 615
Antonius Maximus, 616
Antonsson, O., 595
Antony, Mark, 299, 571, 574, 613
Anubis, 346, 478, 603
Aoede, 357, 367
ape, 205, 356
apexabo, 609
apexaones, 505
Aphrodite, 250, 273, 285 f., 344, 352,

INDEX

357, 544, 547, 549, 558, 575, 577, 594. See Venus
Aphareus, 555
Apicius, 609
Apis, 84, 286, 458, 587, 590
Apocalypse, 21. 6: 338
apocrypha, 34, 292
Apollinarius, 2, 24, 34, 252
Apollo, 76, 80, 84, 108, 115, 180, 182, 186, 196, 210, 218 f., 223, 226, 263, 269, 280, 284, 344, 356 f., 359, 366, 372, 386 f., 389, 396 f., 455, 457 f., 474, 503, 551, 553 f., 556, 558, 560-2, 577, 589, 594, 596, 601; Clarius, 280; Didymaeus, 280; diviner, 476; Philesius, 280; Pythius, 280; Smintheus, 280, 366; Trophonius, 280
Apollodorus, 34, 244, 272, 284, 286, 367, 396, 543, 554 f., 557, 559-62, 589
Apollonius of Rhodes, 272, 576, 599
Apollonius of Tyana, 99, 294
apologies, 4, 25
apologists, 36, 41, 240, 256, 606
aposiopesis, 290
Apostles, 274
Apostolic authority, 25
apotheosis of heroes, 287
appeasement of gods, 484-7, 489, 503 f., 520-2, 524, 582
Appian, 289
Apuleius, 24, 258, 294, 297, 332
Aquila, 354
Aquilius, M.', 89, 289
Aquitania, 276
Arabia, 125, 311, 611
Arabs, 462, 593, 607
Aratus, 370
Arbesmann, P., 577
Arcadia, 357, 365, 396, 555, 557
Arcesilas of Pitane, 34, 122, 309
ἀρχαί, 333
archaism, 23, 251, 598
Arche, 357, 367
Archippus, 561
Archytas of Taras, 34, 121, 308
Ares, 557 f., 593. See Mars
Argos, 576, 586, 588, 600

argumentum ex silentio, 26
Argus, 386, 592, 602
Argus-slayer, Mercury, 478
Arianism, 27
Aristaeus, 366
Aristides, 28
Aristophanes of Athens, 600
Aristophanes of Byzantium, 296, 599
Aristotle, 34, 36, 121, 216, 259, 308, 353, 364, 571
arithmetic, 317, 343
Armenius, 99, 294
Arnim, H. von, 309
Arnobius of Sicca: Arnovius, 5, 241; Afer, 241; Maior, 241; Orator, 6, 241; birth and birthplace, 7, 12; of Greek origin? 5; date of, 7, 10 f., 245, 264; rhetorician, 6; conversion of, 2, 15, 29, 360; baptism of, 275; never a Christian? 18; orthodoxy of, 27, 29, 32, 257, 327, 347; not a Docetist, Ebionite, Artemonian, 615; martyrdom of, 12, 246; learning of, 30, 36; sources of, 34, 543, 550, 585, 587, 600, 616; language of, 251; prolix, 2, 552; style of, 14, 19, 23, 249; method of composition, 546; an apologist, 3; Christian predecessors of, 12, 34; an African patriot, 620; Romanity of, 346; neglected, 4; negative judgments on, 3; A. and Lactantius, 49
Arnobius the younger, 5, 240
Arpocrates, 346
Arrian, 34, 191, 285, 348, 552
Arsinoe, 397, 560
Artemidorus, 616
Artemis, 250, 284, 557, 576, 582, 593, 601. See Diana
Artemisium, 589
Artemonianism, 615
arts and crafts, 207, 209
Ascanius, 184
asceticism, 337
Asclepias, 282, 316
Asclepieum at Rome, 618
Asclepius, 560
Asia, 70, 125, 276, 312

Asinius Pollio, 296
Asopous, 368
Asopus, 587
ass's head, worship of, 47, 204, 355
asses sacrificed, 396, 558, 607
Assyria, Assyrians, 63, 273
astrology, 274
astronomy, 181, 343, 587
ἀταραξία, 214, 279, 324, 586
Atargatis, 286
Atchley, E. G. C. F., 610
Atella, 614
Atellan farces, 517
Athanasius, 603
atheism, atheists, 167, 214, 282, 334, 438 f., 480
Athena, 288, 365, 551, 554, 557 f., 579, 588, 602; Polias, 457, 588, 597; Promachus, 596
Athenaeus, 590, 593
Athenagoras, 28, 42, 277, 363, 606, 610
Athenians, 435, 464, 579
Athens, 433, 457, 476, 578, 600 f.
Athos, Mt., 273
Atilius Regulus, M., 289
Atlantis, 63, 245, 272
Atlas, 181, 208, 284, 343, 358, 560, 577
atomic collisions, 304
atomism, 333
atomists, 282, 309
atoms, 81, 122, 167, 282, 304, 317
attagi, 415
Attalus, King, 537
Atthis, 588
Attica, 288, 432 f., 443, 447, 578 f., 600
Attis, 21, 89, 290, 409, 414 f., 417, 446, 449, 516, 561 f., 564, 566, 569, 571, 573
Atzberger, L., 30, 256
augmenta, 507
augmina, 506, 610
augurs, 278, 405, 546, 564, 570
augury, 312, 335
Augustine, St., 39, 53, 265, 303, 326, 354, 565, 616
  De civ. Dei, 53, 265; 2. 3: 268;
2. 4: 612; 2. 5: 571; 2. 7: 582;
2. 9: 562; 2. 11: 260, 361, 608;
2. 12: 503; 2. 13: 614; 2. 22:
598; 2. 28: 566; 3. 17: 546, 618;
3. 25: 266, 361, 544, 554; 3. 31:
268, 272; 4. 8: 280, 547-9; 4. 10:
363; 4. 11, 363; 4. 12: 367; 4. 14
f., 544; 4. 16: 549; 4. 17 f.: 544;
4. 19 f.: 548; 4. 21: 544, 546,
549; 4. 24: 549; 4. 26: 616; 4. 33:
544; 4. 24: 548 f.; 4. 34: 548; 6. 6:
548; 6. 7: 280, 562; 6. 9: 547 f.;
7. 2: 364; 7. 3: 549; 7. 16: 364-7;
7. 26: 562, 572; 7. 37: 555; 9. 1:
260; 12. 15: 330; 18. 4: 560; 18. 5:
286, 590; 18. 15: 555; 20. 1: 332;
21. 41: 273; *Conf.* 8. 2. 3: 603; *De cons. Ev.* 1. 33: 613; *Enchir.* 6. 18
328; *Enarr. in Ps.* 49. 21: 611
Augustus, 352, 512, 615
Aulus, 458, 591. See Olus
Aurelius, Marcus, 615
Aurora, 398, 561
Auruncus, 372
Aust, E., 280 f., 359, 544, 577
Author of universe, 519
Autonoë, 366
Autronius Maximus, 616
Aventine, 410, 567 f.
averruncare, 283, 372, 607
Averruncus, 372
Axelson, B., 55, 57, 252
Axtell, H. L., 543
Ayala, 503

Baal, 294
Babelon, E., 602
bacchanalia, 284, 427 f.
bacchari, 269
Bacchants, 575
Bacchus, 284, 594
bachelor's lance, 180
Bacis, 108, 298 f.
Bactria, Bactrians, 63, 273, 294
bad, gods, 608; angels, 336; luck, 503; omen, 71
Badham, F. P., 253, 291, 298
Baebulus, 99, 294
Baehrens, E., 307

INDEX   627

Baehrens, W. A., 259
Bagnani, G., 355
Bagradas, 619
Bailey, C., 246, 248, 255, 258, 269, 271 f., 278, 287 f., 296, 305, 316 f., 321-4, 333, 335 f., 353, 365, 548, 564, 617
Bainvel, J., 315
Balbinus, 607
Balduinus, F., 53, 620
banquets, 506, 515
baptism, 304, 325
Barbel, J., 290, 353
barbers, 203
Bardenhewer, O., 8, 34, 239, 241, 243, 245 f., 250, 256 f., 295, 565
Bardy, G., 240, 260
Barth, 256
Barthel, W., 354
Baubo, 433 f., 436, 438, 443, 447, 578-80
Baucis, 562
Baumgartner, M., 321
Bayart, J., 312
Baynes, N. H., 245, 254, 313
Beazley, C. R. 311
beetles, divinized, 78
Beginning, the, 78, 82
belief, 121, 191; in Christ, 304. See faith
Bellerophon, 577
Bellonae, 77, 212, 281, 360
Beloch, K. J., 281
Belus, 99, 294
Benedictines of St. Maur, 266
Beneventum, 546
Berenice, 294
Bernoulli, J. J., 595
Besnard, F. A. von, 56, 240, 267, 333
Bible, 252, 277, 295
Bickel, E., 52, 265
Bie, O., 357
Bigelmair, A., 340
Birt, T., 285, 366
birth, of Christ, 9, 27, 244, 275 (see Christmas); of gods, 80, 390; of Jupiter, 83
birthday games, 110
birthplaces of gods, 553

bishop, of Carthage, 17, 242; of Sicca, 2, 16 f., 240, 242, 264, 268; of Rome, 293
Bithynia, 14, 569
Biton, 600
black bile, 328
black sacrifices, 226, 500 f., 608
black stone, 346, 593
Blanchet, J. A., 544
Blau, L., 315
blessed isles, 587
blind, blindness, 92, 94, 98, 109
Bloch, L., 344
blood, 149, 328, 412
bloody sacrifices, 22, 173, 452, 483, 491, 496, 584, 610
Bobeth, W., 550, 552
Bocchores, 84
body of gods, 198, 511
Boehm, B., 39, 260, 336, 360, 363
Boeotia, 280, 357
Boëthius, A., 57
Bona Dea, 281
books of fate, 534
Borries, B. V., 259
Bortolucci, G., 304 f.
Botsford, G. W., 341
Botticelli, 555
Bouché-Leclercq, A., 279
Bouchier, E. S., 43, 250, 258, 261, 298, 327
Bousset, W., 38, 260, 327, 336
Brahmins, 311
Brakman C., 42, 52, 261, 264, 281, 287, 363, 551, 575, 581
Brandt, S., 14, 23, 243, 246 f., 250, 264, 331, 574
Brimo 429, 443, 576
Brindisi, 313
Britain, 312
Britons, 312
Broadhead, H. D., 252
Bromius, 393
Brown, N. O., 556
Broydé, I., 315
Brunda, 125, 313
Brundisium, 313
Brunner, G., 27, 245, 254, 258, 298, 613, 615

Bryce, H. and Campbell, H., 4, 8, 10 f., 15-7, 22 f., 42, 56, 239, 243-8, 250, 261, 267, 278, 282 f., 290, 303, 306, 308, 315, 324 f., 332 f., 336-9, 342, 345, 350, 353, 546, 577, 581, 584, 597, 603-5, 607, 615
Bucco, 614
Bucures, 286
Bürchner, L., 589
bull, form of assumed by Jupiter, 394, 429 f., 445, 560
Buonaiuti, G., 51
Burel, J., 346
burial, of gods, in sanctuaries, 457 f., 587, 590
Burnus, 381, 548
busticeta, 607
Butas, 34, 427, 574
Butterworth, G. W., 543, 551, 575, 589, 600

caccabulus, 263
Cadmus, 284
caduceus, 50, 217, 365, 554, 579
caduceus-bearers, 433
caducus, 582
caelum, 106, 297
caelus, 106, 297
Caelus, 184, 215, 220, 297, 345, 362, 385, 395, 551
Caesar, Julius, 296, 571
Caesellius Vindex, L., 35, 107, 297
Caesius, 35, 223, 354, 370
Caesius Bassus, 370
caestus, 602, 614
Cagnat, R., 300, 549
calantica, 319
Calaus, 573
calendar, 270
caliandria, 603
Callimachus, 557, 559, 593, 599
Calliope, 368, 434, 576
Callirhoe, 613
Calpurnius Piso Censorius Frugi, L., 35, 368
Calvinism, 30
Calvus, 354
camels, sacrificed, 607

Campagna, 342
Canacheni, 601
Canary Islands, 456
candelabrum, candelabrus, 106, 297
Cannae, 346, 446, 546, 583, 620
cannibalism, 153, 330
Canterus, T., 265 f.
capite censi, 323
Capito, 354
Capitol, Capitols, 82, 387, 419, 458, 476, 524, 545, 598
Capitoline Hill, 376, 591, 615
Capitoline Jupiter, 468, 611
Capitoline temple, 600, 612, 617
Capitoline triad, 283, 600
Cappadocia, 272, 281, 312
Caprotina, 216, 364
Capua, 546
Caracheni, 476
Carcopino, J., 310
Cardea, 548
carduus, 318
Caria, Carians, 396, 589 f.
Carnea, 549
Carneades, 34, 122, 309
caro strebula, 506 f.
Carpentarius, A., 266
Carter, J. B., 366
Carthage, 242, 537, 572
Casaubon, I., 266
Case, S. J., 276
Cassandra, 298
Cassel, P., 602
Cassiodorus, 252
Castor, 84, 182, 285, 344, 356, 369, 386, 397, 555, 559, 576. See Dioscuri
castus, 426, 573
Castus of Sicca, 17
Cassius Dio, 591
Catamitus, 398, 431, 561, 577. See Ganymede
catechetical instruction, 253
catechumen, 18, 279, 566
Cates, W. L. R., 243 f.
Catilinarian conspiracy, 366
Cato the Elder, 205, 251, 297, 300
Cato of Utica, 355, 574
cats, divinized, 78

INDEX

Catullus, 255, 293, 318, 350, 554, 569
catumeum, 505
Caudium, 546
Cecchelli, 239
Cecropians, 433
Cecrops, 457, 579, 586, 588
Celeus, 457, 589
censor, 577
Censorinus, 244, 343, 369
census, Roman, 546
centaur, 560, 564
Cerberus, 437, 581
Cerealia, 186, 346
ceremonies, 401 f., 409, 425-7, 481-539, 585; negligence in, 488
Ceres, 84, 86, 177, 186, 199, 217 f., 223, 226, 285, 346, 352, 356, 365, 398, 426, 428, 430, 433 f., 438, 440, 442 f., 445-7, 450 f., 457, 478, 515, 561, 573, 578, 589. See Demeter
ceroma, 359
cestus, 478, 602
Chalcidicum, 352
Chaldaeans, 63, 294, 384
chance, 118
Charisius, 297
chastity, 114
χειμών, Epicurean term, 605
chiasmus, 283, 297
Chinese, 312
Chione, 560
Chiron, 366, 560
Christ, 20, 27, 47, 49, 64, 84 f., 90, 107, 116, 123 f., 127 f., 145 f., 149, 174, 177, 188, 253 f., 273, 292, 298-300, 304, 314-16, 325, 335, 339, 355, 615; as authority, 175; God, 100, 171; Master, 77; Messenger of good tidings, 111; Preserver, 175; Protector, 90; Savior, 187; Teacher, 89; His disciples, 97; His followers, 338; His friendships, 118; His heralds, 101; love of, 117; miracles of, 123, 338; name of, 125, 146; His powers, 114, 123 f., 146, 177, 338, 606; promises, 116, 124; teaching, 86, 128, 171, 287, 338, 607; works, 123
Christian, abhorrence of incense, 610; doctrine, 598; era, 275; faith, 3, 117, 121; God, 31, 306; literature, 10, 20, 34, 102, 251; meeting places, 10, 407, 586; predecessors, 41; race, 58; religion, 61, 192, 197; ritual, 586; structures, 586; teaching, 33, 519, 606; worship, 77, 566, 611; writers, 102, 407, 596, 610
Christianity, 2, 15 f., 26, 29, 33, 48, 125, 145, 248, 255 f., 274, 276, 287, 325, 340, 353, 449; expansion of, 20, 101, 117, 276, 311
Christians, 9, 200, 205, 273, 282, 300, 305, 347, 355, 395, 424, 452, 544, 566, 584 f., 608; charges against, 19, 58, 68, 192, 268; are innocent, 19; supposedly worship a human being, 46, 83
Christmas, 253, 613, 615
Christopher, J. P., 303 f.
chronology, 243
chronos, 47, 215, 303, 363
Chrysippus of Soli, 34, 122, 308, 398, 561
Chrysis, 476, 600
church, 28, 565; at Sicca, 17; in North Africa, 48
Cicero, M. Tullius, 23, 35-8, 40, 197, 205, 244, 251, 255, 258 f., 270, 273-6, 278-88, 290, 296-300, 307-9, 311, 314 f., 319, 326-31, 333 f., 338, 341, 343, 345, 347 f., 350-8, 360-9, 371 f., 544, 548, 550-3, 556, 562-4, 571 f., 574, 581, 583, 587, 590, 594 f., 598 f., 601 f., 606, 611, 613-7
Cicero, Quintus, 299
Cichorius, C., 368 f.
Cilo, 354
Cimbri, 544
Cincian laws, 180
Cincius Alimentus, L., 9, 35, 222, 244, 369
Cinxia, 212, 216, 360, 364, 462, 593
Cinyras, 396, 427, 458, 557, 575, 587
Circe, 385, 551

circus, 523, 527, 604, 614
Circus Maximus, 617
Cirta, 7
civilizations, decline of, 268
Claros, 280, 601
classicus, 323
Claudius, 571
clausulae, 24, 251
Cleanthes, 324
Clearchus, 589
Clement of Alexandria, 22, 37, 42, 51 f., 256, 261 f., 277, 552 f., 556, 558, 560, 567, 574-7, 580, 590, 596, 600 f.
 Protr. 40, 42, 48, 543, 552, 566, 585; 2. 11: 280; 2. 12: 574; 2. 13: 556; 2. 13: 575; 2. 14: 555; 2. 14: 575; 2. 15: 576; 2. 17: 576, 578; 2. 19: 575; 2. 21: 579; 2. 24: 282, 562, 569; 2. 27: 550; 2. 28: 551; 2. 29: 551 f., 557; 2. 30: 263, 556, 559; 2. 31: 556, 581; 2. 32: 560; 2. 33: 557, 560 f.; 2. 34: 581; 2. 35: 558; 2. 36: 555, 558 f.; 2. 37: 559 f.; 2. 39: 281, 560; 3. 42: 556; 3. 44: 586 f.; 3. 45: 588-90; 3. 46: 593; 4. 47: 557; 4. 52: 278, 299, 597, 599; 4. 53: 594 f., 600 f.; 4. 57: 599; 4. 60: 594; 5. 64: 307; 8: 249; 8. 77: 295; 9. 82: 331; 10: 313; 10. 110: 287; 12. 18: 289; *Strom.* 347; 1. 106: 562; 5. 1: 306; 5. 7: 354; 5. 14: 294, 355; 7. 4: 289; 7. 6: 610; *Paed.* 2. 113: 614; 3. 3: 329
Clement of Rome, 274, 565
Cleobis, 600
Cleochus, 457, 589
Clinton, H. F., 245
Clio, 368
Clitor, 398
Clodius Pulcher, P., 606, 613
Clytaemnestra, 285, 299, 344
cnisae, 605
Cochrane, C. N., 247
Cocytus, 127
Coelius Antipater, L., 616
coemptio, 553 f.
Colombo, S., 18, 41, 53, 243, 245 f., 249, 257, 260 f., 265, 267 f., 274 f., 282, 288, 292 f., 298, 304, 565, 606
Colonia Iulia Veneria Cirta Nova Sicca, 7
columen, 274, 330
comedies, 517, 605
comitia, 340 f.
Commodian, 28, 278
common sense, 180, 375, 545
"common source" theory, 43
communistic marriages, 111, 300
Complices, di, 223
conceit, 114, 116, 119, 125, 129, 132, 142, 175. See arrogance
Concordia, 543 f.
conditional immortality, 301
confarreatio, 553
coniectores, 278
conjecture, 132, 317
Consentes, 223
Conserentes, dii, 427, 574
conservation of matter, 333
Constantine, 8, 243, 247, 555
Constantinople, 596
Consualia, 359
consuls, 523, 528
Consus, 210, 359
controlled experiment, 20, 46, 301, 317
conventicula, 28, 565
conversion, converts, 26, 37, 48, 87, 253-5, 264, 287 f., 295, 354
Cook, A. B., 280, 344, 363, 555, 569, 584
Core, 589
1 Corinthians 3. 19: 252, 305; 8. 7: 345; 11. 8: 607
Cornelius Epicadus, 35, 297
Cornelius Labeo, 38, 40, 259 f., 314, 326, 336, 346, 348 358, 360 f., 363-7, 369 f., 544-6, 550, 553, 574, 585, 604, 608 f.
Cornelius Valerianus, 591
Cornificius Longus, 35, 222, 369
Coronis, 84, 284, 531
Corpus Hermeticum, 310, 315-7, 325
Cortona, 546
Corybantes, 371, 427 f., 575 f., 578

INDEX

Coryphasia, 386, 388
Coryphe, 388
Cos, 272, 583, 586
cosmetics, 154
Costa, G., 267
couches, 89 110, 375, 403, 515. See *lectisternia*
councils of gods, 187, 414, 421
Courcelle, P., 259
covetousness, 153
Coxe, A. C., 15, 41 f., 56, 246, 261 f., 275, 279, 296, 339, 566, 583
Coyle, E., 296
Crassus, 354
Crates of Athens, 368
Crates of Mallos, 34, 221, 368
Crates of Thebes, 368
Cratina, 464, 595
creation, 275, 327; of man, 119
Creator, 50, 129; creator of souls, 149, 168
credulity, of pagans, Christians, 118, 120, 122, 146 f. 304, 309, 465
Creon, 285
Crete, Cretans, 216, 357, 371, 385, 397
Crispus, 354
crocus, 106, 297
Croesus, 556
Croiset, A. and M., 558
Cronius, 34, 123, 293, 310 f.
Cronus, 47, 261 f.
Cross, 27, 293
Croton, 310
Crotonius, 310
Crucifixion, 9, 20, 84, 88, 100, 107, 113, 293, 295, 299
Crusius, O., 576
Cruttwell, C. T., 3, 15, 27, 30 f., 41, 239, 244 f., 247, 249 f., 253 f., 256, 261, 327
crux, 283
Ctesias, 34, 99, 273
cubula, 505
cumin, 26, 335
Cumont, F., 16, 240, 248, 260, 286, 288, 290, 304, 310, 314, 316, 326, 352, 550, 568, 570 f., 573, 575-7, 580, 592, 612

cumspolium, 505
Curetes, 224, 226, 371, 395
curia, 293, 405; *Iulia*, 352; of heaven, 352
curio maximus, 293
Cybele, 564, 568-73, 612 f., 615, 617. See Magna Mater, Mother of the Gods
cyceon, 346, 365, 434 f., 443, 579
Cyllene, 365
Cyprian, St., 12, 28, 41, 239, 246, 248, 251, 255, 349, 363, 610
    Ad Dem. 19, 41, 268 f., 271, 281, 598; *Ad Don.* 268, 564, 613 f.; *Ep.* 272; *Quod idola dii non sint* 278, 369 f., 551, 555, 558, 587; *Test.* 306.
Cyprus, 475, 562, 599
Cyrus, 99
Cythera, 555
Cytherea, 395

Dactyli, Idaean, 224
Daeira, 588
daemones, 31, 74, 257, 263, 278, 290, 320, 586
Dairas, 588
Dal Pane, F., 29, 255, 257 f., 260, 574
Dalechampius, J., 266
Daly, L. W., 365
Damigeron, 99, 294
Danae, 430, 516, 560, 576, 584, 588, 613
Danaus, 560
dance, 155
"dancer," 488, 523 f., 526, 528, 530, 605
Daniel 3: 602, 612
Daphne, 397, 560
Dardanus, 99, 186, 285, 294, 577
Day, the, 88
days of purification, 195, 349
Dea Mena, 364
Dea Syria, 286, 555
death, 128, 146; the enemy, 191
decemvirs, 405
Decharme, P., 259
Decian persecution, 610

declensions, 385
decline, cultural, 38
Decretum Gelasianum, 33 f., 51, 257
Deecke, W., 360
defilement, of sacred ground, 606
Degering, H., 305
Deianeira, 285, 564
deification, of abstract qualities, 21, 375, 543; of emperors, 299, 615; of harlots, 78, 281
deities, 148, 216; of first class, 132
De la Barre, R. L., 266
De Letter, P., 312
Delian, Apollo, 76, 457, 463, 589; archer, 393
delirare, 246
Delos, 84, 272, 280, 285, 589
Delphi, 556, 596, 600 f.
Delphic oracle, 269
Deluge, the, 10, 272, 417 f., 569, 571
Demeter, 285, 288, 562, 578, 580, 589. See Ceres
demigods, 188, 278, 324
Democritus of Abdera, 34, 122, 282, 333
demonology, 260, 315, 336
demons, 49, 91 f., 97, 102, 147, 315, 320, 324, 343, 349. See *daemones*
dendrophoroi, 570
deo commendo, 302
Desires, 212
Dessau, H., 242, 544, 587
Destroyer of death, Christ, 113, 300
Deubner, L., 325, 581
Deucalion, 272, 414, 417, 569
deus = divinus, 307
deus bonus, 302
deus magnus, 302
deus mihi reddet, 302 f.
deus primus, 349
Deus princeps, 279, 349
deus rex, 279
deus rex ac princeps, 279
Deus Summus, 615
deus videt, 302
deverticula, 313
devil, 550
di boni, 39
di Complices, 370
di Consentes, 223

di indigetes, 360
di inferi, 372
di laevi, 39
di minores, 33
di Novensiles, 223
di parentum, 615
di Penates, 223 f., 226
di superi, 372
diabolus, 264, 326
Diagoras of Melos, 282, 400, 562
dialecticians, 150
Diana, 80, 84, 115, 182, 208, 218, 284, 344, 356 f., 387, 389, 393, 400, 457, 462, 476, 478, 557, 577; three goddesses so called, 386. See Artemis
Diana Trivia, 366
Dicaearchus, 559
Dido, 361
Didyma, 589, 601
Didymaeum, 457
dies lustricus, 349
Diespiter, 182, 344, 391, 413, 428. See Jupiter
Digiti, 224, 226, 371
Dindymene, 406
Dio Cassius, 601
Diocletian, 2, 6, 8 f., 12 f., 240, 253, 264, 272, 275, 279 f., 299, 317, 563, 565
Diodorus Siculus, 273, 371, 554, 577, 581
Diogenes of Apollonia, 307
Diogenes Laertius, 289, 296, 324, 333, 562, 589
Diomedes, 297, 357
Diomedes, plains of, 377, 546
Dione, 84, 102, 285
Dionysiac cult, 584
Dionysius Cato, 307
Dionysius Exiguus, 244
Dionysius of Halicarnassus, 244, 296, 325, 340, 343, 366, 545, 574, 577, 580, 590, 614-6
Dionysius the younger, 49, 473, 554, 599
Dionysus, 269, 284, 289, 344, 352, 562, 575, 578, 581, 591, 600, 612; five gods so called, 386. See Liber
Dioscuri, 286, 393. See Castor

INDEX 633

Dis, 343, 396, 436, 440, 443, 447, 450, 455
Dis Manibus, 371
disciples, of Christ, 76, 97
disciplina Etrusca, 336, 343
Discord, 212, 360, 554
diseases, 157, 208, 210, 490
ditheism, 27, 253
divination, 210, 604
divine, attributes, 33; causes, 203; essence, 201, 214; power, 375, 462; right of kings, 271; substance, 144. See anger
Divine Savior, 335
diviner, 74, 76, 208, 278
divinity of Christ, 20, 335
divorce, 117, 213
divus, 110, 299
Dobschütz, E. von, 257
Docetism, 20, 108, 298, 615
Dodona, 280
Dodonian Jupiter, 476
Dölger, F. J., 260, 286, 290, 292, 297, 304, 342, 349, 555, 560 f., 563, 565, 567-9, 573, 575, 580, 583, 586, 594, 609
dogs, on Capitol, 473, 598
dogmatism, 20
dogs, in Capitols, 473; sacrificed, 396, 558, 607
Dolabella, 289
door, of death, 322; of life, 178; to ruin, 140; of piety, 115
Doris, 560
dormitiones, 612
Dossennus, 614
Drachmann, A. B., 282
dramatists, 405
dreams, 15, 17, 93, 120, 247; interpretation of, 278, 294
Drexler, W., 346, 570, 591, 613
drinking, 212
drought, 61, 66, 271, 453, 522
dualism, 330, 359
Duchesne, L., 241, 249, 260
duelles, 276
Dümmler, F., 288, 613
Duff, J. W., 305
Dufresnoy, N., 236

Dyer, T. H., 276
Dysaules, 433, 578 f.

earth, 217, 219, 274, 333, 414, 440, 442 f., 445 f., 503; fixity of, 366
earthquakes, 63, 476
Ebert, A., 256
Ebionitism, 615
ecclesia, 565. See church
Eccli. 21. 16: 338
economics, 275
Edelstein, E. J. and L., 281 f., 284, 288, 290, 292, 339, 346, 359, 552, 556, 599, 603, 608
Egeria, 409, 567
Egypt, Egyptian, 84, 125, 312, 458, 562; divinities, 46, 156, 286, 343, 384, 388; religion, 281; race, 385
Ehlers, W., 547
Eitrem, S., 344, 555, 570, 595, 610
Elamites, 312
Eleatics, 333
Electra, 431, 577
elements, 65, 163, 165, 167, 171, 274, 333
elephant, 87, 596; sacrifice, 607
Eleusinia, 435, 577
Eleusinian, goddesses, 589; mysteries, 432, 446, 577-9; precinct, 457
Eleusinium, 589
Eleusis, 433, 443, 457, 566, 578 f., 589
Eleutherae, 600
Elmenhorst, G., 245, 266, 281
eloquence, 196, 208, 365
Emmaus, 292
emotion, 71
Empedocles, 307
emperor worship, 4, 240, 269, 299, 340
Endymion, 398, 561
Engelmann, R., 588
Ennius, 35, 205, 297, 345, 354, 400, 556, 562
enthymemes, 104
Ephesians, 557
Ephesus, 476, 557, 600 f.
Ephialtes, 557
Ephorus, 34, 221, 367 f.

Epicadus, 107
Epicharmus, 34, 396
Epictetus, 34, 197, 258, 348
Epicurean, ethics, 324; physics, 334; theology, 324, 361
Epicureanism, 29, 37, 167, 255 f., 276, 279, 287, 304, 566, 586, 605
Epicureans, 35, 255, 325, 334, 351 f., 360
Epicurus, 27, 29, 122, 144, 256, 258, 282 f., 287, 296, 317, 324 f., 562
Epidaurus, 284, 357, 431, 618; Aesculapius of, 208, 597
epilepsy, 397
Epirus, 125, 280
Epistula ad Diogn., 315, 592
epulum Iovis, 612
equestrian rank, 549
Equity, goddess, 375
Er, 293
Erasmus, 240
Erato, 368, 602
Eratosthenes, 244, 367, 599
Erechtheus, 435, 588
Erechthidae, 579
Erichthonius, 457, 588
Eris, 360, 554
Ernstius, H., 266
errones, 278
Erythraean Sea, 611
Escher, J., 576
Escher, K., 588
esoteric, ceremonials, 127; learning, 91
Establisher, the, 193; of souls, 169
Estienne, H., 266
Eteocles and Polyneices, 361
eternity, 185; of fire, 405
ether, 216, 219
Ethiopia, Ethiopians, 84, 311 f., 456
Etna, 433, 443
Etruria, 173 f., 508, 570, 590 f.
Etrusca disciplina, 370
Etruscans, 223, 310, 343, 570; divination of, 337; teaching of, 223
Eubuleus, 433, 578 f.
Eucharist, 325
Eudemus of Rhodes, 308
Euhemerus, euhemerism, 34, 38, 48, 282, 287, 400, 430 f., 556, 562, 613
Eumolpidae, 433
Eumolpus, 433, 579, 588
Euphrates, 286
Euripides, 250, 257, 269, 344, 361, 516, 558, 560 f., 564, 584, 588
Europa, 430 f., 516, 555, 560, 576, 613
Eurydice, 576
Eurystheus, 564
Eurythemis, 613
Eusebius, 7, 10, 243 f., 248, 265, 565; *Chron.*, 273, 286; *De praep. Ev.*, 355, 363, 562, 589; *Hist. Eccl.* 245, 253, 272, 275, 310, 312 f., 374, 568
Euterpe, 368
Euxine, 569
Eve, 575
Evenus, 560
evil, 64, 66 f., 161, 164 f., 172, 310, 332; origin of, 65; powers of, 310
Evius, 437, 581
excitationes, 612
expiation, 565, 567
expiatory sacrifices, 336
exta, 610

Fabius, 398
Fabius Pictor, Q., 9, 35, 244, 458, 591, 616
fabula Atellana, 614
faith, 117, 121, 311. See belief
false gods, 380, 550
famines, 61, 275
fana, 278
fanatici, 278
fascia, 319
fatalism, 292
fate(s), 94, 208, 271, 274, 292, 299, 310, 356, 490, 506, 557, 606
Father, God the, 27, 253; of creation, 196; of things, 147, 193
Father Dis, 180
Father Jupiter, 182
Father Liber, 84, 89, 177
Fathers, the, 28
Fatua, 77, 281

INDEX 635

Fauna, 281
Fauna Fatua, 84
Faunus, 46, 77, 84, 184, 280, 284, 345, 356, 409, 411, 545
fear, 127; of Christ, 76; of soul's death, 16
Februa, 364
Februlius, 364
Februtis, 216, 364
Fehrenbach, E., 611
Fehrle, E., 283
Felicitas, St., 544
fendicae, 506
Fenta Fatua, 49, 427
feriae, 275
Feriae Latinae, 342
Ferguson, W. S., 260, 281, 326, 337
Ferrini, C., 271, 341, 553, 563, 579
Fescennine verses, 392, 554
Festugière, A. J., 23, 40 f., 51, 238, 250, 260 f., 293 f., 301, 309 f., 315-7, 320 f., 324-7, 331 f., 336 f., 372, 610
Festus, 319, 323, 341 f., 349, 365, 548, 561, 564, 611, 613 f.
fetials, 179, 341
fetish worship, 29, 87
Ffoulkes, E., 12, 246
fides, 309
Fides, 543
filiation, 327
Finkelstein, L., 353
fire, 121 f., 180, 208, 210, 216, 218, 272, 274, 307, 315, 333, 476, 601 f.; eternal, 405
Firmianus, 2, 240
Firmicus Maternus, 52, 241, 264 f., 281, 294, 329, 363, 365, 367, 551, 555, 557, 560 f., 574-7, 580-2, 592, 603, 606, 615
First Gospel, the, 311
First God, 185, 193; (pagan), 309
Fischer, C. T., 587
fitilla, 505
Flaccus, 35 f., 258, 364, 427, 574
flamen Dialis, 98, 293, 405, 528
Flamininus, C., 546
Flavius Arrianus, 348
Fletcher, W., 263
floods, 63, 66

Flora, 210, 281, 359, 516, 613
Floralia, 516
Florus, 553, 619
Fluonia, 363
Fluvionia, 216, 363
Foakes-Jackson, F. J., 23, 238, 250
Foerster, R., 578
follower of Christ, 49
Fons, 362
fons vitae, 338
Fontus, 215, 362
food, 604
Forculus, 548 f.
Fordicidia, 613
foreign divinities, 615 f.
forging of wills, 50
forgiveness, 407
Fornix of Lucilius, 119, 305
Fortuna, 177, 223, 226, 339
Fortuna Virginalis, 180, 342
Fortune, 477 f.
fortune tellers, 93
Forum Romanum, 272
Fotheringham, J. K., 243
Founder, God the, 198; of universe, 391
Fowler, H. W. and F. G., 597
Fowler, W. W., 281, 284, 293, 342, 617
Francke, K. B., 255, 321, 361
Frazer, J. G., 284, 286, 324, 346, 358, 363, 366, 371, 543, 557, 560 f., 567 f., 588, 601, 608, 612, 619
freedom of will, 176, 293, 315, 338
freemen, 505
Freppel, C. E., 15, 17, 23 f., 30, 42, 238 f., 245-51, 256, 261, 303, 344, 598
fretum, 106, 297
Friedlaender, P., 613
Fronto, 354
Frugiferius, 461, 592
Fulgentius, 367, 556
fullers, 203, 354
Funaioli, G., 296, 364, 591
Furies, 111, 212, 360, 437
Furtwängler, A., 285 f., 288

Gabarrou, F., 15, 18, 37, 41, 238, 241-3, 245, 247-9, 251 f., 254 f.,

257-9, 261, 271, 273, 276, 314, 319, 327, 331, 339, 343, 346, 352, 364, 545 f., 550, 553, 574, 586, 603-5
Gabinius, A., 186, 346, 613
Gaea, 283
Gaetuli, 70, 312
gain, 548
Galatia, Galatians, 125, 570
Galatians 2. 9: 274
Gall, R., 362
Galli, 89, 290, 426, 572 f.
Gallus, 416, 423, 570, 573
Gamaliel, 303
games, 382, 401, 561 f., 522, 524, 526, 604, 617
Ganymede, 450, 516, 560 f., 577, 613. See Catamitus
Garamantae, 276, 456, 587
Garden of Eden, 27
Gaul, Gauls, 70, 246, 290, 312, 598
geese, fed on the Capitol, 473, 598
Geffcken, J., 17, 25, 42, 240 f., 248, 251 f., 256 f., 260 f., 263, 290, 295, 332, 559, 561, 564, 597
Gehenna, 127, 315
Geiger, W., 588
Gelenius, S., 240, 265
Gellius, A., 280, 289, 297, 306, 323, 339, 342, 347, 351, 353, 365, 369, 372, 545, 570, 593, 599, 619
Gellius, Cn., 616
Gelon, 599
gender, among gods, 499; grammatical, 106, 351
Genesis 334; 1. 27: 607; 5: 345; 6-8: 272; 22: 583; 28. 18: 289; 31. 13: 289; 35. 14: 289
genii, 77, 224, 320, 342; of married couples, 180; of a city, 281; of hearths, 379
Genius Iovialis, 223, 226, 370
geometers, 133
geometry, 124, 132, 308, 343
Germans, 63, 275, 312
Gersdorf, E. G., 239
giants, 188
Gibb, J., and Montgomery W., 303
gifts of immortality, 148
Ginzel, F. K., 244

Giordani, P., 304 f.
Glabrio, 354
Glaucon, 336
γνῶσις θεοῦ, 325
Gnostic errors, 327
Gnostic influence, 27
Gnosticism, Gnostics, 27, 41, 254, 292, 298, 310, 314, 317, 325
God, 27, 47, 50, 77, 81, 86, 118, 128, 139, 148, 152, 154, 158, 163, 172, 177, 189, 197, 201, 205 f., 211, 238, 254, 257, 274, 276, 279, 282, 298, 313 f., 316, 318, 325, 329, 335, 338, 347, 351, 353, 598, 604, 606 f., 611; and virtues, 206; as witness, 115; hears, 206; sees, 206; invisible, 26; unknown, 81, 115; of Christians, 565; of the inner powers, 90; of salvation, 191; the Author, 158; Begetter, 128; Beginning, 115, 349; Chief, 35, 119, 148; Creator, 115, 156; creator of souls, 327, 329; the Father, 78 f., 102, 115, 128 f., 141, 148, 177; Father and Head, 157; Father of Souls, 158, 310; Founder, 115, 156; Head of the Universe, 172; Head of virtues, 157; the Head and Pillar, 79; Head and Fountain, 115, 185; Just, 157; Introducer, Master, Founder, 110; King, 156, 162, 175; King and Chief, 148; King of the Heavens, 211; King and Prince, 187, 194; King of the Universe, 151, 174; Liberator, 145; Lord of every power, 113; Master, 75, 138; Most Wise, 157; Parent of souls, 158; Ruler, 75, 100, 115; Ruler and Lord, 188; Salvation, 157; Sower, 156; Supreme, 82, 129, 159, 166; court of, 149; excellence of, 330; gifts of, 211; goodness of, 148; majesty of, 164; mercy of, 125; mind of, 187; modes of, 253; palace of, 173; Providence of, 607; shape of, 205; will of, 32, 148, 164, 174
Godhead, 193
god(s), goddess(es), 147, 198, 275, 351, passim; of agriculture, 288; of

INDEX 637

commerce, 284; of corn, 284; of healing, 284, 604, 616; of light by night, 372; of lightning, 284; of wine, 284; above, 375, 484; breathe, 510; buried, 440, 450; dying, 440; exiled, 58; artisans, 519; experts, 209; farmers, 207; flute players, 207; guitar players, 207; hired, 450; hunters, 207; in the air, 47, 224, 372; hatched from eggs, 84; in heaven, 507; incorporeal, 511; mechanics, 207; musicians, 207; of ill omen, 500; of lower world, 223; of streets, 224; on the left, 378, 546; physicians, 207; sailors, 207; shepherds, 207; soothsayers, 207; woolworkers, 207; wounded, 440, 450; servants of human beings, 47; anger of, 70 f., 200, 205, 220, 407, 424 f., 485 f., 520, 566; importation of, 522; marriages of, 392; names of, 385; sex of, 519
Godet, P., 242
Goethe, 578, 582
Goethert, F. W., 581
Goetz, G., 297, 369
gold, 160
golden apple, 428, 554
Gomperz, T., 308
good, angels, 336; demons, 326; Goddess, 84, 427; gods, 503, 608; luck, 503; men, 159 f.
Goodspeed, E. J., 265 f.
Gorgias of Leontini, 309
Gospels, 27, 49, 248, 253, 287, 290-2, 294
Gospel of Peter, 253, 291
grace, 30
Graillot, H., 346, 454, 568
grammar, 118, 132, 317
grammarians, 117, 133, 150, 297
Granius, 36, 216, 221 f., 364, 458
Granius Flaccus, 35, 258, 364
Granius Licinianus, 364
gratilla, 505
Great Jupiter, 523
Great Mother, 21, 89, 400, 406, 414, 418, 423, 516, 536, 572, 574, 613. See Cybele, Magna Mater
Great Mother (Earth), 217

Greece, 224, 436 f., 446, 464
greed, 153
Greek, language, 196, 251, 385, 427, 605; mysteries, 566; personal names, 5; philologists, 215; philosophers, 34; theology, 605; writers, 34
Greeks, 116, 224, 277, 434, 587, 594, 596, 603
Greene, W. C., 285
Greenidge, A. H. J., 341
Gregory Thaumaturgus, 315
Grillnberger, O., 321
Guinagh, K., 57, 266 f.
Gwatkin, H. W., 248 f., 252, 303, 311
Gyara, 272
gypsies, 602

Habel, P., 598
Hades, 283, 285, 558
Haffter, H., 270
Hagendahl, H., 24, 43, 55, 252, 256, 258, 261, 267, 288, 328
hair on dead, 424, 571
Halimuntian mysteries, 436, 580
Hall, G. N. L., 313
Halliday, W. R., 30, 256, 340
Halm, C., 7, 242, 262
Hammon, 463 f.
hangings, suicide, 213
Hannibal, 186, 346, 536 f., 546, 619
Hanslik, R., 368
Happiness (goddess), 375
harioli, 278
Harmony (goddess), 375
Harnack, A. von, 12, 243, 246, 295, 304, 311
Harrison, J. E., 569
Hartwell, K. E., 250
haruspices, 278, 337, 550
Hassett, M. M., 355
hasta caelibaris, 342
Haug, F., 285
Havet, L., 296
Haywood, R. M., 275
Head and Lord of the Universe, 32
head, bare and veiled in sacrifice, 226
Head of Universe, 159
healing, 94, 97
health, 544; of souls, 126

638 INDEX

Heaven, 149, 414
heavenly powers, 33
Hecate, 184, 215, 345, 362, 576, 607
Hector, 357
he-goat's milk, 422, 570
Heibges, S., 294
Heichelheim, F. M., 284, 361
Heinze, R., 45, 262, 597
Helbig, W., 583
Helen of Troy, 63, 273, 285, 344, 554
Helenus, 108, 298
Helios, 592
Helm, R., 243, 245
Hell, 164, 254
Hellespont, 199, 273, 352
Henna, 443
Hennian grove, 444
Hephaestus, 357, 551, 588
Heptapolis, 368
Hera, 216, 289, 554 f., 558, 562, 593
Heracles, 558-60. See Hercules
Heraclides Ponticus, 587
Heraclitus, 34, 121 f., 307 f., 437, 581
heralds = apostles, 125, 433
Heraldus, D., 244, 266, 279, 325, 361, 565
Herculaneum, 271
Hercules, 80, 84, 86, 89, 180, 182, 187, 196, 222, 285, 344, 369, 372, 406, 455, 558 f., 516, 564, 613; the six, 386; the Theban, 393
Hercules Furens of Euripides, 516, 613
heresy, 29, 33, 277
Herford, R. T., 353
Hermes, 284, 344, 365, 556, 594, 602, 603; Argeiphontes, 551. See Mercury
Hermes Trismegistus, 35, 126, 260, 313, 326
Hermesianax, 371
Hermetica, 260
hermetism, 39, 41, 301, 313, 328, 337, 610
Hermippus of Berytus, 34, 99, 258, 294

Herodotus, 37, 273, 317, 347, 368, 371, 552 f., 556, 589, 593, 600
Herodes Atticus, 599
heroes, 188, 224
heroic age, 508
Herostratus, 601
Herrmann, L., 312
Hesiod, 34, 221, 257, 365, 367 f., 555, 561
Hesione, 577
Hesperides, 428
Hestia, 366, 562
Hesychius, 275, 570, 579
hevia, 575
Hidén, K. J., 251, 619
Hiera, 272
hierophants, 433
Hieronymus, 34, 297, 559, 565
high priest, 339
Hild, J. A., 544 f., 615
Hildebrand, G. F., 56, 239, 305, 570 f.
Hillis, W. B., 578
Hippasus of Metapontum, 307
Hippo of Melos, 34, 282, 400, 562
Hippocoon, 397, 559
Hippolytus, St., 344, 560, 575
Hippothoe, 397, 560
hirae, 506 f.
hirciae, 505, 609
Hirsch, E. G., 353
Hirschfeld, O., 572
Hirtius, A., 10, 418, 571
Hirzel, R., 563
histories, 409, 427, 521
histrionics, 613
Höfer, O., 280, 344, 364, 569, 577, 581, 588
Hofmann, K., 610
Holm, B. J., 243
Holtsinger, H., 583
Holy Spirit, 313
Homer, 34, 257, 344, 371, 555, 557-9, 561, 554, 563, 577, 587, 602, 605
Homeric *Hymn to Demeter*, 589
homo = corpus, 51, 295, 298, 322
Honigmann, E., 590
Honor, Honos, 375, 541

INDEX 639

Hontheim, J., 254
Horace, 35, 258, 278, 288, 307, 325 f., 329, 342, 344, 350, 352, 358, 361, 372, 556, 564, 569, 587
horoscopy, 181
horse racing, 47, 91, 290, 525 f., 530
Horus, 84, 286
Hosius, C., 240, 259, 297
hostis, 314
household gods, 280
Hülsen, C., 313
human, depravity, 77; intercourse, 60; nature, 30; race, 163; sacrifice, 180, 567, 583; sin, 603; soul, 301
Humbert G., 549
humors, four, 328
Hyacinthus, 398, 561
Hyde, W. W., 242, 286, 370, 543, 545, 569, 578, 612
Hyginus, 272, 284, 344, 367, 371, 555, 559 f., 577, 583, 587, 596
Hylas, 398
Hyperboreans, 457, 589
Hyperiona, 385, 393
Hyperoche, 457, 589
Hypsipyle, 397, 560

Ia, 416
Iacchus, 199, 352
Ialysus, 385
Iamblichus, 289, 310, 313
Iasion, 398
Icaria, Icarians, 462, 593
Icarus, 593
Ida, Mt., 285, 598
Idaean Mother, 371, 446. See Cybele, Great Mother, Magna Mater
Idaei Dactyli, 371
idealism, 301, 354
idolatry, 87, 152
ignorance, 128, 165, 171; of pagans, 117
ilia, 506
Ilium, 223
images, 204, 452-480, 522, 585, 592, 596, 598, 603
Immaradus, 457
Immardus, 588
Immisch, O., 579, 581
immorality, 300

immortal gods, 148, 181, 277, 457, 460, 462, 493, 498, 512, 598
immortality, 115, 129, 146, 178, 286, 298, 361, 418; of the soul, 20, 30, 127 f., 139, 142, 147, 246, 249, 315, 323, 325
impassibility of God, 47, 277, 333, 485
imperator, 280, 302
impiety, 115 f., 282, 376, 452
imposters, 125
Inacchus, 286
Incarnation, 20, 27, 100, 107, 254, 287, 298, 347
incense, 22, 89, 189, 211, 240, 253, 412, 452, 454, 480, 483, 491, 507-9, 511, 520, 584 f., 604, 610 f.
incantations, 91, 99
India, Indians, 125, 311 f., 384, 400
indigetes, 21, 84, 110, 299
indigitamenta, 35, 284, 546-9
individua corpora, atoms, 333
ineffability of God, 206
infamy, 614
ingenitae infirmitatis vitium, 27
inhabitabiles, 270
inimicus, 314
initiations, 427, 446, 575
injustice, 376
innate, ideas, 82; perverseness of souls, 161
inner powers, 290
insanire, 269
insanus, 246
insomnia, 153
instinct, 321
intelligence, 137
intercessory prayers, 173, 310
intermediate character, of souls, 128, 144
interpreters of dreams, 74
interventionism, of gods, 167
Inuus, 210, 359
invidia, 306
Ionia, 280
Iphigenia, 442, 582 f.
Irenaeus, St., 28 f., 277, 312, 316, 338
iron, use of, 65
irony, 250

Isaac, 583
Isa. 2. 4: 274; 9. 2: 346
Isiac mysticism, 288
Isidore of Pelusium, 295
Isidore of Seville, 297, 353, 365 f.
Isis, 84, 186, 286, 346, 400, 476, 612
Itali, 395
Italy, 180, 186, 215, 536 f., 555, 557, 591
iter, itinerare, 371
ius fetiale, 341

Jacoby, F., 273, 287
Jairus, daughter of, 292
James, E. B., 325
James, M. R., 311
Janiculum, 44, 84, 215, 283, 351, 362
Janssen, H., 565
January, 362
Janus, 44, 84, 196, 214, 227, 283, 345, 478, 548 f., 602; Matutinus, 362
Jason, 551
jaws of death, 145; of Hell, 164
Jerome, St., 2, 4-6, 8, 12, 14, 18 f., 24, 34, 51, 53, 241, 243, 246, 248, 268
    Chron., 2, 7, 12, 16 f., 240, 311; *De vir. ill.*, 7; 36: 311; 79: 2, 240; 80: 2, 240; *Ep.* 53. 10: 295; 58. 10: 2, 249; 62. 2: 2, 252; 70. 2: 2, 240, 311; 133. 5. 1: 617; *Vita Hilar.* 20: 290
Jerusalem, 312
Jessen, J., 29, 255
Jessen, O., 352, 572, 581
jewelry, 154, 596
Jewish, attitude, 253; fables, 201; teaching, 315; writings, 353
Jews, 283, 312
Joannes Lydus, 362
John 1. 18: 26, 605; 2. 25: 292; 4: 292; 5. 3: 291; 5. 11 f.: 291; 6. 9: 292; 6. 35: 338; 6. 37: 338; 9. 1: 291; 10. 7-10: 339; 10. 9: 339; 11-12: 292; 14. 6: 339; 17. 3: 325
Jones, L. W., 24, 252
Jordan, Heinrich, 271
Jordan, Hermann, 245
Jordanes, 297

Juba, 369
Judaism, 276, 340
Judgment of Paris, 553 f.
Jülicher, A., 23, 250
Julianus, 99, 294
Julianus Pomerius, 268, 329
Julius Caesar, 299
Julius Capitolinus, 607, 614
Jullian, C., 548
Junius Philargyrius, 560
Juno, 31, 177, 182, 196, 215, 224, 360, 363 f., 393, 396, 455, 462, 476, 478, 555, 561, 590, 600, 602; Lucina, 200, 208, 210, 339, 352
Jupiter, 15, 21, 31, 47, 83, 182, 184, 187, 215 f., 220, 222-4, 279, 283 f., 293, 344 f., 357, 363, 368, 370, 385, 388 f., 393, 396-8, 400, 404, 406, 409-12, 414, 417-20, 424, 428-32, 438, 440, 442 f., 445, 450, 455, 464, 466, 473, 488 f., 501 f., 515 f., 524-7, 543, 551 f., 554, 558, 560, 567-9, 577, 590, 594, 600, 603, 612 f., 617; Best and Greatest, 82, 283; Capitolinus, 98, 293, 476; Dodonian, 76, 279; Elicius, 21, 409, 566 f.; Greatest, 392; Hammon, 464, 594; Latiaris, 342; Optimus Maximus, 512, 611; Praestes, 545; Trophonian, 76; anger of, 523; counsellors of, 370; mother of, 428; parents and grandparents of, 83
Justin Martyr, St., 28, 41, 277, 584
    Apol. 1. 6: 282; 1. 9: 592; 1. 13: 610; 1. 18: 315; 1. 30: 290; 1. 43 f.: 606; 1. 62: 607; 2. 4: 610; 2. 6: 606; *Dial. c. Tryph.* 5: 315; 102: 338; 127: 587
Justinian, 545
Juturna, 215, 362
Juvenal, 258 f., 281, 297, 300, 347, 549, 599, 606-8, 614

Kahl, W., 260, 336, 358, 361, 363, 367, 370, 550, 585, 608
Kaaba, 593
Kent, R. G., 609
Kern, O., 289, 299, 371, 578, 589

INDEX 641

Kettner, G., 22, 42, 250, 259-61, 336, 360, 550, 577, 581
Kiepert, H., 6, 242
King, J. E., 308
King of the Shades, Pluto, 433, 583
King of the Sea, Neptune, 463
3 Kings 18. 27: 546
Klebs, E., 289
Kleist, J. A., 244, 293, 315, 565
Klingmüller, 342
Klussmann, E., 29, 255, 287 f., 307
Knaack, G., 569, 574
knowledge, 30, 161, 165 f., 171; of God, 129
Koch, H., 251
Kock, P., 372, 547
Koffmane, G., 565
κοινή, 295
Kolbe, W., 581
Kroll, J., 260, 313, 327, 336, 610
Kroll, W., 39, 45, 260, 262, 267, 281, 286, 294, 298, 320, 358, 360, 363, 366, 544, 577, 581, 586, 590, 596 f., 599 f.
Kronos, 215, 363, 592
Krüger, G., 3, 239 f., 245, 255, 259
Kruse, H., 357
Kübler, B., 293, 323

Labeo, Cornelius, 39, 354 (see Cornelius Labeo)
Labriolle, P. de, 16, 20, 23, 41, 240, 245, 247 f., 249 f., 252 f., 255, 257, 259-61, 276, 352 f.
Lactantius, 2, 12-4, 28, 37 f., 42, 49-51, 238, 240, 243, 246, 250, 255, 259, 263, 271, 316, 553, 563, 579, 616, 618
  Div. inst. 13, 15, 291; 1. 2: 282, 562; 1. 5: 309, 364; 1. 6: 326; 1. 7: 366, 570; 1. 8: 351; 1. 9: 558-60; 1. 10: 554, 556, 558; 1. 11: 356, 551; 1. 11: 357; 1. 12: 363; 1. 13: 357, 555, 562; 1. 13: 362; 1. 16: 362; 1. 17: 242, 556, 558; 1. 18: 356; 1. 20: 281, 359, 367, 545, 547; 1. 21: 286, 343, 371; 1. 22: 247, 264, 550, 574; 1. 23: 345; 2. 2: 586; 2. 4: 264, 278, 352, 598 f., 607; 2. 5: 281, 367; 2. 6: 367; 2. 7: 618; 2. 8: 615 f.; 2. 9: 550; 2. 14: 247, 264, 326; 2. 17: 335; 3. 1: 268, 295; 3. 2: 331; 3. 11: 264; 3. 13: 314; 3. 17: 600; 3. 24: 270; 4. 10: 51, 298; 4. 15: 263, 291; 4. 16: 283; 4. 26: 292; 4. 27: 263, 293; 5. 1: 246; 5. 3: 263, 294; 5. 4: 268; 5. 5: 362, 555; 5. 8: 587; 5. 9: 264, 329; 5. 11: 565; 5. 13: 311; 5. 20: 281, 607; 5. 21: 278; 5. 22: 280; 6. 25: 610; 7. 1: 287; 7. 5: 328; 7. 12: 324; 7. 27: 617; *Epit.* 8: 570; 9: 556, 588; 10: 554; 12: 563; 13: 562; 21: 543; 58: 564; 67: 590; *De ira Dei* 7: 606; *De mort. pers.* 2: 244, 275; 12: 565; 19: 564; 34: 245; *De op. Dei* 247, 268, 353, 356
Lacus Curtius, 272
laeva numina, 360
Lafaye, G., 346, 362, 573
Laius, 561
Lammens, H., 593
Lampridius, 341, 564
Laodamia, 431, 577
Laodice, 457, 589
Laomedon, 396, 558
Lampsacus, 352
lapsi, 610
Laqueur, R., 367, 556, 568
Lares, 142, 224-26, 281, 323, 342, 371 f., 574; Grundules, 77, 280
Larcius Flavus, Sp., 616
Lardner, N., 245, 248
Larisa, 457, 588
Larvae, 224, 372
last day, the, 191
Latin, 24, 196, 385, 400, 608; Christian literature, 565
Latin cities, 580
Latin War, 616
Latinius, T., 616
Latinus, 184
Latium, 44, 362, 395, 555, 607
Latona, 182, 284, 344, 357, 393, 397, 431, 551, 577
Latourette, K. S., 311
latrones, 299, 303

INDEX

Latte, K., 544, 548, 569
laurai, 224, 371
Laurentia, 281
lavatio, 612
Laverna, 212, 360, 396, 556
law, laws, 119, 133; of censors, 180; of death, 164; of fate, 173; of mortality, 146, 168, 173, 509; of sacrifices, 499, 505; of Twelve Tables, 563
lawyers, 117
Lazarus, 292
Leaena, 281
Leandrius of Miletus, 34, 457
learning, process of, 138
Lebadia, 280
Lechat, H., 595
Leckelt, 31, 252 f., 256 f., 321
Leclercq, H., 242 f., 248, 355, 565
Leucophryenian Artemis, 589
Leucophryne, 457
Lécrivain, C., 329, 342, 553
lectisternia, 515, 612 f.
Leda, 182, 285, 344, 393, 430, 516, 555, 560, 576, 584, 613
Leemans, E. A., 310, 313
leges, 271; *annales*, 341; *sumptuariae*, 342
legitimation, liturgical form of, 580
Leigh, M., 256, 303
Lemnos, 395, 551
Lenormant, F., 578
LeNourry, N., 17, 29, 42, 245 f., 248, 251, 255-7, 259, 261, 293, 306 f., 321, 325, 329, 353, 565, 570, 591
Leon of Pella, 34, 400, 562
Leonard, W. E., 269, 287, 317 f., 322 f.
Leonhard, R., 341
leprosy, 291
Lernean hydra, 564
Lersch, L., 54
Lesbos, 556
"lesser gods," 31, 116, 163, 185
Leto, 84, 280, 284. See Latona
Leucas, 601
Leucippus, 282, 333, 560
Leucothea, 358

Lex Calpurnia de repetundis, 368
Lex Cincia, 341
Lex Cornelia, 52
Lex Falcidia et Sempronia, 52
Lex Iulia, 52, 563
Lex Papinia, 52
Lex Villia annalis, 341
libations, 211, 452
libel, 404
Libentina, 381, 548
Liber, 86, 182, 187, 218, 222, 227, 284, 366, 369, 389, 393, 400, 415, 428, 436 f., 446, 450 f., 463, 478, 501 f.; Eleutherius, 476; the Nysian, 436; the Semelian, 436
liber de mysteriis, 40, 567, 575 f., 580
liber de templis et simulacris, 585
Libera, 429, 443
liberal arts, 317
Libitina, 548
libri Acherontici, 35
Licinianus, 364
Liebenam, W., 341
Lietzmann, H., 313
life, after death, 331; eternal, 147
light, 120, 306; of life, 114
Lightfoot, J. B., 240
lightning, 412 f., 524, 531, 600
Lima, 381, 549, 561
limen, 548
Limentinus, 77, 280, 381, 383, 549 f.
Limi, 382, 549
Lindsay, W. M., 548, 555, 561, 567, 580, 610
lions, 355; sacrificed, 607
Lippold, G., 595 f.
Livius Andronicus, 296
Livy, 40, 271 f., 279 f., 284, 289 f., 297, 312, 340-2, 346, 351, 545, 567, 574, 580, 591, 598, 613, 616-9
Löfstedt, E., 24, 252, 339, 604
logic, 124, 317
logicians, 133
longavi, 505, 609
Longinus, 310
Lord, God, 126, 128, 172, 391, *passim*. See God
Lord's Prayer, the, 338

INDEX

Lorenz, T., 24, 251
"lost source" theory, 40
love, 212
Lubentia, 548
Lucan, 258, 288, 312 f., 341, 362, 594
Lucania, 272
Lucian, 21, 37, 587, 597, 605 f., 614
Lucilius, C., 119, 297, 305, 325, 353
Lucretia, 342
Lucretius Carus, T., 18, 24, 27, 29, 35, 37, 243, 246, 248, 251, 255, 258, 268-72, 275, 277 f., 282, 287 f., 291 f., 296 f., 302, 305-7, 309, 314, 316-9, 321-5, 327-9, 332-6, 340, 350-3, 358, 361, 363, 365 f., 371, 545, 548, 555, 564, 566, 587, 592, 596, 598, 600, 605, 608 f., 611, 615, 617, 619; muse of, 199
Lucrii, di, 381, 548
ludi Florenses, 613
ludi Megalenses, 613
ludi plebei, 612
ludi Romani, 612
ludi saeculares, 564
Ludwich, A., 578
Lugli, G., 355
Luke 1.74: 346; 4.13: 292; 4.18: 291; 4.41: 290; 5.12 f.: 291; 6.6-8: 291; 7.21 f.: 291; 7.22: 291; 7.22: 291; 8: 292; 8.2: 290; 8.23-5: 291; 8.26-33: 291; 8.26-39: 290; 8.43 f.: 291; 9.19: 293; 13.21: 291; 13.32: 290; 14.13: 291; 17.12: 291; 21.1-4: 606; 23.45: 295
Luna, 367
lupa, 545
Luperca, 376
Lupercalia, 545
Luperci, 545
Lupercus, 545
lust, 114
Lutatius Catulus, Q., 244
Lycaon, 395, 555, 562
Lycia, 367, 590
Lycophron, 576
Lydia, 415, 556
Lydians, 570

Lynceus, 394, 555
Lysidice, 560

Macar, 556
Macarius, 396
MacCulloch, J. A., 610
Maccus, 614
Macedonia, 64, 125
Macer, 354
Mackail, J. W., 239
Macrobius, 260, 284, 288, 343, 346, 349, 362-6, 369 f., 372, 555, 570, 574, 576, 581, 591, 602, 604 f., 616
macrocosm, 138
Maeander, 589
maena, 410, 414, 568
Magi, 63, 294, 310, 336 f.
magic, 49, 90, 97, 99, 263, 290
magical papyri, 41, 310
Magian, 90, 99
magicians, 93, 173 f., 384
magister, 280
magistracy, 382
magistrates, 405
magmenta, 506, 610
Magna Mater, 290, 365, 562, 564, 566, 571, 583, 604, 617, 619. See Cybele, Great Mother
Magna Mater Idaea, 614
Magnesia, Magnesians, 457, 589
Magnus, L., 308
Maia, 84, 182, 281, 284, 358, 385, 393, 463
Mainland, 587
Malcovati, E., 267
man, 119, 187, 320, 322; compared with animals, 129 f.
Man of Galilee, 287
mancipium, 322
Manes, 224, 371
Mania, 224, 372
Manilius, T., 222 f., 369
Manlius, T., 35
Mantinea, 595
Marathon, 596
Marbach, A., 367, 371
Marchesi, C., 27, 30, 33, 53, 55, 252-4, 256 f., 265, 287 f., 292, 350

Marcion, 29, 277
Marcionites, 29
Marcius, 108, 298
Marius, C., 323, 544
Mark 1. 40-42: 291; 2. 9-11: 291; 3. 1-3: 291; 4. 37-41: 291; 5: 292; 5. 1-16: 290; 5. 6-17: 291; 5. 25: 291; 6. 38: 292; 8. 23: 291; 9. 38: 293; 9. 46: 291; 10. 42 f.: 607; 12. 41-4: 606; 15. 38: 295; 16. 17: 292
Marpessa, 397, 560
marriage, violation of, 555; communistic, 111, 300
Mars, 47, 115, 179, 212, 299, 344, 361, 396, 398, 405, 448, 450 f., 455, 462, 464, 593 f. See Ares
Marsi, 145, 325
Marsyas of Pomponius, 119, 305
Martianus Capella, 281, 360, 364
Martial, 300, 362
Martius Picus, 409, 411
Martyrium Apollonii, 592
martyrs, 15
Marx, F., 305
Masson, J., 248, 282, 296, 306, 334, 336
mastruca, 319
Masurius Sabinus, 593
mathematics, 124, 137
matrimus, 618
Matt. 4. 16: 346; 5. 44: 26, 253, 273; 5. 49: 273; 6. 13: 338; 8. 2-3: 291; 8. 24-7: 291; 8. 28-33: 290 f.; 9. 6: 291; 9. 20: 291; 9. 27: 291; 10. 8: 291; 11. 5: 291; 12. 10: 291; 12. 22: 291; 14. 3: 291; 14. 17: 292; 14. 25-8: 292; 15. 30 f.: 291; 15. 30: 253; 15. 31: 291; 20. 30: 291; 21. 14: 291; 23. 23: 26, 607; 26. 6: 291; 27. 51: 295
Mattingly, H., 275
Matuta, 210
Mau, A., 352, 354
Mauri, 70, 312
Mavors, 464. See Mars
Maxentius, 8
Maximinus, 275
maximitas, 598
Maximus of Tyre, 38. 8: 593

McDermott, W. C., 356
McGiffert, A. C., 21, 27 f., 245 f., 249, 253 f., 298, 311, 330
Mecca, 593
Medea, 551
medicurrius, 365
medicine, 181
Medes, 125, 312
medium quality, of souls, 50, 264
Megaclo, 396, 556
Megalensia, 516, 614
Meiser, K., 619
Mela, 396, 557
Melanippe, 560
Meles, 557
Melesigénes, 557
Meletes, 357, 367 f.
Mellonia, 380, 383, 548, 550
Melpomene, 368
Memoria, 182, 216
memorialia scripta, 35, 593
memory, 216, 220
Meminerva, 216
Menalippe, 397, 560
Mencken, H. L., 251
Menerva, 364
Menippean satires, 601
Mens, 365, 367
merchants, Christian, 276
Mercury, 80, 84, 115, 177, 182, 187, 211, 217, 284, 344, 357 f., 365, 385, 389, 393, 396, 463, 478, 501-3, 554, 594, 603. See Hermes
Mercurius (Hermes Trismegistus), 126, 313
meretrices, 285
Merops, 454, 586
merum, 307
Mesnage, P. J., 242, 248
Mesopotamia, 312
Messalla, 570
Messenians, 386
Mestor, 560
metempsychosis, 317
Methodius of Olympus, 265
Metis, 216, 365, 367
Metrodorus, 34, 122
Meursius, J., 245, 266
Meyer, E., 273, 286, 346, 590
Michaelis, W., 550, 599

Index

Micka, E. F., 12-4, 25, 27 f., 30, 245-7, 249 f., 252-4, 256 f., 259, 261, 274, 276, 281 f., 287, 292 f., 298, 306, 317, 320 f., 326 f., 329-31, 333, 349, 352, 356, 585, 606
Mickwitz, G., 549
microcosm, 138, 320
Midas, 186, 416, 423, 570
Middle Academy, 35, 309
Miletus, 280, 457, 589
military assemblies, 179
militia, 304
militiae sacramenta, 303
Miller, J., 294
Milton, John, 250
milvus, 318
mimes, 516 f.
Mind, 220
Minerva, 86, 182, 196, 216, 224, 288, 357, 364, 387 f., 396, 400, 435, 451, 502 f., 551 f., 558 f., 590, 600, 608; five goddesses so called, 386, 388
Minervium, 588
Minos, 587
Minucius Felix, 12, 42, 44, 48, 51, 53, 246, 255, 261, 316, 347, 349, 584, 620
    Octavius 2: 274; 7: 616; 8: 282; 9: 355; 10: 585; 12: 276; 18: 303; 19: 352, 363; 21: 362, 369, 555, 562; 22: 363; 23: 559, 594, 599; 23: 45, 558, 563, 581, 592, 596; 24: 45, 242, 597; 25: 281, 359, 613; 26: 278, 330, 556; 27: 616; 28: 355, 592; 30: 343; 31: 313, 577; 32: 586; 34: 262, 314 f.; 36: 606; 37: 289
miracles, 188, 253, 263, 290, 326; of Christ, 15, 20, 45, 49, 80-2, 94, 101, 263, 290
misanthropes, 300
misfortune, 157, 490
Mithraeum, 592
Mithraic liturgies, 41, 310
Mithraism, 269, 304
Mnaseas, 220 f.; of Berytus, 367; of Patara, 34, 220 f., 367
Mneme, 367

Mnemosyne, 344, 357, 368, 561
modalism, 27, 253
moderator, 347
Modius, F., 54
Molignoni, G., 14, 247
momen, 323
Mommsen, T., 242, 616
Monceaux, P., 10 f., 16, 243, 245-9, 253, 255 f., 275, 287, 330, 565
monists, 333
monotheism, 46, 340, 356
Montinus, 382, 549
moon, 60, 79, 87, 208, 216, 218 f., 357, 398, 456, 461
Moors, 84, 286
Moricca, U., 10, 14, 16, 243, 245-9, 252, 256, 261, 330, 353
morning ditties, 515
mortal, the, 483
mortality, 72, 174, 201; of soul, 20, 30, 262, 301, 307, 314 f., 324 f., 331, 348
mos maiorum, 271, 613
Mosaic law, 605
Most High God, King, Ruler, 76 f., 90, 109, 177
Mother Ceres, 186
Mother Earth, 163, 502
Mother Nature, 131
Mother of the Gods, 420, 425 f., 462, 415-7, 478, 515, 537, 571 f. See Cybele, Magna Mater
Moule, H. C. G., 15-7, 245, 247 f., 252, 289, 347
Mras, K., 593
Mülleneisen, J., 259, 360, 370
Müller, C., 367
Münzer, F., 289, 369, 616
Mulciber, 478
mundus minor, 320
Munro, H. A. J., 316, 322
Murcia, 549
Murcida, 382
Murley, C., 300
Muses, 182, 208, 220 f., 227, 343 f., 357, 367, 396, 556, 561, 601
music, 124, 132, 155, 181, 403, 520, 563
musicians, 133, 150, 503

mutes, 137
Mutunus, 383, 549
Myrmidon, 398
Myron, 597
myrrh, 611
Myrsilus of Lesbos, 556
Myrtea, 549
Myrtilus, 34, 221, 368, 396
myrtle, 427
Mysia, 556
mysteries, 409, 414, 426, 435, 441, 446, 575; of the Egyptians, 203, 476
mysterium, 303
mythology, 543, 587
myths, 543

Nabuchodonosor, 612
Naenia, 548
Naevius, 297, 354
name(s), of Christ, 114; of angels, 91; of pagan gods, 194, 451
Nana, 415, 422
Nasica, 354
natural science, 404
nature, 19, 65, 74, 87
Nature of Things, 59, 218
natural law, 58
Nauck, A., 560 f.
Nawrath, A., 569
Neander, A., 15, 17, 247 f.
Nebridae, 447, 583
nebrizontes, 584
necessity, 484, 489 f.
Nectabis, 294
nectar, 277, 354
Neilous, 368
Neith, 388, 553
Nemesianus, 324
Nemestrinus, 380, 547
Nenia, 380
neniae, 505
neologisms, 251
neo-Platonism, 30, 41, 277, 301, 315, 337
Nepos, Cornelius, 244, 595
Nepotianus, 242
Neptune, 63, 177, 216, 223, 226, 273, 343, 356, 365, 369, 594. See Poseidon

Nereid, 398
Nereis, 561
Nereus, 560
Nessus, 285, 564
Nestle, W., 308
Nestorius, 298
nether deities, 608
Nettleship, H., 580
neutral character, of the soul, 144, 147, 164, 315, 330 f.
New Academy, 35
New Testament, 25 f., 248, 252, 274, 276, 296, 338
newness, of Christianity, 178; of pagan religion, 182
Newton, A. W., 25, 242, 245 f., 252
Nicagoras (Nicanor) of Cyprus, 34, 282, 400, 562
Nicomedia, 14, 51, 246
Niggetiet, F., 39, 260, 336
Nigidius Figulus, P., 35, 217, 223 f., 362, 366, 369
Nike, 365
Nile, 312, 385, 387
Nilsson, M. P., 578, 607
Niobe, 286, 344
Nisus, 35, 107, 297, 581
Nock, A. D., 16, 248, 314, 315
Noduterensis, 380, 383
Nodutis, 380
Nodutus, 547
Noe, 272
Nomads, 70
nomenclature, 354
nomina, 544, 552
Nonius, 317, 342, 353, 545, 580
Nonnus, 272
Norden, E., 3, 24, 239, 251
Norwood, F. A., 334
Novatian, 29, 277
Novatus, 2, 24, 34, 252
Novensiles, 221 f., 225-7, 284, 368 f.
novi viri, 301, 313, 316, 337
Novius, 614
Noyes, G. E., 296
Numa Pompilius, 21, 35, 125, 312, 343, 346, 351, 355, 409, 411, 413 f., 508, 566-8; religion of, 340
number, 121 f., 137, 139, 308, 322,

INDEX 647

343; of gods, 195, 198; of Muses, 221, 227, 357
Numenius, 34, 123, 293, 310 f., 313
Numicius, 84
Numidia, 6
numina, 39, 269, 359, 361, 544, 552
Numitor, 299
Nycteus, 584
Nyctimus, 555
Nysian plain, 285

Oceanus, 365, 552
Ocrisia, 574
Octavian, 299
Odysseus, 338, 551, 558
Oeagrus, 576
Oehler, F., 8, 15, 24, 56, 241, 244, 247, 251, 265-7, 270, 286, 292, 328, 565, 601
Oedipus legend, 361
Oenopia, 587
Oeta, Mt., 84, 285, 397, 559
offae penitae, 505, 507, 609 f.
Old Academy, 122
Old Testament, 25 f., 276 f., 338, 353, 585, 602
Olenus Calenus, 592
olive, 86
Olus, 459, 587 f., 591. See Aulus
Olus Vulcentanus, 458
Olympia, 595
Olympiads, 8, 243
Olympian, games, 596; Zeus, 217, 465, 468, 595-7
Olympias, 601
Olympus, Mt., 575, 598
omens, 179, 341, 410, 413, 458, 500, 547, 590 f.
omentum, 505, 507
Omnipotent God, King, Master, 83, 147, 482
omnipresence, of God, 82; of gods, 455
omophagia, 427, 575
Omphale, 558
one, element, 167; Father, 32; God, 31, 32, 384
Opigene, 364
Ops, 85, 182, 184, 216, 286, 363, 391

Optatus, 243
oracles, 58, 108, 134, 280, 357, 414, 616
Oracula Chaldaica, 39, 41, 260, 294, 301, 310, 337
oratio, 338
orators, 117, 133, 150, 566
oratory, 132, 208
Orbana (Orbona), 340, 548
Orcus, 332, 440
ordo salutationis, 327
Orelli, J. C., 21-3, 45, 56, 238 f., 244 f., 250, 267, 270, 279, 281, 290, 294, 311, 325, 328 f., 333, 335, 338, 347, 350, 352 f., 359, 365 f., 369, 547, 549, 556, 565, 568, 570, 574, 592, 604, 614 f.
Orestes, 347, 583
Origen, 2, 24, 29 f., 34, 249, 252, 277
  C. Cels. 42; 1.6: 294; 1.7: 314; 1.11: 307; 1.13: 306; 1.17: 577; 1.20: 281; 1.22: 290; 1.23: 344; 1.46: 293; 2.10: 303; 2.26: 295; 3.43: 551; 3.141: 363; 4.20: 274; 4.48: 563; 4.53: 311; 5.57: 311; 8.61: 588; 8.62: 563; *De Princ.* 4.26: 295; *In Gen. hom.* 15.1: 295; *In Iesu Nav. hom.* 8.1: 295
original sin, 27, 253, 292
Ornytus, 397, 559
Orosius, 272 f.
Orpheus, 371, 428, 434, 576, 579
Orphica, 35
Oscans, 364
Osiris, 85, 286, 561, 590
Ossilago, 364. See Ossipago, Ossipagina
Ossipagina, 216, 364
Ossipago, 364, 380, 548
Osthanes, 41, 294, 310, 330
Ostia, 592
Otto, A., 283, 316, 321, 345, 592
Otto, W., 281, 544
Otus, 557
Oudaan, J., 57
Ovid, 37, 258, 272, 284, 286, 290, 297, 322, 328, 330, 342, 346 f., 355, 357-9, 361 f., 366-8, 371,

554 f., 560-2, 567 f., 574, 577 f., 581, 583 f., 586 f., 594, 599, 602, 606-8, 611 f., 617-9

Pacuvius, 283
Paedagogium, 355
pagan, cults, 38, 240, 259, 340, 543; gods, 19, 21, 26, 31-3, 147, 189, 200, 249, 253 f., 257, 269, 282, 337, 350, 358, 375 f., 389, 413, 417, 424, 437, 452, 454, 459-60, 495, 521, 584, 586; gods do not exist, 31, 193, 349; gods formerly men, 85 (see euhemerism); ideas, 249; literature, 37, 246, 400, 553; mysteries, 21; offerings, 610; opponents, 31, 598, 605; philosophers, 20, 29, 123, 276, 354; priestlings, 19, 74; religions, 4, 115; rituals, 22, 74; sacrifices, 26, 58; theology, 519; views, 145; witnesses, 192, 214, 253
paganism, 257
pagans, 118, 120, 126, 305, 395, 407, 424, 438, 440, 544, 549
Palaemon, 358
Palatine Hill, 355, 372, 545, 570
Pales, 210, 223, 226, 356, 359, 370, 545
Pallas Athene, 386 f., 505, 559, 608-10. See Minerva
Palladia, 396, 557
Pamphylia, 312
Pamphylus, 99
Pan, 356
Panaetius, 34, 122, 308
Panchaean gums, 509
Panchaia, 611
Panda, 376, 545
Panda Cela, 545
pannychismus, 577
Pansa, C. Vibius, 418, 571
Pantaenus, 311
Pantarces, 465, 595 f.
Pantica, 376 f.
pantomimists, 405
Panyassis, 34, 396, 558
Paphus, 458
Pappus, 614
1 Par. 13. 8 and 16. 5: 602

paralysis, 92, 94, 98, 109
paraphernalia, 91
parentalia, 521, 615
paries, 105, 296
Paris, 273, 558
Paris, P., 595
Parke, H. W., 269
Parmenides, 307, 333
Parthians, 125, 312
Pascal, 256, 303, 307
Passeratius, J., 266
passio, 277, 322
passions, 71, 125, 407, 453
passivum, 322
Patelana, 380, 547
Patella, 380
paterfamilias, 616
pathos, 322
pati, 322
patibulum, 283, 289
patrician, 142
patrician-plebeian controversy, 323
patrimus, 401 f., 563, 618
Patrocles the Thurine, 34, 397, 559
Patroclus, 357
Paul, St., 274, 298
Pauline Epistles, 292
Paulus, 548, 563 f.
Pausanias, 285, 367, 555, 557, 569, 573, 578 f., 588 f., 595 f., 601
Pavor, 281
Pavores, 77
Pax, 543 f.
Peace (goddess), 375, 407
peace, 65, 407
Pearson, A. C., 560 f.
Pecunia, 382, 549
Peleus, 554, 561
Pellonia, 377, 545 f.
Peloponnesus, 84, 286, 555, 595
Pelops, 344, 396, 398, 557, 561
Penates, 223, 225 f., 369
Penelope, 342
Pentecost, 253, 264, 292
Perdrizet, P., 613
perfection, 128; of souls, 149
Perfica, 380, 383, 547, 549
Pergamum, 619
Peripatetics, 122, 282, 308, 559

INDEX 649

persecution(s), 3, 8, 10, 16 f., 76, 102, 111 f., 114, 189 f., 220, 243, 245, 253, 273, 279, 295, 300, 340, 348, 407, 437, 480, 553, 565, 594, 610; of Diocletian, 304
Persephone, 285, 289, 366, 589
Perseus, 560, 588
Persian Wars, 273
Persians, 70, 125, 384, 462, 593, 596
Pertunda, 380, 383, 547, 549
perturbatio, 277
Pessinus, 346, 406, 416 f., 462, 536 f., 619
pestilence, 61, 522, 604
Peta, 380
petasus, 594
Peter, St., 125, 274
1 Peter 2. 17: 607; 3. 9: 26, 273
Peter, H., 244, 368, 567, 571, 591, 616
Peter, R., 280, 284 f., 360, 364, 372, 544, 547 f., 549
Pétridès, S., 241 f.
Petronius, 297
Pfaff, K., 599, 614
Phaedra, 361
Phaethon, 272, 398, 449, 561, 584
Phaon, 561
Pharisees, 353
Phidias, 288, 465, 595-7
Philemon, 562
Philebus, 338
Philipp, H., 325, 580
Phil. 12. 26: 274
Philippson, R., 296
Philochorus, 559
Philodemus, 296
Philopator, 458
philosophers, 66, 117, 161, 163, 174, 301, 313, 330, 333, 606; beards of, 474, 599
philosophical, investigations, 166; questions, 174; suffering, 324
philosophy, 87, 105, 126, 144, 181, 219, 247; failure of, 15
Philostephanus, 34, 475, 599
Philostratus, 294
phlegm, 149, 328
Phoenicians, 6
Phoenix, 576

Phoroneus, 286, 454, 586
Phrygia, 312, 317, 414, 428, 449, 536 f., 565, 569, 604
Phrygian, cults, 566, 573; goddess, 617; Mother, 186, 538
Phrygians, 125, 346, 415, 570, 572
Phryne, 464 f., 595
physicians, 95, 117, 121, 333, 503
Pichou, R., 330
Pico della Mirandola, 247
Picus, 46, 184, 345
Pierides, 357, 368
Pieriae, 357, 368
Pierus, 357
Pietas, 544
Pietschmann, R., 590, 603
piety, filial, 431; goddess, 375, 488
pignus, 347
pileum, 106, 297
Pindar, 34, 36, 263, 313, 357, 371, 395, 561, 588
pine, sacred, 417, 425 f., 446, 570
pirates, 476, 607
Piso, 186, 221 f., 346
Pithoeus, F., 266
pius, 544
place and space, 80, 169, 282
plagiarism, 48
plague, 272, 275, 523 f., 535
plasea, 505, 507
Platner, S. B., and Ashby, T., 272, 283, 290, 305, 352, 370, 544, 600, 615, 617
Plato, 20, 34, 37, 63, 66, 120-3, 126 f., 134, 137, 146, 148, 163, 176, 245, 258, 272, 274, 278, 288 f., 290, 293 f., 300 f., 306, 308, 310, 313, 315 f., 317, 318, 320, 324, 326 f., 331, 333 f., 336, 338, 343, 363, 366 f., 388; his doctrine of recollection, 137, 301; theory of ideas, 308
Platonic, argument, 321; bowl, 163; dialogue, 345; forms, 319; idea, 322
Platonists, 313 f.
Plautus, 251, 283, 297, 299, 328, 353, 371, 516, 548, 561, 564, 594, 613
pleasure, 484; in misfortune, 347
plebs, 349

Pleiades, 284
Pleione, 284, 560
Pliny the Elder, 270-2, 275, 279, 280 f., 294, 297, 325, 329, 340, 342, 347, 351, 353, 369, 548, 563 f., 574, 580, 584, 591 f., 611, 618 f.
Pliny the Younger, 566
Plotinus, 41, 257, 310, 317, 320, 323-5
Plumpe, J. C., 252 f., 271, 299, 339, 348, 354, 571, 575, 596, 601, 605
Plutarch, 34, 244, 255, 259, 288 f., 342, 351, 363, 371, 397, 559, 562, 564, 567 f., 574, 591, 595, 598, 601, 615 f., 618
Pluto, 255, 343, 365
poets, 133, 150, 200, 278, 402, 404, 409, 416
Pohlenz, M., 14, 247, 277, 320, 326
Polemon, 34, 396, 558
Polias, 457
polimina, 505, 609
Pollux, 84, 285, 344, 369, 559
Polybius, 7, 9, 242, 341, 602
Polyhymnia, 368
polytheism, 287, 356
Pomana, 216, 364
Pompeii, 271, 354
Pompey, 601
Pompilius, 180, 186, 204, 343. See Numa
Pomponius, 35, 119, 305, 614
Pomponius Atticus, T., 244
Pomponius Mela, 285
pontifex, 339, 570
pontifex maxiums, 98, 293, 528
pontificium, 339
Pontus, 272, 312
Pope Gelasius I, 34
Poppaeus Habitus, Cn., 354
popular assemblies, 179
Populonia, 216, 364
Porcius Cato, M., 9, 244, 355
Porphyry, 39, 260, 310, 315, 326, 336, 564, 605
Porta Viminalis, 548
portents, 453
Portunus, 356, 358
Poseidon, 283, 288, 558, 560-2, 579, 594, 597. See Neptune

Poseidon Σεισίχθων, 365
Posidippus, 34, 464, 475, 595, 600
postilio, 562
potestas principalis, 327
Potter, Archb., 561
Pottier, E., 544
Potua, 212, 360
powers, 188
praecones, 295
praeses, 290
praesiciae, 507, 610
Praestana, 376 f., 545
praesul, 605 f., 616
praeteritio, 574
Praxiteles, 464, 595, 597
prayer(s), 75 f., 84, 121, 193, 196, 198, 282, 372, 407, 455-7, 468 f., 489, 565; for the dead, 28, 565; for rulers, 565; in time of war, 606; pagan, 215
Preller, L., and Robert C., 280, 360, 570, 579, 584, 594
presbyter, 18, 249, 264
pre-existence, of Christ, 27; of soul, 321
Priam, 298
Priapus, 478, 603, 607
price control, 275 f.
priests, 199, 405, 564
primal Head, 193
primary, classes in school, 139; causes, 121; divinities, 309
primus, 256
princeps, 256, 279
princeps deus, 294
principale caput, 279
principalis rex, 279
primitive man, 340
prisons, 156, 190, 347
Procles, 593
Procksch, A., 360
Procreator, 80
prodigies, 453, 590
prolepsis, 283
proles, 323
proletariat, the, 142
proletarii, 323
Propertius, 297, 342, 576
prophecy, 25; pagan, 118
prophet(s), 278, 298

INDEX

proscription, 110, 299, 446, 583
Proserpina, 84, 218, 285, 366, 385, 398, 429, 433, 440, 444 f., 447, 501, 559, 561, 578, 580, 582 f., 589
prosicia, 610
Prosumnus, 436 f.
Protagoras, 282, 306, 334
Prothoe, 397, 560
Prov. 13. 14: 338; 14. 27: 338; 16. 22: 338
Providence, 254
provinces, 125
Prudentius, *Ap*. 250: 599; 402 f.: 280; *C. Symmach.* 340; *De Cor.* 10. 655: 302; 10. 157: 619
Ps. 32. 2: 602; 35. 10: 338; 56. 9: 602
psalteries, 478 f.
Psammetichus, 47, 317
Ps.-Barnabas 5. 9: 293
Ps.-Clement of Rome, 29, 277
  Recog. 10. 20-3: 554; 10. 29: 563; 10. 163: 582
Ps.-Cyprian, *De Spect.* 613
Ps.-Justin, *Cohort. ad Gent.* 35 f.: 249
Ps.-Peter, 291, 298
Ps.-Tertullian, *De execrandis gentium diis*, 52
pseudo-deities, 384
psychology, 283; of *Adversus nationes*, 12
Psylli, 145, 325
Ptolemy Philopator, 590
Ptolemaeus of Megalopolis, 35, 458, 590
Pudicitia, 543
Puech, A., 243
Puech, H. C., 293
pulvinaria, 612
punishment, 118, 173; after death, 324
purchase, marriage by, 392
purification, 515; of the earth, 66
purity, of souls, 151
Puta, 380
Pygmalion, 475, 599
Pyriphlegethon, 127
Pyrrha, 272, 414, 417 f.

Pyrrhonism, 21
Pythagoras, 35, 88, 121 f., 126, 134, 289, 308, 310, 313
Pythagoreans, 289, 313, 366
Pythagorean theorem, 319

quadrivium, 317
quacks, 145
Quaestiones, 52
Quasten, J., 563, 602, 612, 618
quindecimvirs, 405, 564, 612
Quintilian, 296
Quirinus, 290, 376, 545, 593
Quirites, 377
Quispel, G., 245, 256
quod deus dederit, 302

Raemers, S., 245
rain, 418, 440, 442 f., 445
Rand, E. K., 3, 15, 17, 239, 242, 245, 256
Rapisarda, E., 4, 17, 27, 29, 43, 51 f., 238 f., 245, 248 f., 251-8, 260-2, 264-5, 273, 277, 288, 292, 298, 301, 303, 307, 313 f., 316 f., 320, 326-8, 330, 332, 335, 341, 344, 349, 358-60, 368, 543 f., 548, 584, 586 f., 596, 605, 609, 611
Rapson, E. J., 312
ratio, 338
rational function, 137
rationalism, 30
Rauschen-Altaner, 246
Ravilla, 354
realism, 356
reason, 64, 130, 147, 174, 219, 309, 338, 488, 512
Reate, 601
recognition, of infants, 307
recollection, 133, 135, 139 f., 319
Redemption, 27, 292
Regulus, 89, 534
Reid, J. S., 296, 334, 336
Reifferscheid, A., 25, 53 f., 241, 252, 265-7, 273, 280, 343
Reinach, S., 573, 592, 594 f., 602 f.
Reisch, E., 583
Reitzenstein, R., 337
religion, true, 115 f.

652   INDEX

reminiscentia, 317
Remus, 545
renewal of things, 66
repetentia, 321
rerum dominus, 328
rerum princeps, 279
res, 295
Resurrection, 27, 93, 254, 292
resurrection of the dead, 93, 98, 109, 126
retorsion, 45
Rex mundi, 328
Rex poli, 360
Rex summus, 347
Reynders, B., 261
Rhadamanthus, 587
Rhea Silvia, 283, 285, 299, 562
rhetor, 255, 264, 269, 275, 295, 307, 566
rhetoric, 6, 13 f., 20, 23, 118, 124, 240 f., 317
rhetorical, display, 105; questions, 24
rhetoricians, 38, 117, 304
Rhinthon, 35
Rhodes, 272, 385
Rhodia, 368
Richard, M., 249
Richardson, E. C., 266
Richter, F., 284
ricinium, 602
Rigault, N., 266
Riese, A., 601
Riess, E., 294
ritualistic perfection, 226
rituals, 401, 603
Robert, C., 280. See Preller-Robert
Robigo, 549
Robigus, 549
Robiou, F., 603
Röhricht, A., 29, 37, 43, 256, 258, 260 f., 273, 306, 313 f., 319, 326 f., 331 f., 338, 343, 360 f., 367, 543, 545, 550 f., 553, 556-60, 562, 566, 575-8, 581, 585-6, 591, 593 f., 595, 597, 599 f., 609
Rössler, C. F., 267
rogi, 607
Rohde, E., 578
Rohden, P. v., 616

Roman, citizen, 275, 546; citizenship, 580; conquests, 64; cults, 42; domination, 398; government, 246, 610; law, 553; people, 418, 534; race, 196; religion, 284, 286, 340, 360, 567; respect for ancestral institutions, 46
Romans, 46, 70, 222, 241 f., 313, 375, 377, 462, 543 f., 563, 583, 587, 590, 594, 603, 613
Romans 2. 19: 346; 12. 17: 26, 273
Rome, 125, 184, 204, 244, 272, 330, 342, 346, 355, 357, 362, 458 f., 523, 534-6, 544-6, 548, 557, 580, 590, 592, 600 f., 604, 614 f., 617 f.; age of, 184
Romulus, 89, 180, 204, 222, 376, 508, 545; Quirinus, 369
Romulus and Remus, 376
Roscher, W., 278, 283, 352, 360, 362, 364, 370, 544, 569, 577, 588, 613
Rose, H. J., 619
Rose, V., 550
Ross, W. D., 308
Rossbach, O., 599
Rostovtzeff, M. I., 275
royal, courts, 149; families, 193
rudes, 354
Ruge, W., 346, 570, 589
Ruler of creation, 128
rumae, 506
rumen, 610
runaway slaves, 278

Sabaeus, F., 54, 239, 264-6
Sabazian mysteries, 428, 576
Sabazios, 576
Sabellians, 364
Sabines, 221, 377, 545
sacramenta, 271, 303; *militiae*, 304
Sacraments, 28, 325
sacred, areas, 375; bull, 590; ceremonies, 456; doctrines of Christianity, 117; grits, 508; grooves, 488; mysteries, 427, 440; rites, 493; stone, 617
sacrifices, 193, 338, 401 f., 452-4, 460, 467, 480-539, 582, 586, 604

Index   653

f., 605, 609
sacrificial rites, 412
sacrilege, *sacrilegium*, 432, 599
Sadducees, 201, 353
safety, 375, 544
Saglio, E., 317, 544, 613
sailing, 66
Salamis, 578
salinum, 342
Salmasius, C., 241, 266, 566
Sallust, 251, 297, 328
salted meal, 211, 412, 452, 584, 611
Salus, 300, 544
salutaria, 302
salutaris militiae sacramenta deponere, 304
Salvation, 113, 115, 117, 148, 178 f., 300
salvation of soul, 333
salvator, Christ, 346
Salvatorelli, C., 17, 238, 248 f., 257
sambuca, 329
Sammonicus, Q. Serenus, 261, 458, 585, 588, 591
Samnites, 546
Samos, 593
Samothrace, 224, 226, 607
Samter, E., 293, 341
Sandbach, F. H., 243
Sangarius, 415, 422, 569, 573
Santee, F. L., 291, 571
Sarapis, 597, 600. See Serapis
Sardis, 396, 558
Sarmatians, 312
Sarpedon, 577
Sahara Desert, 587
Saturn, Saturnus, 44, 46, 84, 180, 182, 184, 196, 214-7, 284, 286, 345, 357, 362 f., 372, 382, 385 f., 391, 393, 395, 397, 412, 463, 478, 549, 555, 562, 602
Saturnia, 362
Saturnian state, 84
satyrs, 450, 560
Savior, 100, 188, 300
Schaff, P., 17, 245, 248, 252, 254, 256 f.; and Wace, 311
Schanz, M., and Hosius C., 240, 259, 297, 305, 567, 574, 587, 614

Scharnagl, J., 241, 251, 271, 277, 295, 299, 317, 355, 361
Scherling, K., 557
Schiff, A., 578
Schirmer, 589
Schmalz, J. H., 251
Schmid, B., 246
Schmidt, E., 618
Schmidt, M., 577
Schmitz, L., 569
Schoeffer, V. von, 589
Schoenemann, K. T. G., 245
scholars, 144, 499
schools, 126
Schneider, K., 281
Schullian, D. M., 242
Schultz, 578
Schultze, E. F., 3, 239
Schur, W., 280, 284, 549
Schwartz, E., 367
Schwenn, F., 288, 346, 567, 569
Schwentner, E., 296
science, 118
scientific questions, 120, 135 f., 150, 169 f., 172, 187, 334
scioli, 310
Scipio Nasica, 571
Scoon, R., 308
Scott, W., 260, 315, 326, 337
Scripture, 15, 25, 28, 248, 252, 276, 295, 306, 339, 565
scripulum, 601
Scriverius, P., 266
Scythians, 63, 70, 312, 462, 593, 607
seasons, 60, 334
seats of blessedness, 149; of gods, 470 f.
Sebadia, 430
Second Coming of Christ, 289
Second Creator God, 327
Second Samnite War, 546
Second Punic War, 346, 604, 617, 619
secta, 313
seduction, 91
Seeliger, K., 555
seers, 74, 522, 524
Seleucid dynasty, 599
seliquastrum, 319

sella, 106, 296
Semele, 84, 182, 218, 284, 344, 366, 393, 450, 554, 581
Senate, 180, 197, 351, 404 f.
senatus consulta, 563
Seneca, 255, 270, 277, 333, 369, 587, 611
Sententia episcoporum LXXXVII de haereticis baptizandis, 248
Septimius Severus, 591
Serapis, 84, 186, 346, 400, 476, 612. See Sarapis
Serenus Sammonicus, Q., 35
Seres, 125, 312, 456
Sermon on the Mount, 292
serpents, 68, 145, 531 f., 618
Servin, L., 266
Servius, 284, 288, 297, 334, 336, 363, 369-72, 549, 591, 604
Servius Tullius, 340, 343, 574
Seth, 286, 355
Seventh Council of Carthage, 17
sex, 21, 197; of gods, 196
Sextus Clodius, 34, 49, 427, 550, 574
Sextus Empiricus, 562
Sextus Pomponius, 305
Shahan, T. J., 256
shape, of gods, 204
Shetland Islands, 587
shipwrecks, 210
Shorey, P., 306
shrines, 375, 452, 458, 507 f., 535, 584, 586
Sibyl, 108, 264, 298
Sibylline books, 564, 616, 619
Sicca, 2, 6, 13, 53, 240-2, 276
Sicels, 6
Sicily, 272, 397, 562, 578
Sichar, 292
signa spirantia, 597
signaculum, 304
Sihler, E. G., 17, 23, 36, 245, 248, 251, 258, 300, 348, 565
silicernia, 263, 505, 609
Silius Italicus, 359
Simo, 354
Simon Magus, 125, 294, 313
simony, 313

simple, the, 140
sin, 292
" single-source " theory, 40
sinister gods, 21, 503, 543
Sisyphus, 559
skepticism, 21, 122, 282, 309
slave(s), 117, 137, 278, 523, 526, 604
sleep, 120
slumber songs, 515
Sminthian mice, 218
Smith, S. B., 267, 269, 287
Smyrna, 557
snake charmers, 325
snakes, 63, 272, 393, 427, 536, 554, 575, 579, 618
Socrates, 88, 119, 289, 300, 306, 319, 338, 352, 446, 583, 595
Sol, 363, 367. See sun
soldiers, 109
solecisms, 104, 106
Solinus, 244
Solon, 245, 272
soothsayers, 74, 93, 108, 112, 210, 276, 279, 300, 383 f., 522, 524, 534, 590 f.
Sophocles, 34, 396, 406, 516, 559-61, 564, 594, 616
sorcerers, 602
Sosibius, 35, 397, 559
sospitator, Christ, 346
soul(s), 50, 120 f., 126, 192, 260, 309, 318, 331; of the universe, 163; divine, 132, 135, 151; immortal, 135, 137, 142, 161, 168; of dead, 224; of wicked, 130; subject to pain, 127
Source of things, 83
Souter, A., 267, 313
sovereigns, 193
Sower of ages and seasons, 83
Spain, 70, 84, 312
Sparta, 396 f., 559
spearhead auspices, 179
species, 119
speech, 217
spelt, 434
Spes, 543
Spindler, P., 251, 258, 285

INDEX

spirits, of the dead, 371
spontaneous generation, 306
springs, worship of, 288
Stabiae, 271
Stace, W. T., 307
Stählin, C., 551, 589
Stahl, W. H., 259
Stange, C., 24, 251
Starnes, D. T., 296
stars, 219, 414, 456
statues, 204, 322, 464, 470, 522, 557, 592, 596 f.; on columns, 615
statuettes, 462
Stengel, P., 578
Stentor, 347
Stenzel, 282
Stepanich, M. F., 345
Sterope, 397, 560
Stertinius Avitus, 300
Steuding, H., 284, 359 f., 362, 365, 371 f., 544, 572
Stewechius, G., 54, 266
Stobaeus, 310, 324
Stöckl, A., 256
Stoicism, 29 f., 249, 276, 309, 324, 332, 336, 361
Stoics, 255, 277, 306, 333 f., 348, 606
Stoll, H. W., 344, 554, 576 f., 579
stones, power of, 294; worship of, 288
Strack, H. L., and Billerbeck, P., 253
stragula, 318
Strato of Lampsacus, 308
straying, the, 186
strebula, 610
strophium, 318
στῦλοι, 274
stupidus, 614
Styx, 127, 437
Suetonius, 299
suffering, 140
suicide, 213, 361
Suidas, 289, 556, 593
Sulla, 446
Sulpicius Camerinus, Q., 616
Summanus, 227, 362, 445, 455, 583
Summus Deus, 565
Summus Rex ac Princeps, 279 f.

sumptuary laws, 46
sun, Sun, 60, 79, 87, 100, 163, 215, 218 f., 378, 385 f., 389, 393, 449, 455 f., 461, 463, 592; reversal of, 126
sun-god, 362, 594
superior demons, 326
superstition, 508
Supreme, the, 147; Being, 148, 159; Benevolence, 175; Deity, 155; God, 142, 163-5, 172 f., 176, 193, 407, 519; King, 32, 149, 169, 189, 454; King and Prince, 196; Power, 149; Ruler, 145
suspicio, 317
Svennung, J., 270
swallows, 597, 601
swan, 394, 450
Swete, H. B., 239
Sybel, L. von, 371, 563
Sychowski, S. von, 243
σύγκρισις, 317
syllogisms, 104
symphoniae, 514, 612
Syncellus, 244
synonyms, 22, 250
Syria, 70, 125, 276, 599
Syrtis Major, 325

tabula rasa, 20, 318
Tacitus, 272, 279, 297, 350, 359, 587
taedae, 505, 609
Tages the Etruscan, 35, 181, 336, 341
Tanaquil, 574
Tangiers, 276
Tarentine poet, 35, 265, 430
Tarn, W. W., 281
Tarpeia, 545
Tarpeian Hill, 590
Tarpeian Rock, 377, 591
Tarquinius Superbus, 590
Tartarus, 143, 428, 436, 562
Tatian, 143, 315
  4: 604; 8-11: 606; 21: 561, 563; 22: 564, 581; 25: 599; 27, 559, 562; 33 f.: 592
Tegeans, 596

Teiresias, 338
Teledice, 286
Tellanae, 580
Tellenian perplexities, 436, 580
Tellus, 217, 220, 515
Telmessus (town), 458, 590
Telmessus (prophet), 457
temple prostitution, 7, 242
temple-robbing, 49, 110, 299, 473 f., 488, 599, 601, 606
temples, 22, 89, 96, 110, 189, 194, 196, 201, 375, 452-480, 505, 524, 531, 535, 544, 584-6, 590, 603; to animals, 78
Terence, 582
Terentius Varro, M., 9, 35, 244, 260, 346, 482. See Varro
Terentius Scaurus, Q., 35, 107, 297
Terpsichore, 368, 602
terra, 365
Tertullian, 2, 12, 15, 24, 29 f., 34, 36, 41, 44 f., 47, 51, 246, 250, 252, 255, 261, 266, 275, 277, 349, 593 f., 610
    Ad nat. 5, 45, 48; 1.4: 262, 304; 1.7: 275; 1.8: 262, 317; 1.9: 41, 262, 268, 271-3, 275; 1.10: 262, 346, 564, 577 f.; 1.11: 262, 355; 2.10: 345; 2.11: 262, 367, 547, 549; 2.12: 262, 363; 2.14: 263, 556; 2.15: 548 f.; *Ad Scap.* 2: 604; 3: 268, 273 f.; 4: 271; *Ad ux.* 1.6: 269; *Adv. Jud.* 7: 312; *Adv. Marc.* 4.8: 611; *Apol.* 45, 262, 340; 3: 262, 304; 5: 271; 6: 46, 262, 341 f., 346, 584; 7: 244, 275; 9: 262, 329, 567; 10: 262 f., 269, 345, 362, 553, 555; 11: 350; 12: 592, 597; 13: 262 f.; 14: 262 f., 555-8; 15: 242, 262, 352, 564, 573; 16: 262, 355; 17: 262, 302; 19: 345, 571; 20: 262, 272; 21: 262, 283, 293, 295, 567; 22: 262, 372, 556; 28-36: 240; 29: 598; 30: 268, 610 f.; 33: 271; 37: 312; 40: 41, 262, 268, 271-4; 41: 278; 42: 279; 47: 249; *De an.* 41, 261, 304, 306, 314; 1: 279; 2: 343, 345; 5: 294, 611; 10: 298; 16: 47; 20: 320; 23: 317, 331; 23: 331;
24: 319; 32: 598; 51: 571; 53: 330; *De cor. mil.* 7: 562; 13: 280, 549; *De cult. fem.* 571; *De exhort. cast.* 338; *De idol.* 280, 548, 594; *De ieiun. adv. psych.* 573; *De monog.* 566; *De orat.* 594; *De pr. haer.* 567; *De pud.* 293; *De spect.* 262, 564, 594, 613 f.; *Scorp.* 548, 567
Tescari, O., 267
Teutones, 544
Thales, 35, 121 f., 207
Thalheim, T., 599
Thalia, 368
theaters, 249, 406, 449, 564
Thebes (Greece), 284 f.
Thebes (Egypt), 594
Thelxinoe, 357, 367
Thelxion, 286
Themis, 356 f., 414, 569
Theocritus, 371
Theodoret, 310, 355
Theodorus of Cyrene, 35, 282, 400, 562
Theodosius II, 596
theologians, *theologi*, 200, 352, 385 f., 389 f., 414, 417, 550
theomorphism, 607
theophanies, 605
Theophilus of Antioch, 28, 42, 345
    Ad Autol. 1.8: 307; 1.9: 286, 554; 1.10: 281, 551; 1.11: 240; 2.1: 596; 2.2: 592; 2.3: 587, 598; 3.6: 315; 3.7: 562; 3.15: 564
Theophrastus, 289, 308
Thesmophoria, 432, 575, 577
Thespiae, 464, 593
Thespians, 462
Thessalians, 398
1 Thessalonians 5.15: 26, 273
Thestius, 398, 561, 613
Thetis, 357, 365, 398, 554, 561
Theuth, 181, 343, 551
Thielmann, P., 270
thieves, 212, 476, 556
things of the world, 118
Third Person of the Trinity, 27
Third Punic War, 242

INDEX 657

Thompson, J. W., 243
Thomson, H. J., 545, 555
Thoth, 603. See Theuth
Thrace, 396, 572
Thrämer, E., 284
three ways, of soul's return, 310
Thucydides, 272, 589, 600
Thule, 456, 587
Thulin, C., 279, 283 f., 376
thunderbolts, 181, 478, 563
thurificati, 610
Thyone, 581
Tiber, 421, 531, 533 f., 567, 618
Tiberius, 275
Tiberius Atinius, 616
Tibullus, 278, 284, 557, 607, 611
tidal waves, 63
time, 117, 215, 592
Timaeus, 163
Timaeus of Cicero, 37; of Plato, 148, 388, 553
Timotheus, 35, 414, 550, 568
2 Tim. 1. 10: 300
Tipoplous, 368
Tiryns, 285
Tisianes, 286
Titanis, 552
Titans, 84, 89, 286, 289, 428
Tithonus, 398, 561
Titus 1.12: 559
Titus Tatius, 376, 545
Tityus, 285
Tixeront, J., 245, 255
Toepffer, J., 588, 595
toga, 437, 581, 615; *praetexta*, 342
Tollinton, R. B., 322
Toner, P. J., 565
τόπος πάντων, 282
Torrey, J., 247
torture, 190
Toynbee, A. J., 268, 323, 551, 554, 559
Trajan, 615
Trasimenus, Lake, 367, 377, 546, 583, 620
Transfiguration, 292
transmigration of souls, 130, 317
transmutation of elements, 59
treason, 563

Trebatius Testa, C., 35, 513, 550, 604, 611
Trebia, 211, 227, 368, 620
Trebonius, C., 89, 289
Trebula Mutuesca, 368
trees, worship of, 288
Trevi, 368
Trieterides, 581
Trinacria, 84
Trinity, 27, 254
Triptolemus, 86, 196, 288, 433, 578 f.
Trithemius, J., 18, 51, 240, 248, 264
Triton, 357
Tritone, 368
trivium, 317
Trojan War, 257, 446, 554, 557, 582 f.
Trophonius, 385
Tros, 613
Troy, 244, 273, 557 f.
Tschiersch, W., 251
Tümpel, K., 569
Türk, M., 584, 591, 599
Tullius, F., 39, 41, 43, 45, 260-2, 349, 358, 361, 363-7, 369 f., 543 f., 550, 556-60, 562, 567, 569, 574-6, 578, 580 f., 585-90, 592 f., 595-7, 599
Tullius = M. Tullius Cicero, 196, 446. See Cicero
Tullus, Roman king, 180, 577
Tuscan rite, 501
Tusculum, 355, 362
tutelar divinities, 211, 594
Tutunus, 380, 383, 547, 549
Twelve Labors of Hercules, 285
twin elements, 167, 333
twin intellects, 138, 309, 320
Tyndareus, 84, 182, 286
Typhon, 294
typhus, 116, 303, 316

Ueberweg, F., 321
Ulpian, 278
unbelief, 191
uncompounded, the, 108, 127, 408, 598
understanding, God's, 132
underworld, 500

undiscoverable, the, 30
universe, 195, 198, 217
unpropitious deities, 212
Unxia, 212, 360, 501
Upibilia, 380
Urania, 368
Uranus, 283, 297, 345, 561 f.
Urbs Saturnia, 44
Ursinus, F., 266, 310
Usener, H., 272, 366
ustrinae, 607
usus, 322, 553
usus = cultus, 350

vagi, 278
Vahlen, J., 267
Valerius, 416, 570
Valentinians, 254
Valerianus, 35 f., 258, 458, 591
Valerius Antias, 35, 258, 567, 571, 591
Valerius Flaccus, 322
Valerius Maximus, 7, 242, 351, 599, 611, 614-6, 618 f.
Valgimigli, M., 267
Van den Gheyn, J., 265
Van Sickle, C. E., 275
vanus, 295
Varro, M. Terentius, 10, 38, 40, 186, 222-4, 251, 283, 297, 299, 340, 346, 349, 351, 353, 358, 363-6, 369, 371 f., 376, 418, 454, 458, 462, 476, 481, 545, 548, 550, 563, 571, 580, 586, 590, 593, 601 f., 604, 609, 616; muses of, 593; chronology of, 10
vates, 278
vegetarianism, 605
Vegetius, 371, 598
Vehling, J. D., 609 f.
Venus, 7, 47, 84, 182, 196, 213, 218, 242, 285, 366, 389, 395 f., 398, 400, 405, 448, 450 f., 455, 458, 463-5, 475, 478, 513, 516, 548 f., 555, 561, 594 f., 600, 602; Armata, 547; Cnidian, 464; Cyprian, 427; Erycina, 242; Libitina, 548; Militaris, 380, 547; temple of, 458; the four goddesses of that name, 386, 476. See Aphrodite

Vergil, 37, 258, 270, 275, 277, 279, 281, 284 f., 287 f., 295, 297, 317, 320, 322, 329, 332, 335, 340 f., 343, 351, 357, 359, 362 f., 372, 544, 553, 555, 560 f., 577, 581 f., 587, 591, 597, 603, 611, 618 f.
Verres, C., 601, 613
Verrius Flaccus, 35, 107, 296 f., 369, 574
Vespasian, 341 ,
Vesta, 217, 365
Vestal Virgins, 299, 405
Vesuvius, 271, 354
vicennalia, 8
Victa, 360
Victoria, 465, 544, 596, 599
Victory (goddess), 216, 375
Victua, 212
Vincent of Beauvais, 52
vintage festival, 515
vinum inferium, 611
violet, 416, 425 f., 570
viscera, 291, 334
virago, 396, 558, 578, 582
viri novi, 260, 310
Virtue (goddess), 375
virtues, 118, 161, 453, 513; of true gods, 453
virtus, 327, 334, 545
Virtus, 544
virtutes, 263, 290, 582, 585
virtutum omnium dominus, 300
vitality, 115
vitiligines, 291
Vitruvius, 274, 297
vivicomburium, 279
vocamen, 271
Volkmann, R., 574
Volsinii, 271
Voltaire, 23, 250
Volturnus, 215, 362
Voss, 238
Vulcan, 177, 182, 208, 210, 218, 356 f., 386; 395, 398, 448, 463, 472, 503, 561, 594, 603; son of the Nile, 385; the Lemnian, 385; the four gods of that name, 386
Vulgate, the, 298, 306

INDEX   659

Wachsmuth, C., 588 f.
Walker, J., 266
Walde-Hofmann, 555, 567 f., 602
Warfield, B. B., 254
Warmington, E. H., 305, 325, 556, 563
wars, 61, 212, 453; against beasts, 63
Warscher, T., 354
Waser, O., 381
Wassenberg, F., 258
Waszink, J. H., 261, 279, 304, 306, 317, 319 f., 330, 343, 345, 545, 571, 596, 598, 611
watchmen, at temples, 473
water, 121, 216, 274, 333; condensation of, 122
Weege, F., 583
Weinstock, S., 368, 370, 372
Weizsäcker, P., 344, 365
Welldon, C. E., 547
Weniger, L., 569
Wentzel, G., 367
Wernicke, K., 366, 554
Wessner, P., 297
Weyman, C., 245, 270
wheat, 447
white victims, 226, 500, 608
Wilman, G., 55, 57, 252, 267, 314, 320, 347
wings of the soul, 146, 325
winds, 461
wine, 22, 46, 84, 86, 135, 180, 278, 284, 307, 342, 409, 415 f., 427, 434, 451 f., 454, 480, 507, 511-3, 520, 569, 584, 604, 610 f.; offered in sacrifices, 513 f.
wise, the, 453
wisdom, 118, 121, 203 f., 214, 219; of man, 119; of this world, 305
Wissowa, G., 269, 280 f., 283-5, 288, 290, 342 f., 346, 351, 357, 359 f., 362-4, 369 f., 372, 544-9, 554, 563 f., 567, 571, 573, 576, 592, 594, 598, 610-3, 615-7
wizardry, 325
wool, 426

word-catching, 197, 250
world, 86, 149, 215, 219, 268; born, 167; immortal, 167; not to perish, 167; on fire, 63, 122; to perish, 167; unbegotten, 169; uncreated, 167; circles of, 129
worship, 28, 585; of dead, 457
wounding, of gods, 208, 251, 287; of Venus, 47
Wright, F. A., 242, 250
Wünsch, R., 325
Wüst, E., 584

Xenophanes of Colophon, 333, 355
Xenophon, 352
Xerxes, 63, 273
xoana, 593

year, the, 215
yellow bile, 328

Zagreus, 289, 576
Zama, 619
Zeno the Stoic, 35, 122, 308, 351
Zeno of Myndus, 35, 457, 589
Zeno, St., of Verona, 344
Zeugitani, 70, 276
Zeus, 279, 283-6, 289, 302, 320, 344, 356, 357, 363, 365, 551, 554, 557, 560-2, 577, 581, 584, 587, 589, 594, 597, 606; Capitolinus, 551; Cassius, 551; Cretensis, 551; of Dodona, 280; Latiaris, 551; Olympius, 551; Pannychius, 551; Propator, 551; Tonans, 551; Trophonius, 280. See Jupiter
Zeuxippa, 397, 560
Ziegler, K., 52, 264, 606
Zielinski, T., 259
zodiacal signs, 65
Zonaras, 591
zone of fire, 99
Zoroaster, 41, 99, 273, 294, 310: Armenius, 294; the Bactrian king, 63, 294
Zoroastrianism, 337
Zosimus, 337
Zostrianus, 99